Spectacular Vernaculars

SUNY Series, Postmodern Culture
Joseph Natoli, Editor

Spectacular Vernaculars

Hip-Hop and the Politics of Postmodernism

Russell A. Potter

State University of New York Press

Published by
State University of New York Press, Albany

© 1995 State University of New York

For information, address State University of New York
Press, State University Plaza, Albany, N.Y., 12246

Production by Diane Ganeles
Marketing by Theresa Abad Swierzowski

Library of Congress Cataloging-in-Publication Data

Potter, Russell A., 1960–
    Spectacular vernaculars : hip-hop and the politics of
postmodernism / Russell A. Potter.
        p.   cm. — (SUNY series, postmodern culture)
    Includes bibliographical references (p.) and index.
    ISBN 0-7914-2625-4 (HC : acid-free paper). — ISBN 0-7914-2626-2
(PB : acid-free paper)
    1. Rap (Music)—Political aspects. 2. Postmodernism. I. Title.
II. Series: SUNY series in postmodern culture.
ML3531.P   1995
782.42164—dc20   94-24990
                                                 CIP
                                               MN

10 9 8 7 6 5 4 3 2 1

*To the Last Poets
who were there first…*

Contents

Contents

Acknowledgments

Before all else, I must acknowledge my indebtedness to my harshest and most perceptive critic, Karen Carr. Her continual critique, and her ability to detect every pose and posture of which I am capable, has prevented this book from being any of the many long-winded pontifications it might otherwise have become. Secondly, I must thank two other readers, each of whom has added a sense of the purpose and direction of this book: Paul Machlin, whose encyclopedic knowledge of the history of music, along with great generosity of mind, have been indispensable, and Michael Collins, whose perceptive ears and lucidly crafty writings continue to amaze and influence me. I also owe a debt of gratitude to the series editor, Joseph Natoli, who supported this project from its earliest stages, and to Carola Sautter, for guiding it through SUNY Press.

In the research and preparation of this book, I have had the help of many people, most principally my research assistant, Michael T. Miller (word to The P.O.E.T.!), along with Kebba Tolbert (MC Tevski), Rob Caruso (musician, filmmaker, and video director extraordinaire), Jason Oberfest, Chris Chamberlain, and all the students in my January 1993 hip-hop class at Colby College. Thanks are also due to those in the hip-hop nation who, without knowing me personally, have given generously of their time and knowledge, including Chuck D, Harry Allen, the staff at DefJam Records, DJ Timebomb, Charles Isbell, Phil Julian, Jerome Glassman, and everyone else on the funky-music e-mail list. The work of other scholars has of course been indispensable; among all those whose writings I benefitted from I would like to send major shouts out to Paul Gilroy, Dick Hebdige,

David Toop, Tricia Rose, Houston A. Baker Jr., John Pareles, Jon Michael Spencer, Nelson George, Ben Sidran, bell hooks, Amiri Baraka, Donald B. Gibson, Henry Louis Gates Jr., Angela Spence Nelson, Geneva Smitherman, and Ronald Jemal Stephens. Last, but far from least, I would like to thank the people who first turned me on to hip-hop: Quentin Stith, who rapped out rhymes to a tabletop beat in my 1987 poetry course at Syracuse University—and Misha Elmendorf, whose whiskey and smoke-filled room of jazz, hip-hop, and blues was a crucible for so many of the ideas in this book. Like so many things, scratch the surface of an author and you'll find a collectivity—this text, like all others, is a "posse cut" in a heteroglossaic mix. Peace.

Introduction—Coming to Terms:
Rap Music as Radical Postmodernism

It is sadly ironic that the contemporary discourse which talks the most about heterogeneity, the decentered subject, declaring breakthroughs that allow recognition of otherness, still directs its critical voice primarily to a specialized audience, one that shares a common language rooted in the very master narratives it claims to challenge. If radical postmodernist thinking is to have a transformative impact then a critical break with the notion of "authority" as "mastery over" must not simply be a rhetorical device, it must be reflected in habits of being, including styles of writing as well as chosen subject matter.

—bell hooks, "Postmodern Blackness"[1]

It's after the end of the world. Don't you know that?

—Sun Ra[2]

The broader cultural debates about postmodernism have in recent years become almost a kind of cottage industry—fueled both by fascination and loathing, as critics alternately extol the "postmodernity" of some text or social phenomenon, or decry the intellectual bankruptcy of a "postmodernism" that they regard as a sort of willful intellectual meltdown. As a result, it has become almost conventional to insist that there are multiple postmodernisms, and for each new text to claim for itself a different textual genealogy made up of the books, texts, or cultural happenings that *it* prefers to regard as characteristically *postmodern*. It can seem a wearying gesture, but nonetheless it needs to be made—in part precisely because it is all too easy to wave the banner of "multiplicity" in front of every confounded reader, as if complexity all by itself were an occasion for critics to abdicate judgment and jump into a happy free-for-all of floating signifiers. For "postmodernism" is all too often read as the idea that *nothing is at stake*, a signpost on the way to relativistic chaos, whereas I share with many other writers the sense that a great deal is at stake, and that what is perceived as relativism is really an attempt to confront some of the most troubling contradictions of contemporary culture.

One influential model of this troubled dichotomy is Theresa L. Ebert's discussion of "ludic" and "resistance" postmodernism.[3] "Ludic" postmodernism, as its name implies, is the postmodernism of play, of free fall, of delight in irresolution; "resistance" postmodernism, with which Ebert aligns her critical practice, is a model of critique which, while aware of the complex interdeterminations of social and textual subjectivities, draws deeply on Marxism's insistence on the correlatives of material conditions, and seeks quite explicitly to "resist" what it sees as humanistic pluralism. However compelling and useful Ebert's dichotomy may be, I would like to immediately undercut it by suggesting the possibility of a *play* that in its ethos and effects is a form of *resistance*. That is, rather than polarize postmodernism, in the manner of Monty Python, into "silly" and "serious" camps, I would like to suggest that *play*—and not only in obvious forms, such as parody and satire—is potentially a powerful mode of resistance.[4] Play certainly can be an idle distraction, but it can also be the mask for a potent mode of subversion, and indeed I argue in this book that hip-hop culture in particular, and African-American culture in general, is precisely such a form. What needs emphasis here, however, is that there *is* something at stake in constructions of postmodernity, that political questions are *not* rendered moot by postmodern indeterminacies, that indeed postmodernism has as profound an ethical dimension as any *modernism*.

Another question about postmodernism, and one that has been played upon by many critics, is what exactly it is *post*. And, while there remains an inevitable slippage into chronology, I think the central problem of postmodernism is that its own *time* is deeply and repeatedly *untimely*. Bennet Schaber and Bill Readings put it this way in the introduction to their book, *Postmodernism Across the Ages*:

> For us, the postmodern marks a gap in the thinking of time that is
> constitutive of the modernist concept of time as succession or
> progress. This is something we feel strongly about. It commits us
> here to resisting a number of existing images of the postmodern.
> We do not resist in the name of truth or purity, but in order to
> refuse that the postmodern be given a truth, circulated as current
> and legitimate coinage.[5]

Here we have a different kind of *resistance*—a resistance to the very
kind of history that would anoint the bearers of pre-, present-, and post-.
And there is what I would identify as a central trait or trope of the postmodern: its refusal of fixed or progressive models of time. As much
"not yet" as "not *then*," decidedly *after* a kind of time that constitutes
itself as progressive (even if that time is still ticking); perhaps running
in grand Viconian cycles of eternal return, perhaps preferring the kind
of local interruption of time that takes place in a musical *sample* of
previous recordings. Not that this sort of postmodernism has no roots,
that it is not susceptible to a diachronic survey—but rather that its
succession is always in (and indeed *about*) dispute, as Schaber and
Readings might say, *illegitimate*.

　　How exactly hip-hop culture can be seen as *postmodern* has
everything to do with this same peculiar splitting of time. In one sense,
African-Americans have good reason not to give too much credence to
"progressive" time, since for four hundred years most of the economic
"progress" in the United States has disproportionately benefited its
white citizens. Yet at the same time, there has been an unyielding
hunger and thirst for the *promise* of the future—what bell hooks calls
"Yearning"—coupled with a bitter awareness of the *presence* of "past"
oppressions. This split in time, in turn, has potent connections to the
inner-spatial "double consciousness" articulated almost a century ago
by W.E.B. DuBois: that African-Americans, even as they have sought to
build from within a full sense of self-authenticity, have had to exist in a
nation where the fundamental symbolic structures continually place
them in the position of "Other." As Paul Gilroy demonstrates compellingly in his book, *The Black Atlantic: Modernity and Double
Consciousness*, there are potent yet obscured common genealogies at
stake here—including but not limited to the philosophical dialectics of
master/slave relations, the reflexive constructions of "whiteness" and
"blackness," and indeed the metastasis of parts of the racialist epistemology of eugenics in the current ascension of cultural studies.[6]

Gilroy, who has a healthy suspicion of the simplistic relativism of some avatars of postmodernism, prefers to see these black cultural formations as oppositional *modernities*, rather than *post*modernities. Yet precisely because these formations inhabit recurrent moments of resistance, situated both in and as "breaks" in progressive time—and because, in their intrinsic structures, they constitute both a counter-aesthetic and counter-ethos to the fuzzy humanism of many modernist movements—I feel strongly that they are more accurately described as *postmodern*. In particular, even within black modernisms, there has been, as Gilroy describes it, "both an imaginary anti-modern past and a postmodern yet-to-come."[7] The chronological bifurcation, analogous to double consciousness, is profoundly different from the one-way street of the vast majority of "modernist" movements, and constitutes the core of a full-blown postmodern sensibility that in its fundamental structures refuses the terms of Eurocentric modernisms (which themselves owe much more than they often care to admit both to the conceptual terms of "blackness" and to particular black expressive arts).

In this sense, it could be said that *all* black artistic movements are postmodern. In fact I would argue that, while in a very general sense such a statement has its truth, in actual historical practice postmodernity has marked a particular *part* of the cycle of African-American arts, a part intimately related to its material situation. For there is history at stake here, not only the history of the structures of resistance, from spiritual songs to Calypso stick-dancers to Public Enemy's S1W security force, but the already double(d) history of "white" appropriation, commodification, and dilution of black artistic expressions. From the minstrel shows of the nineteenth century, through the "swing" jazz cover bands that cashed in on the Jazz craze of the '30s, to the white musicians who appropriated jump Blues and called it rock-n-roll, African-American arts have always been dogged by the backhanded compliments of exoticization and commodification. A great deal of value has been placed on black arts, but this value has been largely negotiable only in terms of white dollars. Conscious of this recurring act of appropriation, African-American artists have again and again wrenched new time out of old, refusing and interrupting the commodification of their work. And, while much of this has been represented by its chroniclers as a species of *modernism* (and here I am thinking of moments from the Harlem Renaissance to Bop to the Black Arts move-

ment), each has been pointedly sited on cultural*breaks*—breaks with
pre-existing black traditions that had been appropriated and retailed to
suit mass (read *white*) tastes, and at the same time *returns* to previous
moments within the black artistic continuum. The resulting radical
now, based on the irruption of unaccounted histories and as-yet unful-
filled futures, itself constitutes a *gap* in progressive time, a gap which
both draws from and gives voice to the frustrations felt when the artistic expressions of black diasporic communities are once again taken
out of the control of their originators and producers.

Despite these potent and suggestive connections between black
vernacular artforms and the modalities and ethics of postmodernism,
there has been a longstanding—and oftentimes justified—suspicion of
the part of black writers and philosophers over what (if anything) postmodernism could possibly offer for the kinds of critical histories they
were engaged with constructing. As recently as 1989, it was possible for
Cornel West to allow, in his essay "Black Culture and Postmodernism,"
that "the current 'postmodernism' debate is first and foremost a
product of significant First World reflections upon the decentering of
Europe."[8] West, as one of the leading black philosophers of our time,
saw both the parochial and ludic elements of postmodernism as signs
of its insufficient engagement with black culture, even as he gestured
towards "a potentially enabling yet resisting postmodernism."[9] Yet in
the light of critiques and analyses by scholars such as bell hooks and
Paul Gilroy, it has become increasingly evident that what had earlier
been articulated primarily as the subcultural resistance of black
artforms has in fact had a long and intimate relation with the founding
dialectics of "Western" modernism. At the same time, 'postmodernism'
as a field of discourse has widened, moving a considerable distance
from Jean-François Lyotard and his circle of abstract intellectual
vanguardists. While some now disparage what they see as 'vulgar' postmodernism, perhaps what has in fact happened is that the earlier
coterie of postmodernists has been forced to reckon with more material formations of postmodernism, many of which are no longer willing
to wait for their cue.

So 'resistance postmodernism,' as I hope to articulate it in this
book, is not simply a theorization of a more political postmodernist
stance; it proposes (against the grain of many self-announced 'resistance postmodernists') that the material and social forms *resistance*
takes in a specific cultural context exceed and may well be indifferent

or even hostile to some of the academic formulations of postmodernism. And, in the case of black cultural histories, the reason for this hostility lies not solely or even primarily in what is too readily construed as a reactive hearkening towards a pre-modernist worldview, but in a deeply historical and resonantly informed *vernacular* articulation of *anti*-modernism. Too many ostensibly 'radical' intellectuals are so filled with the conviction of their own radicality that they can only conceive of rejection by the people in whose name they articulate resistance as a *reactionary* move. The 'organic intellectual,' raised as a hopeful sign, is dropped all too quickly when he or she refuses to walk in step with the announced theoretical vanguard. Particularly in the case of black cultures, where there has been, as Paul Gilroy hints at, a vernacular ethics, a vernacular history, and a vernacular version of 'modernism,' it is vital to recognize that there are material inheritances—such as slavery—whose reverberations need not be recorded by a seismograph in a sealed laboratory, but can be and are felt in the everyday life of black diasporic cultures.

All of this comes down to almost a single proposition: the historical experience of slavery—which by no means ends with the "emancipation" proclamation—makes a fundamental difference in the cultural and philosophical modes of expression of black cultures. Black cultures have inhabited the contradictory space of what Gilroy calls the "slave sublime," have glimpsed the fundamental rottenness of European modernism from its very intestines long before Europe noticed any trace of indigestion. Living, talking, making music, and writing in the subjectivity of resistance that was built—*had* to be built—against the economic and philosophical bulwarks of slavery and colonialism, black cultures conceived *postmodernism* long before its "time" as construed by writers who had to wait and take their cue from Derrida, Foucault, or Lyotard. This is not to (re)make the particularist argument that black postmodernisms, because earlier or more visceral, are therefore superior—but it is at least to stake a claim that they are of equally fundamental importance. More importantly, I do not want to advance any notion that black postmodernisms, because *lived* or *felt* are in any sense less *thought*—a problem which inhabits many claims as to the value of black artforms. Instead, I would say that European and black traditions (which are now of course also European, as well as American, Caribbean, and so forth) stand of different sides of a specific historical ideological formation, one which rationalized slavery in the name of "higher" pursuits, and underpinned the vast ethical disaster of raising an "Age of Reason" on the profits of an unjustifiable trilateral trade in slaves, sugar, and rum. Slavery, as Gilroy insists, can no longer be seen as merely incidental to capitalism, or to the philosophical movements which have attended or been produced by capitalist societies. Black history carries the subversive truth that contemporary rationales for poverty, ghettoization, and trickle-down economic policy that justify the increasing wealth of a few on the backs of a growing black underclass are also part and parcel of this ongoing capitalistic hegemony, and black arts are the signal site for the return of these repressed realities.

Black diasporic cultures, immediately linked to this economy of enslavement, have re-articulated the West from its pre-history on up, starting with the reading of the enslavement of the Jews in Egypt that underpins the whole worldview of the tradition of spiritual song. In so doing, they were most emphatically *not* seeking to turn time *backwards* (the past of Jewish slavery being read *as present*) but rather to focus an intense energy on an as-yet utopian future—and yet as much an earthly utopia much as a heavenly one. Building culture out of remembered fragments, linked together with anagogical syntheses appropriated from the slavemasters' cultural past, and yet intensely directed towards a visionary and personal future—*this* is the modality within which black modernisms have arisen, and from which, in ages of renewed despair and struggle, black *post*modernisms have proceeded. Black modernisms, of course, have never been hermetically sealed off from European or Euro-American modernisms, and indeed the substantial debts of modernism to black cultures are as yet only partly tallied—but what is most significant here is that the untimely sense of *time* so fundamental to postmodernism arrived considerably earlier within black diasporic cultures—and has as a result had antecedents and results distinct from, though not at all unrelated to, those of European (post)modernisms.

So what time is it? With this question, rappers situate themselves within a black diasporic timezone, outside the "official" time of calendars and digital watches; for hip-hoppers, as for the Last Poets, "time is running out."[10] Or perhaps it has already *run* out; as Sun Ra says, "it's after the end of the world." Flavor Flav's gargantuan timepieces, like Dali's wilted watches, mark a surreal incursion, a time radically at odds with the modernist world. Hip-hop's triad of graffiti, dance, and rap are post-apocalyptic arts, scratches on the decaying surfaces of post-industrial urban America; they are not monuments to some romanticized "human spirit," but fundamentally anti-monumental arts. If there are analogous moments in European chronologies, they are not in Joyce's Dublin or Eliot's London, but in the carcereal dementia of Piranesi's Rome, or the situationist juxtapositions of Debord's Paris. Hip-hop's time is post-apocalyptic, and its landscape is the Society of the Spectacle, in which the ultimate commodity form is that of the spectacularized image. Rather than, as most modernist texts would do, reject such a society and yearn for a return to a world made whole by art, hip-hop aims for a world made *hole*, aporic, fracturing the fragmented, graffiti on the graffiti. If there is a communality in hip-hop—and I think there can be no doubt there is—it is the communality of the recognition that "it's like that, and that's the way it is"—that the time for naive idealism is past, that the world's in a non-stop state of emergency that no amount of rose-colored rhetoric can amend.[11] Instead of grand projects cut from a single block, hip-hop rebuilds art from parts, mobile and recombinant.

Debord saw the spectacle as the ultimate commodity form, and thus the central currency of a post-industrial age. The spectacle is "capital to such a degree of accumulation that it becomes an image," and marks "the moment when the commodity has taken the total occupation of social life."[12] Resistance to such commodification seems futile in such a model, and yet it continues to occur. From the historical position of post-industrial, postmodern urban arts, the recognition that everything is or will soon be commodified has instead served as a spur, an incitement to productivity; within specifically African-American arts, it is a move with a long history. For every musical form that black culture has produced has been appropriated and commodified by white culture in the name of a very particular kind of *spectacle*, whether it be a minstrel show, a big band concert, or a rock-n-roll extravaganza. Black Americans, having experienced the violence of slavery's subjugation, have had the singular historical experience of having their blackness made into a spectacular commodity of great value, even as they themselves have been denied the profits of such commodification.

As middle-class Americans have danced their tango with the society of the spectacle, they have, it is true, become aware of its vacuousness. And, at each step, many have turned to African-American culture for something to spice up the bland gruel of their existence. And, aware that their cultural capital bore an inverse relation to their material wealth, Black Americans have frequently deployed the arts of Signifyin(g), giving white audiences what they thought they wanted, while at the same time giving themselves what they needed: a mode of communication which could signal solidarity. None of these relations are, in the end, reducible to their material components (though the profit sheets of the major record companies can bear ready testament to "who stole the soul?"); they are instead *spectacular* relations, cultural exchanges along an uneven, class and racially-inflected social faultline: you take your stereotype and I'll take mine. Hip-hop culture is the ultimate incarnation of this spectacularized cultural exchange; never has black rage been more up front; never have consumers been so ready to buy. Many such purchases, no doubt, will be recontained by the very commodity structures that enabled the exchange in the first place; for some consumers, a hip-hip CD may be simply a safety-sealed black rage in a handy 5 x 5 inch package. Yet despite this, hip-hop's message of disaffection and rage has many other points of resonance in post-industrial America, and can readily be the catalyst for identification *across* racial lines. As bell hooks puts it,

> The overall impact of the postmodern condition is that many other groups now share with black folks a sense of deep alienation, despair, uncertainty, loss of a sense of grounding, even if it is not informed by shared circumstance. Radical postmodernism calls attention to those sensibilities which are shared across the boundaries of class, gender, and race, and which could be fertile ground for the construction of empathy—ties that would promote recognition of common commitments and serve as a base for solidarity and coalition.

In this sense, I would put hip-hop forward as one form of radical postmodernism, a postmodernism whose representational strategies, while complex and contradictory, do not for that reason lose their liberatory potential. While its rhetorical and musical structures clearly come out of African-American vernacular traditions, its audience has from the start crossed racial and regional lines, and the substantial sales figures of hip-hop albums by groups such as Public Enemy, De La Soul, and A

Tribe Called Quest clearly indicate that their audience includes both black and white listeners of a wide range of social classes.[13] As Chuck D has remarked, hip-hop has come to mark more of a generational line than a racial one, and indeed this is one reason why it is so threatening to the dominant race-class system; it invites identification across forbidden lines, and demonstrates widespread disaffection from the machinery of capitalism at a time when the free market is widely hailed in the media as the great economic savior.[14]

Lines of race, gender, and social class are not the only ones hip-hop crosses; particularly in the early '90s, it is increasingly clear that hip-hop has become a transnational, global artform capable of mobilizing diverse disenfranchised groups. Following the diasporic byways of the black Atlantic, which as Gilroy has demonstrated have been pivotal cultural vectors for centuries, rap music has surfaced in a wide range of cultural and intercultural sites.[15] Contact between West Indian and East Indian communities in England has produced the so-called Bhangramuffin (from 'Bhangra,' the traditional rhythm-driven music of Punjabi émigrés, and 'ragamuffin,' a cognate of "reggae" used to describe the rapid-fire dancehall toasting popular in Jamaica today) style exemplified by artists such as Apache Indian; in Paris, the Sénégalese rapper MC Solaar has established himself with his mixture of New York attitude and smooth rapid-fire French; in South Africa, the traditional rhythms of resistance have joined with hip-hop-inflected vocals of groups such as Prophets of the City. In this sense, while hip-hop's time signature is "after the end of the world," it *locus* is simultaneously local and global; the end of "the" world, after all, may be only the beginning of worlds, of a realization that the declarative determinisms of "the West" or "America" or "the Contemporary" are no longer possible. While this sense is no doubt for many a *tragic* one, most postmodernisms take it rather as a point of departure, a new possibility. For one, the line between what was at one time construed as "high" or canonical culture and what was set aside in the same move as "popular" culture, can no longer be drawn with any certainty; indeed the very act of drawing such a line at all appears suddenly as an *ideological* rather than an *aesthetic* act. Problematizing this act has been one of the central themes of many postmodernist artforms.[16]

Despite these promising rifts and openings, much of the criticism that surrounds and frames the debates over postmodernism has remained foreclosed, set under the hermeneutic seal of a new vocabulary of technical terms drawn from psychoanalysis, Marxism, and philosophy, and linked to a heavy-handed, often plodding academic apparatus. The dissolution of "high" culture has, to date, been proclaimed primarily in a language which only those already within the world of academic postmodernism can readily understand.

If the claims that postmodern theorists make about the insupportability of any clear boundary between ostensibly privileged knowledge and 'popular' knowledge are valid—and I think they are—they are claims that these theorists have largely failed to enact. While the insistence that 'theory is necessarily a practice' is often advanced as a defense, it is rendered ludicrous by the ways in which many postmodern theorists have to date regarded culture at large only as a kind of grand field of objects for analysis. Architecture, television, film, and music have all provided grist for the academic mill, and yet the wonders that they disclose, rather than recirculating across cultural boundaries, have too often been recontained. In the absence of the ostensibly discredited "high" culture, the analysis of the popular has taken its place, forming a new élite community of discourse. As Steven Connor puts it,

> [We are told that] the waning of the cultural authority of the West and its political and intellectual traditions, along with the opening up of the world political scene to cultural and ethnic differences, is another symptom of the modulation of hierarchy into heterarchy... [and yet] something [happens] in postmodernist theory...which names and correspondingly closes off the very world of cultural difference and plurality which it allegedly brings into visibility.[17]

Yet despite this apparent closure, there exist many strata of discourse within which postmodernisms continually cross and recross the boundary zones which many of its theorists are so reluctant to transgress. For one, there is a fair amount media coverage—albeit much of it negative—of the broad outlines of postmodernist debates. The arguments over the dissolution or reconstruction of literary canons (to take an example) are widely reported—whether in the television coverage of Stanford students shouting "Hey ho, hey ho, western culture's gotta go" or the traveling roadshows of such avowedly anti-academic proselytizers as Camille Paglia or Dinesh D'Souza (for whom such a dissolution is either a joyful bonfire of academic vanities or a cause for decrying the 'decline of Western Culture').

These scattered moments when academic postmodernism enjoys its 'fifteen minutes of fame' can hardly be taken as the ground for a sense of 'postmodern culture' at large. To do so would only replicate the logic of academic postmodernism, which thinks of itself as its own ultimate enactment of "the" postmodern. On the contrary, if postmodernism has any validity at all, then it must be a phenomenon that broadly suffuses contemporary cultural practices. To date, most postmodern theorists have re-enacted the very thing Marx criticized the old rationalistic philosophies for doing: they have sought to bring philosophy 'from heaven to earth' (or even, in the case of the study of "popular culture," from 'earth' to 'heaven'), calling for "materialist" critique and yet never conceiving (as Marx only dimly conceived) that the people and practices which they sought as the *object* of their study were already *subjects* in their own right.

Some academic theorists—among them marxists, feminists, and cultural historians—have recognized this problem, and have consciously sought to provide different models. In this cause, attempts have been made to see certain cultural phenomena—whether it be the emergence of the IWW in the 1930s, Star Trek fanzines, or group activities ranging from gangs to skateboarding—as examples of indigenous resistance instigated by 'organic intellectuals.' The problem of the objectification implicit within academic discourse has, however, proven difficult to overcome; the inhabitants of the cultural zones under scrutiny are rarely in a position that enables them to critique the "knowledge" that is made of those zones. Even when the one doing the studying is a member of the community, the difficulty of regarding one's own culture as somehow *remarkable* (as well as the suspicion suddenly cast on anyone whose task is to regard their friends and neighbors as objects of study) is almost impossible to overcome, as Zora Neale Hurston discovered when Franz Boas sent her to Eatonville, Florida to collect folklore. "To see myself as somebody else"—as Hurston puts it—requires a kind of Zen mind few people possess.[18]

What is a committed postmodernist to do? How can one write and speak of the contemporary while at the same time working within academic discourses which continually reinforce the demand that the productions of the present be looked at *as objects*, that they be defined, commodified, and described to the point where one becomes a stranger to one's own time? I do not want to suggest that there is no solution to this problem, but I do think that it must be continually borne in mind. Another closely related difficulty in writing across and among the many cultural practices that comprise the contemporary moment is neither to overvalue nor to undervalue any particular part of it. The necessity forced upon archaeologists in their study of cultures long dead is both to extrapolate from partial findings (and every dig, however rich, is partial) and yet not to place too great a significance on the accidents of survival; a culture's most valued practices may have left only the slightest trace, and yet their refuse heaps may be perfectly preserved. The person who wishes to write of the contemporary must similarly be able to extrapolate from inevitably partial experiences among the multiple cultures while at the same time resisting the urge to hold forth any one thing as a static synecdoche for the vast and intricate webs of cultures.

Despite the difficulties involved, the urgency of this task is great, as all of us live in a world where both the oversupply of information and mutual unintelligibility among cultures are increasing at a fantastic rate. This is not to say that any particular cultural practice—and one could include academic as well as hip-hop language—bears a responsibility to be easy to understand; some work, some interaction with the cultural communities at stake will always be required of any reader or listener. Yet what *will* be lost if academic discourse and contemporary artforms such as hip-hop drift out of each others zones of intelligibility is an understanding of the numerous and vital connections which already exist between them. Hip-hop, far from being a simple object which a postmodernist project could 'bring to light' or offer up as exemplary, is itself an active, ongoing, and highly sophisticated postmodernism—a postmodernism which in many ways has gone farther and had more crucial consequences than all the academic books on postmodernism rolled into one.

For instance, postmodern theorists have spent a great deal of time talking about the ways in which identity, far from being reducible to essentialized categories such as race, class, and gender, is in fact more of a patchwork of overlapping—and in some cases, *conflicting*—identities. Yet despite the many books echoing this theme, in the spectacularized world of the mass media, essential identities continue to have ample airplay; hip-hop's engagement with this world is direct and ongoing. Well aware of the power of media such as television and radio, rappers have managed to bum-rush the Spectacle, to hijack the media by its own devices. If violent black males in hoodies are stirring up fear on the evening news, rappers will represent with guns in their hands, "sending out mad shots, making devils run naked."[19] Yet check under the hoods and you will find a different message, a message of solidarity with other African-American communities, a message of survival against the odds. It's what N.W.A. calls "the strength of street knowledge"; there is power in language, the power to make oppressors tremble, and more: the power to make them think.

While this might seem in some ways to signal a still *more* essentialized, exoticized blackness, I would say instead that it Signifies on white fears about black culture; its building blocks are stereotypes, and yet the ultimate effect of heaping them up is to render the stereotype untenable. Furthermore, the identities represented by rappers are themselves direct embodiments of capitalism's deep contradictions; inveighing against white capitalism, rappers call out the praises of Jeeps, BMWs, Gucci watches, and fat bankrolls; criticizing white standards of beauty embodied by hair straighteners and blue contact lenses, many rappers end up pointing the finger at black women more than the cosmetic industry. And yet at the core, even these material icons, like graffiti-bombed subway cars, remain in transit both towards and against the larger capitalistic system; as Boots of the Oakland rap group the Coup puts it,

> Capitalism is like a spider
> The web is getting tighter
> I'm strugglin' like a fighter . . .
>
> . . . just when I think I'm free
> It seems to me the spider steps.
> This web is made of money,
> made of greed, made of *me*
> Or what I have become in a parasite economy...
>
> —The Coup, "Not Yet Free"[20]

In their material icons, as with their political messages, hip-hop texts themselves are no less conflicted than the multiple cultural positions which produced them. Thus a rap that attacks American militarism and racism, such as Ice Cube's "I Wanna Kill Sam," is also marked by homophobic metaphors; a rap that dramatizes the plight of the Los Angeles ghetto (e.g., N.W.A.'s "Straight Outta Compton") goes out of its way to diss women with misogynistic epithets.[21] In liberal circles, it's commonplace to lament that rap's revolutionary potential is "marred" by these subtexts, but in the heteroglossaic space of hip-hop, there is no way to filter out the "noise"—in a sense the very desire for some kind of "pure" revolutionary spirit, unmarred by other struggles, discloses a kind of pre-modernist nostalgia for a world in which ethics and politics are less conflicted. One of the tasks, then, of this book is to resist this very kind of reading—not in the name of a pure or authentic cultural space, but rather to oppose the discourse of "purity" itself. This is indeed a move which many rappers also make (Chuck D, in "Fear of a Black Planet," intones "Who is pure? What is pure? Is it European? I ain't sure"), although it is almost always deployed, as in this example, against white, Eurocentric culture.[22]

Yet hip-hop, even as it makes politicized incursions against the dominant, is founded on the verbal play of signification; in this sense it is does not exclude the "ludic" from its modes of resistance. When Chuck D proclaims that he will "cock a doodle do a riddle," or Humpty Hump declares "I use a word that don't mean nothin', like loopted," the dichotomy commonly assumed between "play" and "seriousness" collapses.[23] Indeed, as I will argue in greater detail below, the history of the African-American mode of Signifyin(g) is a history of a serious unseriousness, a power/play, a verbal game in which the stakes continually escalate. Thus, the postmodernism of hip-hop pushes the boundaries of the political, in the process redefining the very structures of resistance.

Another question that has vexed theorists of postmodernism—especially those who are committed to a political struggle—is the dichotomy between theory and practice. Many political postmodernists are haunted by a sense that their theoretical work, despite its intellectual efficacy, does not actually intervene in the reproduction of the dominant ideology. Some of these anxieties derive from a sense that the language of postmodern theory itself forms a kind of barrier, excluding from the discourse of postmodernism the very subjects who are presumed to be most implicated in it; other anxieties come from a sense that critical practice, however powerful, is marginalized within the academy and society as a whole. Indeed, these anxieties are in many ways justified—but only to the extent that academic practice fails to enact its own possibility. Intelligibility is political—but then again, so is *un*intelligibility; academia may be marginalized in some ways, but in others it can readily mobilize new discourses, never more effectively than in the necessarily heteroglossaic space of the classroom.

Hip-hop's poetic and musical practices offer an exemplary case, militating against any such simple dichotomy. Its Signifyin(g) lingo, continually shifting and expanding, serves as a kind of permeable membrane, admitting anyone willing to listen and learn; indeed some rappers such as Chuck D and Ice-T have argued that hip-hop is at its most revolutionary when it enters the ears of white teenagers. At the same time, its multimedia presence—including and perhaps most importantly the blaze of media criticism—serves as a continual engine; hip-hop's activity stirs media re-activity, which in turn spurs hip-hop activity still further. Thus, as George Yancy has observed, hip-hop is "fundamentally a form of praxis," an everyday and ongoing militancy; in Ice-T's terms, it's a "cultural movement" that is a direct product of "city life"[24] It is tempting, indeed, to think of hip-hop music as the missing *practice* which theories of the postmodern have gestured towards—but in fact such a conception would only re-enact the very dichotomy that I would like to problematize, by implying that these 'practices' are somehow naive, somehow lacking their own indigenous theories.

That this assumed naiveté is such a widely-held presupposition is symptomatic of the ways in which the theory/practice line itself has class and race connotations which have a long history; ultimately they are connected to the romanticized 'simplicity' or 'naturalness' of black culture for predominantly white audiences that dates back at least to the 'minstrel' shows of the mid-nineteenth century. The ideological slippage from the privileged dichotomies of racist ideology takes the form of a series of displacements that can be traced rather in the manner of a series of "Miller Analogy Test"-like couplets: Practice is to theory as action is to thought, as "primitive" is to "sophisticated," as natural is to artificial, as physical pleasure is to intellectual contemplation. Within such an ideologically charged series, it's all too easy for hip-hop to be dismissed—both by "liberals" who regard hip-hop as a form of pandering to the stereotypes of the violent black male—black hate as a titillating gift-box that ticks but does not explode—and (ironically) also by African-American intellectuals who, wary of the fact that hip-hop is often taken by whites searching for a simple synecdoche of "blackness," would prefer to substitute Ornette Coleman's jazz or Toni Morrison's fiction.[25] Indeed, there has been considerable class tension *within* African-American cultures, as exemplified (albeit in diluted form) in the sitcom *Fresh Prince of Bel-Air*, where a 'streetwise' Philadelphia kid (played by rapper Fresh Prince) goes to live with his snobby upper-middle class relatives in their ostentatious Bel-Air home.

Given that hip-hop's problematics of race and class take place on the level of language, I think this entire question is best addressed through an analysis of the possibility of resistance *via* language. One exemplary text—though not one I would wish to invoke without caution—is Henry Louis Gates's *The Signifying Monkey*, which he explicitly names a *vernacular* theory.[26] Gates's central contention in this book is that African-American texts have had a very highly developed theoretical framework from the start, a framework which like African-American culture itself has roots which can be traced back through novels, poems, slave narratives, and tall tales back to West African interpretative rituals and protocols. The caution I would attach to this work—which I will elaborate later as I engage with hip-hop culture itself—is that to assume a singular, unified, and transhistorical African-American vernacular is to do violence to the complexity of the histories through which African-American culture—and "American" culture in general—have taken form. Speaking in the "vernacular" has not always been a valued mode of resistance, and is not necessarily empowering, even today.[27] There is, in any case, no single African-American "vernacular"; the vernacular of the Afro-Caribbean inhabitants of Barbados in the seventeenth century is not the same as the Rasta-Jamaica patois of Bob Marley, and neither of these is the same as the everyday vocabulary of a young girl in the South Bronx in the late 1970s. The point of this linguistic heteroglossia is only amplified when other cultural forms, such as art, music, dress, and body language are taken into account—and in any case is compounded still more by differences of social class and gender. Within this tissue of overlapping and at times contradictory vernacular cultures, to valorize a particular voice or tradition as *the* African-American vernacular becomes a romanticized quest for an unattainable grail; such a quest can only succeed by erasing historical difference.[28]

Nonetheless, I do not think this crucial point should obscure Gates's other argument, which can readily be rephrased in the plural: that African-American vernacular cultures have always been as theorized, and as capable (perhaps *more* capable) of *irony* and abstraction as "Western" culture (which itself must also be seen as the fictional conflation of difference that it is). Indeed, the practice of *Signifyin(g)*, which Gates demonstrates compellingly lies at the heart of much vernacular African-American language and art, is a theorized practice which is fundamentally ironic, fundamentally *postmodern*. Signifyin(g), briefly put, is both the trope of pastiche and a pastiche of tropes, and its most central trope is that of the sly exchange of the literal for the figurative, and hip-hop is its most profound and lively incarnation. I will illustrate this point directly with hip-hop in the chapters that follow, but for now suffice it to say that in this sense, at least, African-American cultures have been producing postmodernisms of their own for centuries.

If postmodernist art can be said to be haunted by a sense of belatedness, a sense of living in the ruins of the abandoned structures of modernism, then it should come as no surprise that African-American art in general—and hip-hop in particular—has come into its own at just this juncture of history. The incipient aesthetic of art constructed from debris has haunted societies at just those points when their brightest dreams have gone down in flames. For many African-Americans in the United States, the disappointment of the political and economic dreams of the civil rights movement of the 1960s, along with the worsening economic situation of the inner cities have combined to bring about a similar sense of life on the edge; for rappers, the ghetto is best evoked by images of Vietnam (for Ice-T, it's "the killing fields," "the home of the bodybag"; for Ice Cube, it's a "Concrete Vietnam"). If Blues is the 'classical' music of African-American culture, and Jazz is its 'modernism,' then hip-hop has a powerful claim to be regarded as their postmodern successor, not so much on account of chronology as on account of what Bakhtin calls "chronotopes"—the linked prismatic synecdoches of cultural history.[29] Hip-hop's central chronotope is the turntable, which Signifies on its ability to 'turn the tables' on previous black traditions, making a future out of fragments from the archive of the past, turning consumption into production. With this mode of turning and re-turning, hip-hop's appropriative art (born of sonic collage and pastiche, reprocessed via digital technology) is the perfect backdrop for an insistent vernacular poetics that both invokes and alters the history of African-American experiences, as well as black music on a global scale.

Yet even as I use this term—"black music"—I encounter the difficult but central question of the terminologies of art and identity. While
I use the term "African-American" where it is appropriate, I also use
the term "black," by which I mean not only African-American peoples
and cultures, but the full continuum of the multiple and interlinked
African diasporic cultures in the Americas, the Caribbean, Africa, and
Europe. Too often, as Paul Gilroy has demonstrated, cultural formations which move across multiple borders are nonetheless treated as
isolated national phenomena. Gilroy has shown, beyond any doubt I
believe, that what he calls the "black Atlantic" is a densely intercon-
nected cultural formation which, despite and in some cases *because* of
discontinuities, continues to mobilize, encode, and transmit cultural
matter—without which, none of its particular diasporic outposts can
be understood. Gilroy does not capitalize "black," and in this way
marks his difference from the kinds of conservative and essentialistic
conceptions of "black" that have formed and fueled some black nationalist movements. Yet I am continually conscious, as I hope my readers
are, that throughout the Americas and Europe, racial inequality and
injustice continues on a massive scale. Having cast off the telltale robes
of *political* apartheid, racism hides behind ostensibly autonomous
formations, such as economics and demographics, the more reprehen-
sible because the more insidious. In such a climate, it is inevitable that
polarizing dichotomies of race will continue to be central, and indeed
the spectacular politics of race, within and against which hip-hop is
struggling, are fundamental to its emergence. Some writers take it for
granted that postmodernist theories, because they proclaim the
erasure or complication of racial dichotomies, seek to evade or grant
dispensation for racist ideology, but on the contrary I see radical postmodernism as a powerful weapon against such ideologies.[30] Radical
postmodernism gives us a third option, neither the essentialized racial
identities cherished by separatists on all sides nor the erasure of difference which is so dear to so-called "liberal" theorists who still dream of
a "melting pot" society, but a concrete "double" and perhaps even
multiple consciousness—the awareness that "white" is no less a construction than "black," and that cultural differences emanate not from
hermetically-sealed universes, but from an insistent and ongoing *mix*.
So while the term "black" designates a very specific cultural
formation, this formation itself exists in a particular kind of historical
bind: culturally speaking, it is highly permeable, and is continually

crossed and recrossed by language, music, and visual arts. Yet on a
social level, as a result of the economic and social structures of racism,
"black" and "white" are rendered impermeable—two different neighborhoods, two different boxes to check on a form, two different spectacularized opponents. The struggle against this ongoing racism
pushes its way up through music, not only because (as Gilroy observes)
music is so central to African diasporic cultures, but because most
other outlets for its mediation or expression have been blocked. Un-
blocking those routes, connecting across racial polarities, is perhaps
the most revolutionary work of hip-hop music and culture; as KRS-
One puts it, "Black and white ain't the real fight, that's the only thing
the media hypes."[31] This move, moreover, is one that must become as
central for "whites" as it has been for "blacks"; perhaps rather than
hoping for an end to the kind of double-consciousness first described
by DuBois, we should be working to spread it around. The central trope
of "white" is, I think, the luxury *not* to think doubly, to see the world
through the one-eyed vistas of privilege, rather than having to account
for one's own identity within and against a fundamentally multiple
culture. Making this latter kind of consciousness not only possible but
necessary may be the only way to re-open the lines of communication
that the economic apartheid of the '80s and '90s has severed; to the
extent that hip-hop (along with Ska, Reggae, and other diasporic
African musics) carries messages across the polarizing lines of racism,
it has the potential to accomplish just that.

Finally, I must account for my own position—or, more accurately,
positions—in relation to both hip-hop and postmodernism. Both
formations have their own protocols for making such an account—hip
hop has its ubiquitous name-, place-, and date-tagging ("Ice Cube,
motherfucker, comin' at cha in the nine-tray"; "South Bronx, South
South Bronx"), and postmodernism has its reflexive self-accounting in
terms of race, gender, class, and sexuality. These modes, whatever their
rhetorical protocols, have a great deal in common; both are highly
contingent, aware of the multiplicity and flux that surrounds any act of
self-accounting, and both recognize themselves as *performative* acts,
acts of self-staging. Yet beyond these stage directions, it's crucial to
account for the material cultural discourses which inform and support
any text, especially in the context of hip-hop culture, which is shaped
both within and against commodity formation. Hip-hop CD's and

university-press books both come from within very specific discourses and places of production, and both (though for different reasons) often express an underlying anxiety about how the pressures of commodification affect their 'product.'

For cultural critics, the exemplary question is that posed by Michel de Certeau in *Heterologies*: "From what position do the historians of popular culture speak? And what object do they constitute as a result of that position?"[32] And again: "The uncertainty about the boundaries of the popular domain, about its homogeneity over against the profound and always reinforced unity of the culture of the elites—does it not signify that the popular domain has yet to exist, because it is impossible for us to speak without annihilating it?"[33] Which is to say that it is rarely, if ever, in the interests of 'insurrectionary knowledges' (such as hip-hop) that the historians or chroniclers of "culture," as constituted by the knowledges of semiotics, anthropology, or literary theory, have spoken. The ultimate interest of these knowledges, which dominate the discursive spheres of academia, is quite frequently not to *preserve* the cultural phenomena that they study, but to (re)constitute these phenomena as the *object* of pre-existing knowledges, or perhaps (at best) of new or modified modes of academic knowledge. Amiri Baraka framed much the same problematic in relation to jazz and white jazz critics when he wrote in 1967 that:

> What had happened [in the 1940s] was that even though the white middle-brow critic had known about Negro music for only about three decades, he was already trying to formalize and finally institutionalize it. It is a hideous idea. The music was already in danger of being forced into that junk pile of admirable objects and data that the West knows as culture.[34]

This difference is particularly significant in the case of hip-hop, for as Jon Michael Spencer has observed, both rappers and scholars partake of a discursive universe where skill at appropriating the fragments of a rapidly-changing world with verbal grace and dexterity is constituted as *knowledge*, and given ultimate value.[35] This parallel emphasis is echoed within rap's own discursive terminologies; a particularly skilled rapper is known as a 'teacha' or a 'professa,' who 'drops knowledge' on the mic and gives her/his opponents 'schoolin.' Yet unlike a college professor, whose competence is underwritten by degrees and certificates, a rapper's competence is constituted primarily by her or his continuing skill at the ongoing practice of rapping; indeed many rappers, such as Sister Souljah, explicitly deride academic expertise: "The experts, the scientists, Ph.D.'s / Souljah pays no homage to a paper degree."[36]

The *knowledge* which rappers draw on is not only their own-day-to-day experience, but also the entire recorded tradition of African-American music (as well as other African, American, and European musics, from Manu Dibango to Kraftwerk to Spandau Ballet to the Incredible Bongo Band)—which it re-reads and Signifies upon through a complex blend of strategies, including samplin', cuttin' (pastiche), and freestylin' (improvisation). Thus, to an even greater extent than has been the case with earlier African-American artforms, hip-hop constitutes *itself* as a knowledge, complete with its own discursive forms, both citing and siting its own tradition(s). For such an established 'cultural movement' as hip-hop, it would be an act of *violence* to appropriate its indigenous knowledges and practices merely in order to annex them to academic modes of knowledge. And nonetheless, that is exactly what much scholarly writing about rap has done; this book itself opposes but cannot entirely escape this problematic.

Thus the question is not: "Of what significance could I (or the ubiquitous academic "we") declare rap to be?," but rather, "What are rap's own modes of signification, intelligibility, and reference?" And how might they constitute a postmodern politics of resistance? These questions cannot be answered without reference to the networks of power/knowledge within which hip-hop circulates, which must include television coverage of the Los Angeles uprising, MTV, the controversies over 2 Live Crew, Ice-T's "Cop Killer," and Snoop Doggy Dogg, the 1994 congressional hearings on gangsta rap, the 5% Nation, and the local hip-hop scenes in New York, Miami, Oakland, Los Angeles, Houston, Detroit, Philadelphia, and other major urban areas. As with other cultural productions, there is no essential inside/outside, only enactments of who or what is "in" or "out". Academics only remain "outside" if they fail to realize that whatever their material privileges and shelf-load of degrees, their planet and the hip-hop planet are one and the same, and if the music doesn't seem to speak to them, perhaps it's because they just haven't been listening. As recent work by scholars such as Houston A Baker Jr., Tricia Rose, Paul Gilroy, and Cornel West amply demonstrates, hip-hop and academia *do* have a great deal to say to one another, particularly within black studies, but also within cultural studies as a whole. Rappers and producers, for their part, have been an increasingly visible and proactive force on college campuses; Public Enemy's Chuck D sets aside a part of each year to travel the college lecture circuit, and rappers such as Sister Souljah, KRS-One, and Queen Latifah have also lectured at major universities. College towns are also primary sites for rap in performance, especially since the mid-'80s wave of paranoia about violence at rap concerts, which closed many major stadium and indoor venues to rap artists.[37] Finally, college radio has supplied the only substantial nationwide airplay for rap music, which except for Los Angeles' now-defunct KDAY and a small number of maverick stations that program a few hours of rap a week, has very little radio exposure outside of New York City.[38]

I hope this book enters into the mix, bringing academics, performers, and all who care about society in a postmodern, post-industrial world together, dropping some knowledge and breaking down some barriers. I hope, too, that it does something to dispel the pernicious notion that rappers are somehow non- or anti-intellectual, or that in describing the crises facing urban America and the world they are somehow glamorizing or advocating the conditions of which they testify. On the academic side, I hope that no one will any longer be able to think of music *or* poetry in the late twentieth century without assigning rappers a primary place, both out of an awareness of the urgency of their message, as well as on account of the tremendous poetic power and variety of their expression. And for rappers themselves, and everyone in the vast and growing hip-hop nation, I hope this book will help make evident the multiple connections between hip-hop's insurrectionary knowledges and the historical and societal forces against which they are posed, and in so doing expand and strengthen the depth of our determination to "fight the powers that be."

Chapter 1

Gettin' Present as an Art:
A Signifyin(g) Hipstory of Hip-hop

R&B disco, pop country jazz
All thought hip-hop was just a fad
But here comes Grandmaster Flash non-stop
And right after Flash, Run DMC drop
Now they had to pay attention to the scale
Where other music failed, hip-hop prevailed
See, rap music has gone platinum from the start
So now in '89 we gettin present as an art . . .

—KRS-One, "Hip-Hop Rules"[1]

Signifyin(g) Histories

Can hip-hop be defined? Or is definition a kind of death, a refusal of the change that any evolving artform must embrace? These questions are particularly urgent for a musical/verbal artform which is as deeply imbricated in the politics of identity, authenticity, and reception as is hip-hop. Whether one sees postmodern culture as marked by the 'free play of signification' or a politicized struggle for meaning in the face of indeterminacy, hip-hop is a paradigmatic instance; at once carnival and contest, it is a cultural crossroads through which everyone passes—whether in a Lexus with the windows rolled up and the a/c on, or in a Jeep loaded with speakers blaring out phat bass lines. For those who have grown up in, or moved into its discursive and social world, there's no need for commentary (Ice-T: "I'm through explaining

25

this shit")—as for everyone else, well, "something is happening here, but you don't know what it is—do you, Mr. Jones?"[2] So what exactly is going on? Certainly, with so many doctas, professas, and teachas 'in the house,' somebody can explain it all?

Hip-hop is all too often conceived of by casual listeners as merely a particular style of music; in one sense they're right, though the question of *style* has far more political significance than they may attribute to it. For others—including many musicians and music fans—it is not music at all, but rather from-the-gut "street" poetry or (as with many of the performers quoted in a recent issue of *Musician* magazine) just so much noisy, mindless boasting. Leaving aside the historical ironies of middle-aged rock-n-roll fans using the same arguments their parents once used about the Rolling Stones (that's not music, it's *noise*), it is clear that hip-hop continues to pose a problem for the old categories of music; it has recently reached the point where country and soft-rock stations make "no rap music" part of their promotional campaigns. Despite the fact that its audiences today are more diverse in terms of race, class, and region than any other music, the reception of hip-hop continues to be a central element in highly polarized arguments about race from both white and black communities.

Before engaging, however, with the postmodern politics of audience, reception, and (sub)culture that hip-hop incites, it is crucial to locate the music (as well as other elements of hip-hop culture such as graffiti, clothing styles, and verbal comedy) in the specific cultural histories within which it, like previous African-American artforms, has emerged. Precisely because the media debates over the "dangers" of rap music ignore these histories, it is crucial that they be recovered, and indeed it is one of hip-hop's own central strategies to re-invoke its own history as well of the history of African-American and black expressive culture in general. Hip-hop's continual citation of the sonic and verbal archives of rhythm and blues, jazz, and funk forms and re-forms the traditions it draws upon, and without specific attention to this process of cultural recycling and production, its central place in the ongoing 'culture wars' cannot be understood. Hip-hop, moreover, draws not only upon African-American traditions, but upon its dense interconnections with black diasporic music, from dancehall to Afro-pop, from soca to UK funk.

It has only been about seventy years since the first commercial recordings of African-American music were issued on the "race" labels of the 1920s. Yet even at that early date, the multiple threads of tradition were already interwoven; field hollers, arhoolies, and spiritual songs had evolved into the blues, New Orleans jazz, and ragtime—and already these traditions were continuing to evolve alongside and against their commercialized doppelgangers, from minstrel shows to vaudeville to Broadway. "Race" records, part of a system of musical apartheid that had its origins in "black" and "white" theater and carnival circuits, at first featured black women vocalists, whose repetoire included not only blues but show tunes. The market for such records grew rapidly, and by the late 1920s (when new electronic recording technology enabled record companies to set up "field units" to travel the country in search of new music), "race" labels had expanded to cover a wide variety of African-American music, ranging from Delta blues to Chicago honky-tonk, from New Orleans jazz to Memphis jug bands.

Thus, early on, African-American traditions were able to draw upon recorded music as one of their key sources of continuity and communication; not only did rural and urban styles cross-influence one another, but the practice of making performances that copied, referred to, or set themselves in variation against previously *recorded* works became widespread. And, just as Henry Louis Gates Jr. has documented with African-American *written* traditions, the vernacular, aural/oral traditions of black music produced and framed these variations through the modes of Signifyin(g).[3] While Gates outlines some quite specific modes within which verbal Signifyin(g) operates—and which I will discuss in detail in chapter 3—it also functioned on a musical level, and it is on this level that the structural variations and styles of African-American music have developed. Simply put, Signifyin(g) is repetition *with a difference*; the same and yet not the same. When, in a jazz riff, a horn player substitutes one arpeggio for another in moving from key to key, or shifts a melody to what would be a harmony note, or "cuts up" a well-known solo by altering its tempo, phrasing, or accents, s/he is Signifyin(g) on all previous versions. When a blues singer, like Blind Willie McTell, "borrows" a cut known as the "Wabash Rag" and re-cuts it as the "Georgia Rag," he is Signifyin(g) on a rival's recording.[4]

Thus, African-American music is fundamentally *at variance* from "Western" music, with its obsession with the precise reproduction of written notation, and indeed *at variance* from itself; when New Orleans jazz evolved into swing, or the hard boppers broke from swing, or the "cool" jazz school drifted away from hard bop, these new forms were Signifyin(g) on their precursors. Within African-American modes of expression, to "break" with the past is itself a tradition; to "cut" or "bite" on one's precursors is to invoke them; to deviate is to remain true. Given this, it is little wonder that the twentieth century has witnessed the Africanization of music on a global scale; what becomes more remarkable, in fact, is the strangely hostile reception many listeners have given rap music. On the one hand, as Amiri Baraka observes, for many white listeners the only good African-American music is a *dead* one; indeed collecting old jazz and blues records and commenting on them has become an old Euro-American tradition.[5] On the other hand, mass culture, dominated though it may be by homogenized and sanitized cultural products, has always embraced exactly what it most feared; in this sense, hip-hop (to Signify on a phrase of Ice Cube's) is "the music ya love ta hate."[6]

To understand the status of hip-hop within its own Signifyin(g) traditions, it is crucial to know the histories of recorded (and performed) African-American musics, since without these histories the musical and verbal texts against which hip-hop music has (re)marked its difference would be obscured, and the double valences and resonances of the Signifyin(g) weave would pass unnoticed. The historical and social significance of Signifyin(g) itself cannot be underestimated; it stands as the principal bridge between two kinds of distinctly African-American stances: on the one hand, a reverential feeling for the past, a sense of ancestral voices; on the other, a deeply agonistic sense of social and verbal rivalry. Gates postulates two separate modes of Signifyin(g) corresponding with these two social functions: "motivated" Signifyin(g), which is parodic and agonistic, and "unmotivated" Signifyin(g), which is empathetic and reverential.[7] Despite the fact that the difference between these two modes is often hazy, the distinction is still worth making, as it offers a model for two different modes of reception, *both* of which are continually at work in the articulation, the (un)-folding, of hip-hop's musical praxis.

Given, then, that Signifyin(g) histories are always already *double*, there would be little point in constructing a linear 'history' of hip-hop; instead, I will set forth a series of historical vectors, which (re)trace the crooked pathways by which the musical and verbal texts of the past (both distant and recent) eventually found themselves embedded in the liquid amber of hip-hop.[8]

1. Tramps

Lowell Fulsom first recorded the song "Tramp" in Los Angeles in 1965–66, and it was released shortly afterwards, reaching number 52 on the pop charts.[9] In his version, the song is a monologue, spoken and sung in the voice of a man who boasts to his lover that, while she may call him a tramp, that he's "a lover" and that "lovin' is all I know to do." Fulsom quotes his absent interlocutor only to brush aside her name-calling, and to undercut her accusations ("Heh...call me country, right from the woods, I'll answer when ya call me") with his assertions of (implied) sexual prowess, adding that he has a "big bankroll" and "three Cadillacs" to boot. Fulsom's monologue itself 'tramps' over the words of an unequal speaker, a woman whose words are quoted only to be implicitly devalued.

Fulsom may have been surprised, in 1967, to hear a cover version of his song cut by Otis Redding and Carla Thomas (then the reigning 'King and Queen,' as the album cover billed them, of Memphis Soul).[10] This version transformed Fulsom's monologue into a *dialogue*, the reported speech into a playful bantering between the sexes. This kind of banter, which at times approached the agonistic extremities of the 'dozens,' was itself hardly new to the African-American tradition. It went back at least as far as 1930, when Lonnie Johnson and Clara Smith cut "You Had Too Much" for the Okeh label.[11] Johnson and Smith engaged in a 'spirited' debate over which one was drunker than the other, each using increasingly vivid figurations of drunkenness in an effort to out-trope the other. To transform the Fulsom monologue into such a playful bantering song may well, for Otis and Carla, have been an instance of 'unmotivated' or empathetic Signifyin(g). Yet to Fulsom, their interpretation 'made fun' of his song, and according to some reports he was far from pleased; from his point of view it was a parody, and a highly 'motivated' one at that.[12]

To engage with the question of who is Signifyin(g) upon whom in these two versions, it may be helpful to compare them in detail:

Fulsom version:

Tramp? You can call me that . . .
I don't wear continental clothes . . .
Stetson hats . . .

[Chorus]   *But I'm a lover…heh heh…mama was…papa too*
                I'm their only child…lovin' is all I know to do.

heh…call me country…right from the woods
I'll answer when ya call me,
heh, baby, that is, if it makes ya feel good.

[Chorus]   *But I'm just a lover…mama was…papa too*
                But I'm their only child. . . lovin' is all I know to do

Now what if ya called me . . .
heh, I'll even go for that.
'Course I keep a fat bankroll in my pocket, baby.
You know I own three Cadillacs . . .

[Chorus]   *'Cause I'm just a lover…*(etc.)[13]

Thomas-Redding version:

[Carla Thomas]   [Otis Redding (sung lines in italics)]

Tramp!

                                  What you call me?

Tramp!

                                  You didn't!

You don't wear continental
clothes or a Stetson hat . . .

                                  But I'll tell you one doggone thing. It
                                  makes me feel good to know one thing…

                                  I know, I'm a lover

It's a matter of opinion, baby

                                  That's alright…Mama was

so?

                                  Papa too!

hmmm.

                                  And I'm their only child,
                                  Lovin' is all I know to do.…

You know what, Otis?

               What?

You're country!

               That's alright!

You're straight from the
Georgia woods!

               That's good!

You know what? You wear overalls!
Them big ole brogan shoes . . .
And you need a haircut, tramp!

               Haircut? Woman, you too
               Oooh, I'm a lover....
               mama was, grandmama, and papa too

Doesn't make you one!

               Oh, that's alright.

               But I'm the only son of a gun
               This side of the school [?]

               Tramp!

That's right, that's what you are!

               baby...brand new hat...[?]

You're a rat and a tramp!

You know what, Otis, I don't care
what you say, you're still a tramp!

               What?

You haven't even got a fat bankroll in your pocket. You probably
haven't even got twenty-five cents!

               I got six Cadillacs, five Lincolns, four
               Fords, six Mercuries, three T-birds,
               Mustangs . . .

> *oooh I'm a lover....*

Prove it by me!

> my mama was...my papa too

What?

> I'm a tell you

Well, tell me!

> *I'm the only son of a gun*
> *This side of the...*so long!

You're a tramp, Otis!

> No!

I don't care what you say, you're
still a tramp!

> Don't call me that!

Looka here, you ain't got no money!

> I got everything!

You can't buy me all those minks
and sables and all that stuff I want!

> I can buy you rat [?], frog[?], squirrel,
> rabbit, anything you want, woman!

Look, you done go outta the Georgia
woods to catch them, baby!

> Oh, but you're ruthless!

You still a tramp! A tramp, Otis,
just a tramp! You wear overalls.
And you need a haircut, baby!
Cut off some o' that hair off your
head!

You think you're a lover, huh?[14]

   In Otis and Carla's version, Carla not only gives voice to the hitherto absent interlocutor, but provides undercutting commentary on

the male singer's claims, commentary which reiterates her doubt as to his sincerity (and, for that matter, his sexual prowess).[15] Carla's commentary fills the rather lengthy (in Fulsom's version, two full bars) pauses between the spoken lines leading up to the chorus. And, while she picks up on many of Fulsom's tropes, she elaborates them and personalizes them through a variety of Signifyin(g) strategies. Fulsom's "Call me country...right from the woods," becomes Thomas's "Otis...you're country, you're straight from the Georgia woods!"; she adds her own details about Otis's shoes, overalls, and need of a haircut. Redding, for his part, offers formulaic defenses ("That's alright") to her accusations, and turns the vocal fervor of the chorus up at each turn; Fulsom's "only son" becomes Redding's "only son of a gun." In the final verse, where Fulsom had boasted of his "three Cadillacs," Redding ups the ante to "Six Cadillacs, five Fords, six Mercuries, three T-birds, Mustangs"—but this doesn't impress Thomas, who rejoins with "I don't care what you say, you still a tramp!"

Thomas and Redding's version thus not only makes Fulsom's monologue into a dialogue, but shifts its weight through Signifyin(g) on its tropes; a male boast becomes the site for a female toast, and Fulsom's hoochie-kootchie man persona is sent packing. His bravura was to suffer still further under the dual assault of women rappers Salt 'n' Pepa in 1987. Salt 'n' Pepa's version samples the Thomas/Redding version with a tape loop of the 'Memphis Horns' chorus, as well as a sample of the single word "tramp!" from the early part of the song. Hip-hop drums and some funky instrumentation are added, along with a (now barely audible) male voice that lingers in the choruses, where it protests "Tha's alright baby, I'll be your tramp, you know what I'm sayin'? Fat rings, thick gold chains, you know what I'm sayin', gold on my *teeth* . . ." But once the intro ends and Salt 'n' Pepa begin their rap, this voice hardly stands a chance; they don't even bother to address him directly. In their version, the song is instead addressed to *women* in the audience:

> Home girls, attention you must pay
> So listen close to what I say!
> Don't take this as a simple rhyme (*Tramp!*)
> 'Cos this type a thing happens all the time.
> Now, what would you do if a stranger said, 'Hi'
> Would you diss 'em, or would you reply?

If you answer, there is a chance
That you'll become a victim of circumstance
Am I right, fellas? Tell the truth
Or else I'mma have to show an' prove
You are what you are, I am what I am
It just so happens, most men are

Tramps!
(male voice, sampled) What you call me?
Tramp!
What you - what you call me?
Tramp!
What - what you- what you call me?
Tramp!

[male voice: "Yeah, I'll be your tramp"]

Have you ever seen a dude that's stupid and rude
Whenever he's around, he dogs your mood
I know a guy like that, girl
He thinks he's God's gift to the world
You know dat kind, excited all the time
Tramp!
With nothing but sex on the mind
I'm no stunt, on me you can't front
I know the real deal, I know what they want
It's me (why?) Because I'm so sexy!
It's me (what?) Don't touch my body!
'Cos you see, I ain't no skeezer
But on a real tip, I think he's a…*Tramp* (etc.)

[male voice: "This is gettin' ridiculous. Don't waste my time!"]

On the first date, he thought I was a dummy
He had the nerve to tell me he loved me
But of course, I knew it was a lie, y'all
He undressed me with his eyeballs
Tryin' to change the whole subject
'Cos everything he said pertained to sex

So I dissed 'im, I said 'Youse a sucka!
Get your dirty mind out the gutter!'
You ain't gettin paid, you ain't knockin' boots
You ain't treatin' me like no prostitute
Then I walked away, he called me a teaser
You're on a mission, kid! Yo! He's a...*Tramp* (etc.)

[male voice: "Now why you gotta be all that, damn! You know
what I'm sayin'? I'm tryin' to talk to you, you tryin' to diss me,
you know what I'm sayin'? Now if I rolled on you, I'd be
wrong, right?"]

Shut up, Tramp![16]

Salt 'n' Pepa Signify upon the Thomas/Redding version by completely fragmenting it, building their rap among its disjointed pieces.
The male voice, dominant in Fulsom and comically punctuated in
Thomas/Redding, is completely marginalized here, appearing only as a
one-dimensional comic foil (a similar technique has been used by
many other women rappers, including Roxanne Shanté and BWP
(Bytches With Problems)).[17] Salt 'n' Pepa switch off voices, but only to
create an open, conversational frame, not to diss each other (though
there is a hint of rivalry in the last verse). The slowed-down, slightly
scratchy Memphis Horns plug in and out at the chorus, ending in a
"wicki wicki" scratch; Carla Thomas's sampled voice breaks in with the
word "Tramp" at various moments during the verses, sometimes joined
by Salt and/or Pepa. If Fulsom's version is monologic, and the Thomas/
Redding cover dialogic, Salt 'n' Pepa's is *heteroglossaic*, two to the
power of (at least) three (including Spinderella, Salt 'n' Pepa's DJ).
Even the samples, which through their familiarity invoke the larger
tradition of African-American music, are anything but what they were.
There is a Signifyin(g) difference between emulation/citation (again,
Gates's *unmotivated* Signifyin(g)) and literal *sampling*, which in its
replication of a ghostly aurality is ever po(i)sed on the edge between
mocking pastiche and reverential invocation of musical ancestors.
    Sampling, then, is not intrinsically either positive or negative—
and, for that matter, the multivalent lines of Signifyin(g) upon African-
American (and other) musical traditions, cannot be readily separated
into "motivated" or "unmotivated" categories in the sense that Gates

uses these terms (indeed, the entire Signifying Monkey paradigm hinges precisely on the inevitable possibility of mistaking one for another). Such "motivation" is to a great extent in the ears of the consumer, not in the turntables of the producer; Lowell Fulsom may think Otis and Carla are mocking his song, and Carla Thomas may or may not appreciate being sampled by Salt 'n' Pepa. Sampling, as EPMD might say, is always "business, never personal"; as an element in a new musical construction, the sampled material, whatever it was, becomes something else, an element in a far more complex discursive structure. Rap has even reached the point where rappers sample other rappers; Chuck D is a particular favorite.

In a sense, the hip-hop practice of "sampling" pre-recorded sounds constitutes its founding gesture: an incursion against the author-function, a midnight raid on what Houston A. Baker Jr. calls "the 'in effect' archive."[18] It also constitutes a reversal of the traditional modes of production and consumption that have fueled the music industry in its exploitation of African-American music. The rap DJ evolved from the party DJ, whose ostensible role was merely to play pre-recorded music for dance parties; like their audiences, these DJs were *consumers* of pop music. Yet by taking these musical sounds, packaged for consumption, and remaking them into new sounds through scratching, cutting, and sampling, what had been consumption was transformed into *production*. Such a cut-and-paste valuation of the hitherto unvalued put hip-hop in a unique relation with commodity capitalism, and concomitantly with cultural production in general. If consumption could be productive, it could never again be regarded as merely passive; at a stroke, hip-hop framed in acutely materialistic terms a question that had hitherto been though merely philosophical. Or perhaps, in a still more revolutionary sense, hip-hop simply made visible (and profitable) a productivity of consumption which had been there all along, albeit in a more diffuse form.

2. Earthquake on Orange Street

The shift from consumption to production can ultimately be traced back to the Afro-Caribbean traditions of Jamaica, which in many ways stands as the link between identifiably African elements and European musical conventions. The question of hip-hop's relation to Afro-Caribbean music has been given too little attention; aside from a chapter in Dick Hebdige's *Cut-n-Mix* and a brief article in the *New York*

Times, most critics have preferred to pursue the roots of rap in funk, soul, and "rhythm and blues."[19] Yet in many ways both the narrative and musical connection between hip-hop and Caribbean musics are the most central to its musical identity. For one, the making of an indigenous music out of materials made ostensibly for *consumption* (records) was certainly practiced in Jamaica long before it reached the South Bronx. Jamaicans, living within listening distance of U.S. radio stations, heard the rhythm-and-blues music of the '40s, '50s and early '60s and liked what they heard. Yet because of their poverty, much of the population had little access to the musical instruments, amplifiers, and other sound equipment necessary to *make* such music on their own. The pioneers of ska took American R&B records, especially instrumentals, and played them over amplified sound systems at parties, mixing in shouts of encouragement to the dancers. Later, when the first recording outfits were set up by sound system men such as Prince Buster, their recordings reflected these heteroglot beginnings; over a chorus of upbeat horns playing a slowed New Orleans-style shuffle, Buster boasted and cajoled, calling out challenges to his rivals on Kingston's music row:

> Man, stand up and fight if you're right!
> Earthquake on Orange Street! [20]

Buster was one of the first sound-system men to go into the recording studio; while the older DJs like Duke Reid still valued imported American R&B singles, Buster and the new generation of producers made their own records, subtly altering the rhythmic emphasis, flattening the jump beat into more of a shuffle, and intermixing the 'burru' rhythms of Rasta drummers like Count Ossie.[21]

The earliest Jamaican-produced records were mostly 'specials'— discs pressed in very small quantities for the exclusive use of the sound-system men who had footed the bill for their recording. It was only later that these records were commercially distributed, mostly through licensing arrangements that enriched the producers (though not necessarily the performers). Yet even as these records moved back from the place of production and were re-marketed for popular consumption, they returned again as sites for production, through the 'talk-over' or dub records that were produced from the late sixties onwards; these records featured b-sides with only the instrumental

tracks, b-sides that could in turn be used as the basis for new recordings, talked-over at system parties or on the radio, or as the soundtrack
by the new school of dub poets such as Linton Kwesi Johnson. And,
while the toasts of the early sound system men had consisted primarily
of topical rhymes or exhortations to the dancers, the lyrics from the
mid-sixties onwards, along with the poetry of the dub poets, voiced
social protest and suffering.[22] By the time ska began to shift over to the
more thoroughly Afro-Caribbean forms of rock-steady and 'reggae,' the
music had become thoroughly identified with the "concrete jungles"
and other impoverished areas of Jamaica, an identification which
singers such as Bob Marley helped create, and used as the basis for
creating a global voice for the disenfranchised in the 1970s.

That much has been widely known, but what is less often noted is
the strong similarity between the rhetorical and narrative conventions
of ska and reggae with those of hip-hop. Of particular significance is
the early "rude boy" style, which glorified the angry, young, tough-
living kids of West Kingston; there are striking similarities, both
cultural and musical, between the 'rude boys' of ska and the 'gangstas'
of hip-hop. A case in point is Prince Buster's well-known series of songs
on the "Judge Dread" theme. Each song contains a courtroom vignette
narrated by Prince Buster as Judge Dread; before him come a number
of 'rude boys' who plead their crimes.[23] In the first of several 'sequel'
songs, when a rude boy brings "a barrister from Europe," Judge Dread
is particularly incensed, dealing out as harsh a sentence to the barrister
as to the defendant; one unlucky rude boy is sentenced to 'four thousand years imprisonment.' The next song in the sequence (all of which
share the same upbeat horn riffs), "Judge Dread Dance," uses the
courtroom drama as the pretext for a new witness, who turns out to be
the horn soloist who plays the dance's theme. Buster finished the series
with his "Barrister Pardon," in which Judge Dread releases the prison-
ers, followed by a celebratory ska dance; there are also a number of
answer records, including Derrick Morgan's "Tougher Than Tough"
(produced by Buster's arch-rival Leslie Kong), and Lee "Scratch"
Perry's "Set Them Free,' in which Perry comes before Judge Dread,
mentions the defendants by name, and makes a lengthy plea for mercy
based on their poverty and lack of education; this record runs out,
however, before the judge can offer a reduced sentence.

Even before the 'rude boy' craze, Prince Buster had injected gangster machismo into his mixes; in one early cut, "Al Capone," Buster

tells his listeners "Don't call me Scarface! My name is Kerpown-C-A-P-O-N-E Kerpown!"[24] As the poverty and oppression of Kingston's slums increased, so did the gangster/rude boy ethos, which eventually laid part of the foundation for Marley's political reggae of the later '60s. Compare all this with the courtroom drama which N.W.A. stages in their now-infamous cut "Fuck tha Police": The courtroom opens with "Judge Dre in full effect," and the various "niggaz" in the court step forth one by one to give their "testimony." Not only is "Dre" an accurate dialect spelling for the Jamaican patois "dread" (final stops are often dropped in the patois), but the rude boys, now gangstaz, have effectively turned the tables; this judge, like Lee Perry, is on their side, and the trial ends with the white cop being dragged off cursing his accusers. I do not mean to suggest here that Dr. Dre took his name or the song from obscure old ska recordings (though he well might have); even the courtroom drama has other analogs in U.S. popular song—but only to observe that the narrative framing of power relations *via* music adapted remarkably similar strategies in both hip-hop and in the early days of ska.[25] Part of this similarity may be due to similar social inequities, but it is also clear that many of the influences at work here came via the Jamaica–New York–Los Angeles connection. U Roy, Big Youth, and other Reggae talkers produced major hits in Jamaica in the early- to mid-'70s, delivering a powerful message with tracks such as U Roy's "Wake the Town" (1970). Kool DJ Herc, one of the pioneering DJs of hip-hop, came to New York from Jamaica, where as a child he had heard and seen the system men.[26] In fact, the Jamaican connection is hip-hop's strongest claim to specifically African roots, since not only the narratives and the basic technology, and the concept of talking *over* recorded music arrive via this route, but also the rhythmic, cut 'n'mix sound that is at the very heart of the hip-hop aesthetic.

Jamaican music continues to be a central influence on hip-hop, particularly through the faster and more insistent "dancehall" sounds that have come to dominate the scene since Marley's death. Some artists, such as KRS-One, used Jamaican-style rhythms in their raps (listen to his chorus, "Wa da da dang, wa da da da dang / Listen to my nine millimeter go bang" on BDP's early cut "Nine Millimeter"); other rappers brought in dancehall collaborators to add some regga flavor up their hip-hop mix. KRS-One himself cut a single with Shabba Ranks, and similar collaborations took place in the early '90s between Queen Latifah and Scringer Ranks, Ice-T and Daddy Nitro, Q-Tip and Tiger, and Patra and Yo-Yo. In the mid-'90s, many hip-hop crews literally *embody* the black Atlantic continuum; groups such as Mad Kap, the Fugees, and the Fu-Schnickens have a dancehall or "ragamuffin" rapper as one of their lead members, and one, "Worl-a-Girl," includes women from Jamaica, the United States, and the United Kingdom. When Patra remakes Lyn Collins' seminal "Think (About It)," or Worl-a-Girl cuts a new version of Prince Buster's "Ten Commandments" (reversing the terms and listing the "ten commandments of 'oman to man" rather than Buster's "ten commandments of man to 'oman"), the cultural phonelines of the black Atlantic are 'ringing off the hook,' and the odds are that this connection will remain open.[27]

3. Sound of the Funky Drummer

One of the deepest veins of ore that hip-hop has mined is the soul/funk tradition, from Junior Parker to Isaac Hayes, and the uncontested Papa-lode of that vein was (and is) James Brown. Yet however prevalent JB samples were in the mid- to late-'80s, back in the days of '79, his brand of hard-working soul filled only one of the many crates DJs hauled from show to show; Grandmaster Flash and Afrika Bambaataa—to name two— took equal delight in cutting up "white" music (Neil Diamond, the Rolling Stones, Simon & Garfunkel, the Pink Panther Theme, Thin Lizzy, the Beatles) as they did in sampling funk or soul tracks. The radio playlists of the '70s, it should be recalled, had not yet fallen under the musical apartheid of "format" radio; it was still possible to hear Stevie Wonder or Miles Davis on a "rock" station—or to hear the Doobie Brothers or Rod Stewart on a "soul" station; in any case, DJs like Bambaataa took pleasure in fooling the crowd, getting them to dance to music they would rarely play on their own.[28]

Nonetheless, James Brown was an early and powerful influence on hip-hop. He had already enjoyed one of the longest careers of any black vocalist, and despite his occasional tendency to ramble, he set the standard for high-energy beats, as well as classic message songs such as "Say It Loud, I'm Black and Proud," and "Funky President." Yet Brown's broadest influence, perhaps, was not his voice, but his band, which at one time or another included Fred Wesley, Bobby Byrd, and Catfish and Bootsy Collins. It was November 20 of 1969 when Brown brought the band into the studio to record what would later be known as "Funky Drummer"—and become the single most-sampled beat in hip-hop. It was one of Brown's last sessions with his old band (within a few months he dropped his veteran sidemen and replaced them with the Collins brothers). Brown's drummer for this session was Clyde Stubblefield, and it was Stubblefield's drum break three-quarters of the way into the seven-minute cut that gave it its name. The distinctive syncopated 4/4 beat of hip-hop is there loud and clear, along with Brown's repeated interjection "Ain't it funky now!"[29]

In the earliest days of hip-hop, DJs would mark off the drum break on a record; with two copies of the same record, it was possible to 'cut' back and forth and produce a continuous rhythm track. Later, "breakbeat" albums were compiled, with longer samples built from tape loops and ample room for cueing them up; digital technology eventually rendered even these compilations obsolete, as even a low-end sampler could grab and repeat four bars of *anything* you could feed it. Digital samples also enabled the slowing down ("shrinking") or speeding up ("stretching") of classic beats; one can now order a compact disc featuring such cuts as "Funky Drummer 110 bpm" or "Stretched President 121 bpm."[30] An astonishing list of the break beats given on one of the earlier DJ compilations is given by David Toop:

> *Super Disco Brakes*, a four-volume set of poorly transferred disco classics mixed with [disco promoter Paul] Winley product, contains tracks like 'Funky Nassau' by West Indian group The Beginning of the End...'Funky Drummer' by James Brown, and other b-boy source material by The Meters, whose New Orleans fatback funk was one of the main roots of hip-hop beats, Creative Source (disguised as Creative Service), the JB's, and The Blackbyrds. Some of the major breaks records are included—Magic Disco Machine's 'Scratchin',' Dennis Coffey's 'Scorpio,' Captain Sky's 'Super Sperm' and Bob James's 'Mardi Gras.' There are two African tracks , 'Soul Makossa' (Winley was the first to jump on the New York craze for Manu Dibango's Cameroon Afro Quelque Chose) and Easy Dancin' by Wagadu-Go (reputed to be the Nigerian highlife star Prince Nico). Grouped together on volume three are Gil Scott-Heron's disco hit 'In The Bottle,' a track from Lightnin' Rod's *Hustler's Convention* (basically a Last Poets record, but credited to Alan Douglas on *Disco Brakes*), and the legendary 'Apache.'[31]

This bizarre smorgasbord of pirated, misattributed, and recompiled tracks (assembled, appropriately enough, by one "DJ Jolly Rogers") was

only one attempt to appeal to the rapidly-changing and highly compet-
itive DJ market for breakbeats to slap on for a hip-hop party. Hip-hop
had begun its raids on the musical *archive* of the past, and for the time
being music licensing organizations weren't paying much attention.

Since the era of this particular compilation, rap DJs have continued their raids not only on African-American musical traditions, but on
every form of discourse, ranging from newscasts, talk-shows, movie
dialogue, sound effects, television themes, and answering-machine
messages. Yet beyond what might be merely a fragmentary citation or
duplication of these "samples," the hip-hop culture has Signified upon
them, rearranging them to produce a new art, what might in itself be
called a *transvaluative* art. A drum break, only enough to fill a measure
or two in the "source," becomes reconstituted as an entire seven-
minute rhythm track; a scream, a howl, or an electric-guitar twang
becomes a rhythmic accent on the second or fourth beats of a four-beat
measure (James Brown's shout in Public Enemy's "Fight the Power";
Jimi Hendrix's wailing guitar in digital underground's "The Way We
Swing"). "Scratchin" the pre-recorded sound, originally done on a
turntable by the DJ, is now done electronically as well, taking a horn riff
and turning it into a howl of percussive sound, a grinding back-n-forth
beat. Single words, excerpted digitally from speech, can be assigned to
keys on an electronic keyboard; one rap producer programmed all
eighty-eight keys with different intonations and voicings of the word
"bitch," creating in effect a new verbal-electronic instrument.

The double-edge of sampling can be most clearly seen at play in
rap cuts where spoken-word samples are employed. Malcolm X, Martin
Luther King, Huey Newton, and Dick Gregory are among the positive
African-American voices heard in rap, most often in introductions, but
often throughout songs as a chorus or rhythmic accent. This is not a
new practice by any means; from the earliest days of commercial
recordings of African-American spiritual music, such as the Reverend
J.M. Gates' "Death's Black Train is Coming" (1926), it was a common
format to issue "sermon" recordings in which a sermon or monologue
was framed within two choruses of sacred song.[32] A similar format
appeared around the same time in "hokum" blues, which used double-
entendres ("You Can Play With My Pussy, but Please Don't Dog It
Around") and comic dialogue to build an exaggerated sexual narrative.[33] Typical examples are Big Bill Broonzy's "Terrible Operation
Blues," which frames a staged "operation" ("Doctor, doctor, what's

that?" "Oh, don't you worry, that's just a doctor's *tool*," etc.) with a musical chorus, or the comic interludes of duos such as Butterbeans and Susie or Harris and Harris, who often did 'guest' appearances on blues recordings.[34]

This chorus–spoken word–chorus format carried over, as David Toop notes, into the 'love raps' so common in '60s and early '70s soul, such as Laura Lee's "Guess Who I Saw Today?," Irma Thomas's "Coming from Behind," and on into Barbara Mason's "Another Man" (c.1983).[35] At the same time, inspirational spoken (not rapped) messages on political and personal issues continued to play a part in Black music; among the best known are James Brown's "King Heroin," "Public Enemy #1," and "Rapp Payback (Where iz Moses?)," but there were numerous other recordings of a similar kind, ranging from Isaac Hayes's mixtures of soul-lover and tough-guy to Lou Rawls's 'Dead End Street.'

The first generation of 'old school' rappers, rather than sample earlier spoken word recordings, preferred to cut up drum breaks and melodic riffs, though an occasional James Brown "aaaw" found its way into the mix. It was not until rap's productive series of changes in the mid-'80s—aided by new digital sampling technology—that *samples* of spoken materials became common. Most of these were fairly straightforward, rarely consisting of more than a few words, such as Bobby Byrd's ubiquitous "I'm Comin'." In part, this was due to DJ's preference for short, percussive sounds, in part due to the limits of technology; aside from mixing in tape or vinyl, digital samplers capable of storing more than a few seconds of music were not readily available until the mid-'80s. Afrika Bambaataa claims that a record he cut with Soul Sonic Force in 1983, "Looking for the Perfect Beat," was the first record to use digital sampling.[36]

Yet another crucial breakthrough in terms of what sampling could do to the hip-hop mix came in 1983, when former Sugar Hill house drummer Keith LeBlanc cut snippets from speeches of Malcolm X and produced the track "No Sell Out."[37] While some were outraged that "Minister Malcolm's" words would be sonically mingling with hedonistic dance music, there were many who realized the political potential of such a technique; fortunately, Dr. Betty Shabazz, Malcolm's widow, was among them, and the recordings received her seal of approval.[38] Before long, samples from Malcolm X, Martin Luther King, Jr., Stokely Carmichael, and other black leaders became hip-hop commonplaces, even spreading into late-'80s techno dance mixes.[39]

Such samples soon became a straightforward way to signal political awareness; the tone and context into which these samples were inserted tended to reflect their content; the Signifyin(g) mode here was generally "unmotivated" and respectful.

Of course rap also Signifies in a fairly unambiguously *motivated* way by sampling everyone from Hitler to George Bush; with the proper tape loops and edits, it is relatively easy to render anyone's words ridiculous (though it certainly helps if they are worthy of ridicule beforehand) . The industrial-rap group Consolidated, for instance, samples George Bush and cuts his voice in with that of a newscaster, producing sentences such as "Every morning, I receive an intelligence briefing from THE KNIGHTS OF THE KU KLUX KLAN" along with "I don't...I don't...I don't care what the facts are."[40] Similar samples have been used by other political rappers, such as Laquan; the rapper Paris even went so far as to alter a sample of George Bush, changing "our outrage against Iraq" to "our outrage against the poor" in order to make explicit Bush's attitude towards urban Americans.[41] Thus, samples have the capacity to strengthen and consolidate a tradition (as when rappers sample identifiable fragments of cuts from James Brown, Isaac Hayes, Otis Redding, or the Last Poets), but also to mark the profound *alienation* of the voice from its "original" speaker(s) and interlocutor(s), making an art of taking things out of one context and inserting them in another.

The effect, for instance, of a sample from *either* Hitler or Martin Luther King (Shazzy, in her "Intro" cut to *Attitude: A Hip-Hop Rapsody*, samples *both*) is going to be vastly different on listeners who were born long after the '60s, still longer after the '40s; the historical contexts which made both voices intelligible are absent, and many of these listeners may be unable to readily supply them.[42] When I play a rap by Paris in a classroom, for instance, with the sample, ""Stick 'em up, motherfucker, we've come for what's ours," most of my students (born well after the glory days of the Black Panther Movement) have no idea who is speaking. Without prompting, some think it is the rapper himself; others say "it must be from some movie" (popular choices include *Lethal Weapon* and *Boyz N The Hood*). Fortunately for them, Paris has filled the liner notes to this recording with biographical and historical articles on the Panther movement (though of course no one is compelled to read them, and they are thus absent from many actual listening situations (parties, clubs, and [if it were possible] radio).

Thus, even when it can be said that a verbal sample is being inserted into a recording in a profoundly 'unmotivated' way, there is no way to guarantee that all the record's potential listeners will receive it in an empathetic manner. Empathy, after all, requires knowledge; when I play a hardcore political rap for my students, most of them feel threatened, as many of them are unsure exactly who Paris is threatening when he says he'll bust "Fat Tom's" cap with a tech-9 (both African-American idiomatic phrases such as 'bust a cap' (= blow someone's head off) and brand names of semi-automatic weaponry such as 'tech 9' are obscure to many of them).[43] Through the noise, both the music and the heteroglossaic din of rap language, many people don't get the message at all; like listeners sampled on Ice Cube's *The Predator*, they react simply to the anger: "I'm scared!" "I think we hear…violence."[44]

4. Adventures on the Wheels of Steel

When pressed to name the "first" hip-hop recording, most people who know something about 'old school' music will name the Sugar Hill Gang's "Rapper's Delight," which was released in 1979. There are numerous variations on the story of how Sylvia Robinson rounded up (or created) the Sugar Hill Gang: that she picked them up off the streets, that she hired someone she heard rapping at a pizza parlor, that their rhymes were all borrowed from Grandmaster Caz, that in fact the Fatback Band's "King Tim III" was *really* the first hip-hop record, and so forth; true or not, these anecdotes have long been part of hip-hop mythology. Yet what most listeners don't realize is that "Rapper's Delight" is not a hip-hop record at all, but a rapping novelty single. As David Toop puts it, "Rapper's Delight" was a sort of "translation"—or, more precisely, a *crib*—of hip-hop. There were rhymes, sure, and a disco backup track, but the most crucial elements of hip-hop practice—turntable scratches and cuts from record to record, audience call-and-response, breakneck battles on the mic—were all absent.

Hip-hop's remaking of consumption as production was the first thing lost in this translation; despite its appropriation of Caz's rhymes, "Rapper's Delight" was first and foremost a *thing* to be consumed, not a *practice* in action; its relation to hip-hop actuality was like that of a "Live Aid" t-shirt to a concert: a souvenir, a metonymic token. Hip-hop was something goin' down at 23 Park, 63 Park, or the Back Door on 169th Street; you could no more make a hip-hop record in 1979 than you could make a "basketball game" record or a "subway ride" record. As a vernacular practice, hip-hop depended on its audiences, its sites, and its technologies to construct a zone of sonic and cultural bricolage which was produced as much by the dancers or listeners as by MCs or DJs; no two jams were the same, and such unpredictability was built into its antagonistic aesthetic. At best, a record could offer a *trace* of one or another jam—as did the tapes Grandmaster Flash used to sell for a dollar a minute—at its worst, as with the Sugar Hill Gang, it was a Disneyland simulacron, a robotic hip-hop recreation.

Nonetheless, despite the lack of connection between the Sugar Hill sound and that of the street, it was an influential recording, even at street jams; whatever had happened before was now haunted by the knowledge that its imitation could be sold for big bucks.[45] "Authenticity" as constructed by the b-boys and b-girls was decentered by the acts of mass consumption that received "Rapper's Delight" *as* hip-hop. The problem, as Walter Benjamin puts it, is that "technical reproduction can put a copy of the original into a situation which would be out of reach for the original itself"; in such a situation, questions of "authenticity" turn into a struggle between the contexts and cultures of the producers (both the street DJs *and* Sylvia Robinson) and those of consumers (both the South Bronx breakdancers and club-hopping disco fans).[46] The *reproducibility* of the record radically increases the probability that it will be (mis)taken as an accurate sample of the productive culture as a whole, since it can now be consumed far outside of its indigenous sites of production.

In the case of "Rapper's Delight," despite the fact that all the established DJs and MCs knew how distant its sound was from what they themselves produced, they imitated it anyway; the "Sugar Hill sound," built around elaborately remixed multi-track masters pre-selected by Sylvia herself and watering down the strong language of street boasts into "party time" inanities, became *the* sound of hip-hop on record well into 1982. Hip-hop in the parks and clubs went on as before, though now alongside new, larger venues whose patrons were a mix of b-boys and punks, but when it was time to go into the studio, there was *that* sound again. Sylvia even had the nerve to take Grandmaster Flash, whose cutting and scratching skills were the stuff of legend, into the studio and *assign* him a twenty-four-track master tape to use as the basis of his first Sugar Hill single.[47] Even when a few of the better-known DJs established the use of scratching in studio sessions, the overall backing track was still a homogenized studio tape. It wasn't until 1982 that DJs like Flash and Bambaataa really got a chance to prove their capabilities in a studio, and the results were the first tremors of the earthquake that would eventually render the "Sugar Hill sound" obsolete.

Finding a way to put hip-hop's indigenous modes of production onto the very vinyl that it founded itself on cutting into pieces was no small task, but if anyone could do it, it was Grandmaster Flash. "Adventures on the Wheels of Steel" was Flash's record, a DJ record (since most of the rapping on it was cut by Flash from earlier records). Flash took no fewer than six instrumental cuts to use as his breakbeats, and every one of them he brought into the mix from a turntable instead of a twenty-four-track master. Dropping the needle down on Chic's "Good Times" or the Sugar Hill Gang's "8th Wonder," he immediately lifted, dropped, and lifted again without missing a beat. Namechecks were provided by cuts from his own earlier records (the Furious Five's "Birthday Party"), Blondie's "Rapture," and an old radio sign-on for "The Official Adventures of Flash" [Gordon].[48] Cowboy provided his signature "Say ho, ho!" call-and-response, and in an inspired moment, Flash cut in a snippet from what sounds like a fairy tale record: "Why don't you tell me a story?" pleads a child's voice; "Well, it went pretty much like this," answers a male voice in a condescending tone; in an instant Flash breaks in with a blast of nine heavy percussive scratches that tear up the audio fabric and kick into yet another perfectly timed backbeat. "Adventures" was more than a sonic bricolage, it was a tactical neural implant, a short circuit in the inner wiring of the music industry, a tone-poem to chaos that brought the street back into the studio.

The impact of "Adventures" was immediate and sent everyone in the business back to the drawing boards. What Sylvia Robinson and her peers had never understood, Flash had realized and put into practice: hip-hop was not able to *record* itself until it could sample its own previously recorded selves, until the audience for *records* knew as well as the club crowds the precise *situatedness* of each of its outbursts. The doubleness implicit when Flash or Bambaataa cut up an old Bob James or James Brown track was lost when, in the studio, these aural recyclings were replaced by the spiffy, polished-chrome sounds of disco. Bambaataa took his listeners back to school via a slightly different path; he worked *within* the multi-track environment, but remade it to his specifications. Using keyboards to move bass lines and beats from Kraftwerk or Queen into the mix, he added a multi-layered *vertical* bricolage: electronic game noises, chants, sound effects, and scratches piled one atop the other, creating a funky, raw yet polished sound that would later be known as "electro-funk"; "Planet Rock," which hit big in 1982, was his founding gesture.[49] Whether through a return to "street" rawness or a re-appropriation of such formerly inaccessible technologies as multi-track tape and digital samplers (often through *both*) hip-hop was on the verge of the first of many cycles of collapse and re-invention, which was also—inevitably—a central moment in ongoing anxieties about authenticity, consumption, and a broader listening audience.

5. Just Living in the City is a Serious Task

Despite a tradition of social commentary that stretched back to the Last Poets and earlier, despite the hard-hitting cuts such as Brother D's "How We Gonna Make the Black Nation Rise," Flash's "The Message," or Run DMC's "It's Like That," most hip-hop in the early- to mid-'80s was not outwardly political; while many groups cut a "message" rap or two, few if any were looking to make a career of them. Yet the worsening situation in the inner cities, aggravated by Reagnomic cuts in urban aid, with the concomitant increase in both affluence and arrogance among the moneyed classes, added a new element of urgency to hip-hop. Performers such as Run DMC and LL Cool J made their claims to fame on stripped-down breakbeats with rock guitar accents that appealed to a large, multiracial audience that bridged the growing social rift; as one of the few artforms to do so, its capacity to communicate the sense of crisis was unparalleled. Yet on the west coast, while the necessary elements were certainly present, there was as yet no performer or group capable of serving as the catalyst for these raw energies.

The initial rumblings were there, nonetheless; like many earthquakes, this one was first felt in Los Angeles. L.A., as sociologist Mike Davis has documented, had been a magnet for blacks and Latinos seeking well-paying industrial jobs in the postwar boom years; as those jobs vanished, it was rapidly becoming a city of dreams deferred.[50] Seeing the landscape of South Central in a film like John Singleton's *Boyz N the Hood*, it is not hard to turn back time a bit; the modest, stuccoed bungalows whose doors and windows are now covered with iron bars would have had a fresh coat of rosy paint, flowerboxes in the window, maybe a new Frigidaire whirring away in the kitchen. The long slide from working-class community to ghetto was greased with effectively racist seniority systems, corporate relocations overseas, white flight to outlying areas, and (eventually) bank and insurance company red-lining. The kids who grew up in South Central in the '80s looked out over a horizon of possibilities that was framed by police barricades; the L.A.P.D. was one of the most openly racist police departments in the nation, with an unmatched record of beatings, shootings, overzealous raids, and harassment.

Early west coast rap, like the east coast hip-hop scene it started out imitating, was upbeat, funky, and fun; most of its rhymes were as hedonistic and unapologetic as a busload of Valley Girls.[51] A few early message raps, such as Captain Rapp's "Bad Times (I Can't Stand It)," notable for the sheer number of issues it crams into six minutes (beatings, robbery, unemployment, nuclear waste, nuclear war, El Salvador, AIDS, and drugs among them), made some waves, but if anything the scene was more commercialized, more above-ground than anything a self-respecting South Bronx b-boy would be impressed by.[52] Yet the worsening economic situation, combined with political frustration at Reagan's re-election, took its toll, as did the reign of L.A.P.D. Chief Daryl Gates, who was everything his predecessors were only more so; Gates's boys were known to bust ass, and got so excited during one raid that they trashed an entire building, spraying "L.A.P.D. rules" on the walls.[53] Slowly, surely, west coast rappers began to see hip-hop as a medium through which to bring a sense of resistance and power to their communities. In 1985, Toddy Tee came out with his cut, "Batterram," which dramatized the arbitrary use of a powerful battering ram designed to cave in reinforced steel doors on supposed drug dealers' houses; that same year the Future MC's "Beverly Hills Cop" and Kid Frost's "Terminator" hit the streets. These latter two cuts, despite their titles' rather bald attempt to cash in on current hit films, were filled with vignettes of social commentary in a style reminiscent of Flash's "The Message"; the list of grievances was being aired, but as yet the manifestos were unwritten.[54]

The political messages of these cuts notwithstanding, their sound and production values were still pretty much old school, flavored with a west coast proclivity towards electronic funk; their lyrical urgency was undercut by their musical predictability. Yet at that very moment, east coast old school hip-hop was about to be overthrown; at the head of the new school were artists united in their desire to replace techno-excess with a stripped-down sound closer to the beat of the streets. When Jam Master Jay cut up Bob James's "Mardi Gras" on Run DMC's "Peter Piper," he wasn't doing anything Flash or Bambaataa hadn't done before—but he was doing it *on a record*, and that made it revolutionary. Similarly, kids with LL Cool J's bag of egotistical tricks (if not his lyrical skills) were rapping at every house party, but for LL to make it to vinyl with no more accompaniment than a drum machine, a snip of rock guitar, and a couple of cowbells was something never heard before. Hip-hop's subtractive mathematics of style had never been so fully put into effect; it didn't take long for perceptive west coast ears to pick up the frequency. By 1986, Ice-T had thrown out the "cold wind" sound effects and was cranking out "6 in the Morning" over a raw, solo beatbox:

> Six in the mornin', police at my door
> Fresh Addidas squeak across my bedroom floor
> Out the back window I made my escape
> Didn't even have a chance to grab my old school tape[55]

Ice-T wasn't the only one who left his old tapes behind; by 1986, almost all of the first generation of hip-hop had seen their stars fade. Melle Mell went back to small-time theft; the "Basketball" court emptied out as Kurtis Blow deflated overnight; even Dick Gregory's wholefood diet couldn't save the Fat Boys from taking the express train to oblivion.

The hungry young rappers and DJs who took their place wanted a harder beat with more bass but no synth; rock guitars gave it an edge, and sirens, screeching tires, and fast-paced dialogue gave it a street-theater soundtrack. For some groups, the change was so fast as to make for unexpected ironies. On the jacket of one of its singles, the World Class Wreckin' Cru had thanked the L.A.P.D. for providing security at its concert; by 1987 its refugees (among them Dr. Dre and DJ Yella) were at the center of a loose collective known as Niggaz wit' Attitudes; within a year they would be cutting "Fuck the Police." Meanwhile back east, LL was rapping over his own siren samples, "Bigger and Deffer," while the Beasties were making their tongue-in-cheek punk-hop collages; in the wings, Chuck D and Flavor Flav were in the studio with Hank Shocklee and Eric "Vietnam" Sadler, who were about to make a sound 'louder than a bomb.' Within the brief span of two or three years, hip-hop had gone from being party music with PSA add-ons to an angry, minimalist-with-a-vengeance rhythm of revolution; the change was so sudden that at least one fan was heard to protest that Public Enemy wasn't hip-hop at all, but "black punk rock."

And so it was, but with this difference: it was no longer at the edge but at the *center* of hip-hop culture and attitude; whereas before music critics went to some lengths to remind listeners that there was a serious message in that stuff they were dancing to, they now had to go out of their way to explain that "rap music" (as it was still frequently referred to in the press) was not *only* the music of angry, political, polemical poets and gat-toting gangstas with an attitude. Of course hip-hop had been both all along—and *more*—though in the media theater of the Spectacle you are only allowed one costume change a year. Despite that, the tables were turned, even as the broader audience generated by acts like Run DMC and LL Cool J was hooked; this was audience participation night, and as Ice-T once rapped, "I'm not runnin' from ya, I'm runnin' at cha!"

The soundtrack that emerged from the implosion of the old school had many forms; like the range between Flash's back-to-the-street basics and Bambaataa's multi-track techno extravaganzas, LL's minimalism and the Bomb Squad's infamous "bring the noise" squall were not opposites but complementary parts of a music that had made art out of cultural detritus. The message, too, had its range, from the raw resentment of "Fuck the Police," through the tactical ambivalence of Chuck D's poetic riddles, to the laid-back didacticism of Salt 'n' Pepa's "Let's Talk About Sex." It may seem odd that hip-hop's turn towards a more politicized, uncompromising ethos ended up *broadening* its audience—but no more odd, perhaps, than the fact that the Sex Pistols' uncompromising nihilism and anti-commercialism turned out a smashing commercial success. Somewhere deep down in the ethos of bourgeois culture there is an insatiable thirst for the different, the dangerous, and the dislocated, and hip-hop located that nerve. Whereas most American kids were utterly oblivious to the class politics of British punk, they could not miss the racial politics of rap's messages. To the tensions on every side in the '80s, hip-hop gave an insistent and uncompromising voice.

One of the least compromising of these voices undoubtedly belongs to Boogie Down Productions leader KRS-One. Give some early-'80s hip-hop like Whodini's "Friends," the Boogie Boys' "Fly Girl," or 2 Live Crew's "2 Live" a spin; over bleepy beats and synth, the rapper's words slide along like Luther Vandross over silk sheets. Then someone hands you an obscure tape from Rock Candy records, and you say "What the heck?" and cue it up: the track begins with the sound of clashing metal reverberating in a skeletal, irregular beat, calling to mind Einstürzende Neubaten's "Stahlversion" (which consists entirely of sledge hammer blows to a metal bridge). A few moments later, however, fractured scales emanate from a dislocated portable organ, while the pounding intensifies. Is this the soundtrack to a Satanic thriller? A recording of a music-therapy session in a mental hospital? Suddenly, without warning, the beat arrives, and a percussive chant superimposes itself on the sonic chaos: "Because we've got to advance, we've got to advance / 'cos nothin' in our lives ever happened by chance..." It's the underground, the raw ghetto sound, it's one of Boogie Down Productions earliest recordings, a verbal-sonic collage instigated by the "Grand Incredible Scott La Rock" and the no less incredible KRS-One (Kris Parker).[56] The BDP sound broke over the South Bronx in '86 like a sonic boom. Nuclear war, despair, information overload—as KRS says, "we have elevated far beyond the Rapper's Delight."[57] BDP brought back knowledge raps with a gangsta edge, rolling over fun-and-games rappers like a bulldozer over a playground.

Despite the shooting death of Scott La Rock, KRS-One carried on; his second recording, *By All Means Necessary*, featured a cover photo that did photographically what Keith LeBlanc had done sonically; with an uzi in his hand, KRS peered out through the curtains in a retake of the famous photo of Malcolm at the time when his house was fire-bombed. KRS was soon regarded as the premier political rapper on the east coast; by 1989 he sat at the head of a growing BDP empire (posse members Ms. Melodie, Harmony, and D-Nice were all at work on solo projects), and took seriously his role as hip-hop historian and authenticity sound-check:

> I've come to show a different look
> And that look is the whole of rap
> Not just the commercial pap
> But the underground, that raw ghetto sound

From which rap music was found
So you can't deny it, you cannot refute it
I be rockin' that ghetto music

—KRS-One, from "Ghetto Music," by BDP[58]

As always, KRS raps this message over a relatively simple machine-generated drumbeat and handclaps. In the gospel according to Parker, while hip-hop has both commercial and "underground" sounds, it is fundamentally "ghetto music," "raw" (as opposed, he implies, to more "cooked" commercial rap). Rap music, in this sense, was not so much *founded* as *found* (a claim strikingly similar to that made by the medieval troubadours and trouvères, whose name means "those who find"); it is "found" in the ghetto, and its sounds, as well, are "found" via a combination of electronically generated sounds and samples from earlier (predominantly African-American) musical traditions. Because it is "founded" on the experience of the ghetto, it cannot be "refuted," and will not be "denied"; like many other rappers, Parker sets forth an ironically constructivist definition of rap's "authenticity," a standard of ghetto aesthetics that echoes Ice-T's "ear to the street" test of authenticity.

Conclusion

From these fragmentary and multiple tangents, several things are clear: (1) That the fundamental practice of hip-hop is one of *citation*, of the relentless sampling of sonic and verbal archives; (2) That the distinction between "consumption" and "production" is rendered untenable, with profound implications for questions of audience and authenticity; (3) That hip-hop's inventions and re-inventions insist on their *situatedness* within a long and complex musical continuum. Hip-hop *sites* itself as a product of African-American urban cultures at the same time it *cites* the sonic past in order to construct a radical present. This present, like the past(s) of which it is constructed, resists by its very temporal liquidity the pressures of commodification (Ice Cube: "can't bury rap like you buried jazz").[59] It is musical, kinetic, sartorial, and verbal style; it is process as well as product ; Ice-T plays upon the notion of "product" (drugs) in his cut "I'm Your Pusher"—only now the 'product' is the music.[60] It is also firmly localized, whether in broad categories such as "new school" or "old school" rap, posses such as

Native Tongues, the Juice Crew, Boogie Down Productions, or the Flavor Unit, or in the numerous hip-hop *sitations* of the [neighbor]-hood (e.g., BDP's "South Bronx, South South Bronx" and N.W.A.'s "Straight Outta Compton"). Finally, hip-hop's coherence and continuity are a result of its practice of its improvisations upon language itself, which form the verbal corollary of musical samples, repeating *with a difference*, troping dopes, and serving as a crucible for reformation and *de*formation of language. This verbal Signifyin(g) is not, in the end, fully separable from the sonic Signifyin(g) out of which it grew, but its practices constitute the fundamental backbone of hip-hop's political incursions; as a rapper who's about to cap another shouts, "It's time to get some schoolin'!"

Chapter 2

Postmodernity and the Hip-hop Vernacular

This vernacular of mine joined together my parents, since they spoke to each other in it…for this reason it is clear that my vernacular had a part in my generation, and so was one of the causes of my coming into being.

—Dante Alighieri, *De Vulgari Eloquentia*[1]

The "vernacular" in relation to human beings signals "a slave born on his master's estate." In expressive terms, the vernacular indicates "arts native or peculiar to a particular country or locale." The material condition of slavery in the United States and the rhythms of Afro-American blues combined and emerged from my revised materialistic perspective as an ancestral matrix that has produced a forceful and indigenous American creativity.

—Houston A. Baker,
Blues, Ideology, and Afro-American Literature[2]

It's my vernacular that's simply spectacular.

—Saddat X, "Ragtime"

1. One or many vernaculars

Despite all the preceding analysis of hip-hop music and its development, the questions asked at the outset remain only partially answered. What is hip-hop's relationship to or among black vernaculars? Just what exactly is a vernacular, anyway? Is there even a coherent linguistic situation that can be referred to as *vernacular* despite differences of race, class, and historical circumstance? Such a proposition seems hardly defensible at first, and yet there is an uncanny resonance between the situation of the late Troubadours' Provençal, Dante's Italian, the bluesmen idealized by Baker, and Saddat X—all are poets in a language without a nation, or rather, with a nation that exists outside of or against a nation, a culture whose condition is that of exile, wandering, and resistance to a dominant power.[3] Within these counter-nations, the vernacular functioned for its speakers as a badge of identity, a tongue inseparable from their histories, a language that in its speaking called them together as a nation, whether via Dante's construction of a courtly Italian at a time when there was not yet an Italian court, or through George Clinton's aural invocation of "One Nation under a Groove" as an oppositional and potentially transnational black nation.

Still, the history of vernacular speech has been bound up since Dante's time in the history of nation-states, and indeed once there *was* an Italy as a political unity, the texts of Dante, Petrarch, and Boccacio were called upon to serve as the foundation for Italian culture. This process continued throughout Europe, with each emergent nation staking its own claim on its "native" tongue, often as not accompanied by campaigns of violence against those who, while within the "borders" of the state, did *not* speak the new official tongue. This violence continued, inevitably, with the project of colonialism, in which the colonizing languages were used as instruments of cultural erasure and appropriation: taught in the schools and instituted in the courts, children beaten for not speaking it, its knowledge and use demanded as a condition for access to positions of power. Even within these new national languages, differences in syntax and pronunciation underwrote class difference; there was no one English, but many Englishes, each of which kept a certain region or class "in its place."

Thus, for the past seven centuries at least, "native" European languages have been instruments of nationalism and colonialism, languages of domination, which although still vernacular in the sense that they were languages learned from infancy by the populations of European nations, were everywhere marked and regulated in the service of power, no longer languages of household slaves (for as Baker reminds us, vernacular comes from *vernaculus*, a slave born in his/her master's house) but languages of mastery. In a very important sense, these languages, particularly in their standardized written forms, are no longer vernaculars at all; the tongues of the former "barbarians" are now the tongues of imperialism. And, among those whose labor or lands have been exploited in the name of Empire, a multitude of languages, a global heteroglossia within which the words of the colonizers and those of the colonized are intermingled and transformed into new kinds of vernaculars.

Yet this heteroglossaic space is not merely or mainly "diverse" (in the sense that "diversity" is often invoked as a happy celebration of difference), but a matter of contending voices, contending forces; it is an arena for an ongoing struggle between colonizers and colonized. As Marlene Nourbese Philip puts it,

> In the vortex of New World slavery, the African forged new and different words, developed strategies to impress her experience on the language. The formal standard language was subverted, turned upside down, inside out, and sometimes erased. Nouns became strangers to verbs and vice versa; tonal accentuation took the place of several words at a time; rhythms held sway. Many of these 'techniques' are rooted in African languages...the havoc that the African wreaked upon the English language is, in fact, the metaphorical equivalent that coming to the New World represented for the African.[4]

Although Philip is primarily describing the situation in the Caribbean, her claims apply equally to the linguistic histories of North America, for while black vernaculars in the United States are perhaps less strongly marked by elements of African syntax or accentuation, they are if anything *more* marked by the continual struggle over appropriation and reappropriation.

Whatever, then, the elements of variance in a given vernacular, there are clearly two general classes of vernacular languages, classes whose difference is both a product and a producer of the postcolonial experience. On the one hand there are hegemonic vernaculars, such as "Received Standard English" (the term that postcolonial critics use to highlight the arbitrary status of the privileged "standard" dialect of English); posed against them, appropriating and subverting their claims to "standardness," are what I would call *resistance vernaculars*, since even to speak these vernaculars is in a crucial sense to make inroads against the established power-lines of speech. Hegemonic vernaculars were appropriated early on by the emerging European nation-states, and constructing and enforcing their "standardness" has has been a central nationalistic project at least since the early modern period. Like Dante's "noble Latian vernacular," these privileged dialects were based on forms common to regional variants of the "mother" tongue, and sought to replace internal differences with standard constructions and vocabularies. In so doing, they secured the fiction of the "unified" state, not only through making this language the "official" one for state documents, but also through the canonization of national literatures and "great" writers.

More recently, the nineteenth century saw in the United States a vastly expanding educational apparatus, both via free public elementary education and the establishment of land-grant and other public universities. In both these areas, the "standard" dialect was reinforced, and its mastery became the pass-key to housing, employment, and "respectability." The codes of this new "standard" marked and enforced the divide between rich and poor, black and white, immigrant and "native," urban and rural. More recently, through radio and television, the standardized phonology of Spoken RSE (based on the geographical, racial, and class demographics of certain consumer markets (generally, Midwestern, white, middle to upper-middle class) whose purchasing power the large media conglomerates seek to reach) has further expanded the reach of the hegemonic "vernacular."

In contrast, the forms of English that have generally been referred to as Black English, Black Vernacular English (BVE), or African-American English are read/heard by many middle- and upper-class Americans, both black and white, as a sign of lower class status, education, and/or intelligence. The hegemonic system has established, via education and mass media, an engine of linguistic assimilation that has marked *class* difference above all else, and in so doing has forged a barrier which has served to divide communities among themselves. Nowhere is this anxiety of assimilation more marked than in the case of African-American cultures, where not only speech but clothing, style, and mannerisms have been polarized along class lines. Starting back in the days of Reconstruction, there has been a painful division between those who have sought to gain self-respect via the existing hegemonic signifiers (such as Booker T. Washington) and those who have, in whole or part, rejected this strategy (such as W.E.B. DuBois).

For Booker T. Washington (and indeed for most nineteenth-century black writers), using the vernacular was if anything *disempowering*. The black vernacular was not at the time even regarded by most whites as a distinct speech, but primarily as a collocation of error, of deviance from "standard" English. Indeed, many influential blacks regarded the black vernacular as a dreadful curse, and disparaged it in terms surpassing even those of white racialists. Gates offers the example of the nineteenth-century pan-Africanist Alexander Crummel, who attacked the black vernacular as "meager," "harsh," "characterized by a lowness of ideas," and "the speech of rude barbarians."[5] For Crummel, "proper" English was a divine gift, and the way out of slavery was paved with great authors such as Chaucer and Shakespeare. The association between the "master's tongue" and the oppression of slavery was clearly not, in Crummel's time, a tenable one—not because it was not accurate, but because the cultural struggles of colonized peoples (whether in Africa or the U.S.) had not yet reached the strategic *turn* from which such a critique could be mobilized.

Aside from these difficulties, in the nineteenth century, black vernaculars posed (and to an extent, still pose) a difficult problematic of reception. The most high-profile public presence of these vernaculars, among whites, was in minstrel shows, where its difference was framed either as *comic* (as a sign of error, stupidity, or exaggerated jollity) or *tragic* (what Zora Neale Hurston called "the sobbing school of Negrohood").[6] Despite the fact that the minstrels, like popular jazz in the early decades of the next century, contained in their musical texts and subtexts particles of actual musical and poetic expressions of the African-American experience (there were in fact a number of black owned-and-operated minstrels), these particles were deployed via stereotypical poses that refused any claim to a subjectivity on a par with their largely white audiences; all the irony, the humor, *depended* upon the assumption of inferiority.[7] As writers as opposed as Washington and DuBois perceived, neither the "comic Negro" nor the "tragic Negro" were particularly empowering, and prior to the popular distribution of more grassroots African-American artforms (such as the blues), it is little wonder that few writers hazarded the vernacular—at least outside of fictional dialogue where a certain claim of "realism" could excuse its use.

Many black educators, making a strategic choice to eschew the vernacular, sought to scrub it out of the mouths of youth with a toothbrush not unlike the one every Tuskegee Institute student was required to own in the name of oral hygiene; if climbing the class ladder meant learning the class dialect, then it was time to start learning.[8] And, while BVE has for some time now been recognized as a legitimate language in its own right, and formed the core of a multiplicity of literary, musical, and dramatic artforms, an awareness of the continuing set of biases its usage invokes has made many cautious of its use. Even the Nation of Islam (which despite its rejection of the conciliatory stance taken by those who followed Booker T. Washington's model, inherited some of Washington's insistence on the symbolic relationship between neatness, diction, and self-respect) encouraged its young preachers to employ a formal, standardized English. In a suggestive passage in his *Autobiography*, Malcolm X slips briefly in and out of black English in order to offer his readers a graphic example of both his familiarity with and *distance from* this speech:

> Shorty would take me to groovy, frantic scenes in different chicks' and cats' pads, where with the lights and juke down mellow, everybody blew gage and juiced back and jumped. I met chicks who were fine as May wine, and cats who were hip to all happenings.
>
> That paragraph was deliberate, of course; it's just to display a bit more of the slang that was used by everyone I respected as "hip" in those days. And in no time at all I was talking the slang like a lifelong hipster.[9]

African-American poets and fiction writers, too, have struggled with this same question: whether to write English as most of them grew up hearing and speaking it, and risk being taken as comic primitives by white readers acculturated (via minstrel shows, vaudeville, and radio) to regard Black English as a tragicomic sign of inferiority, or to write in a manner closer to the standard literary prose of the times, and abandon both their ancestral voices and the verbal realism by which so much writing was and is judged. Thus the vexed question of authenticity in the history of African-American writers and speakers has been caught in this double bind: whether to seek recognition by playing the game by the existing rules, winning applause in the echo of which was a certain hollowness, or to take up their own vernaculars and risk reinforcing white stereotypes.[10]

Thus, as noted in the preface, to speak or write in the vernacular has not been, until much more recently, an act which could assure

African-American authors much in the way of power or recognition. A large part of this difficulty, of course, lies in the fact that "literature" was (and often still is), linked with a romantic/modernist ideology of the transcendence of particularities; African-American writers were often deemed "literary" by established critics precisely to the extent that their blackness was subsumed within a universalizing, humanist framework—or, in the name of a different sense of the "authentic," to the extent that they enacted an exoticized *blackness* against a backdrop of jungle drums or smoke-filled nightclubs.[11] The former model of literature was intimately linked with critical practices, such as the formalism of the "New Critics," which explicitly rejected the contextualizing of literature, especially via the identity of the author, and thus tended to devalue texts that insisted on foregrounding the politics of race, whether in their form or content. The latter model was that of a belated romanticism which looked to black culture for the quintessence of either the "primitive" or the "modern"—sometimes both—ultimately, an avatar of the larger cult of the "noble savage" where the spectacle of the subaltern is mobilized for the moral "benefit" of the dominant. Despite the affective and pathetic elements of this model, it was deliberately chosen by some black writers, such as Charles Chesnutt, who sought to undermine stereotypical tales (such as Joel Chandler Harris's *Uncle Remus*) by Signifyin(g) upon them.[12]

Yet the cultural category of "literature," as set forth by the formalist critical canons, was only part of the picture, and its biases would have been of little significance had they not been supported and echoed by other elements of the hegemony of the "American" state, among them business, education, and the de facto apartheid that have combined to make assimilation the price of middle-class status. Education, then and today, works to instill received standards of usage and style, not simply for their own sake, but in order to reproduce class values; like school uniforms, "good" grammar is supposed to instill and/or guarantee a certain bourgeois gentility. Indeed in a sense instilling such class values is precisely the ideological work education is called on to perform—and African-Americans as a consequence have faced an internal conflict if they wanted to hold on to the very language that educators sought to de-privilege, if not eradicate. The erasure of the vernacular, and its replacement with the standard, is in a very important sense a central technique of education, and thus it is not surprising that African-American vernaculars continue to be de-privi-

leged in the circles of the white oligarchy; Tipper Gore's anti-rap
diatribes are only the latest installment in the series.

At the same time, however, as black vernaculars were de-privi-
leged in education, business, and within a certain school of literary
realism, blues and jazz musicians—and more than a few African-
American writers as well—were not only speaking the vernacular, they
were making a living by doing so.[13] Such is the contradictory status of
many vernacular practices; even as they are condemned and banned,
their verbal productions have often enjoyed wide popularity; in the case
of African-American vernaculars, this irony was redoubled. When Duke
Ellington was forced to use the back entrance of a club in which he
himself was performing; when a black writer who provided "jive"
scripts for a white radio deejay was fired for reading his own lines over
the air; when Big Bill Broonzy, a bluesman already established in
Chicago clubs for over a decade, was described on the liner notes to his
first "folk" (i.e., white-listener-targetted) album as though he had never
left the plantation—in all of these instances, the double status of
African-American vernaculars was underlined with a vengeance.[14]

Yet vernacular languages, "black" English included, are not
merely *doubled*, but multiple. The streetwise slang of young kids
"straight outta Compton," the gospel 'surge singing' of Ethel Perkins
and Equila Hall (recorded in 1954 outside of Selma, Alabama), the
measured staccato of a young attorney from Nigeria who now lives in
New Jersey, the rapid-fire Jamaican patois of Shabba Ranks—all these
are black vernaculars, as radically different from each other as any of
them are different from the so-called standard. Each emanates from
and signals a particular place, a particular time; in the inflections of
each are traces of ancestral voices that speak of a mixture of tongues
wrought not by a tower of Babel but by slavery's ships. And all are
changing, changing even as they are being spoken; indeed, nothing has
the dual potential—to go out of style tomorrow or last for centuries—
of a vernacular trope.

This multiplicity of black vernaculars must also be seen within
the larger frame of the difference(s) that they mark, and of their
profound links with the situationality of discourse. Not only are the
majority of those who employ vernaculars equally capable of employ-
ing "standard" forms when the context demands it, but also a great
number of "shades" in-between a "pure" standard and a "pure" vernacular (as if such things existed). A single BVE speaker may use one style

and vocabulary when calling her grandmother on the phone, another when chillin' with her homegirls at the park, and still another when speaking with a relative stranger at a bus stop. Furthermore, since all these vernaculars are themselves sited not only within black communities, but also disseminated through interpersonal contact and media presence, they are imbricated in the speech of any number of heteroglossaic situations. Numerous words and constructions from black vernaculars have entered into the "standard" dialect, and have intermingled in the new urban heteroglossia of Spanish, Japanese, Korean, Portuguese, Vietnamese, and other languages. One result of this mix is that almost any speaker of English in the United States practices a greater or lesser degree of language and/or dialect shifting; indeed some rappers such as Mellow Man Ace ("The Brother With Two Tongues") have made such shifting their trademark. A young white suburbanite in Colorado may flavor her speech with hip-hop lingo; an up-and-coming black rapper from Cleveland may pick up the Jamaican patois he has heard only on recordings; rappers as diverse as Japan's Scha-dara-Parr or the Senegalese/French rapper MC Solaar may bend their vernaculars and intermix them with American ghetto slang.

Given this situation, it would no doubt be a romanticization to speak of a single, monolithic "African-American Vernacular." Instead, the multiplicity of vernaculars must be framed as a condition *of the vernacular*; that is, the vernacular (to Signify on a phrase of Luce Irigiray's), is *that language which is not one*. Indeed, the very idea of a single uniform tongue, whose regularity and similarity would somehow subsume difference, is a creature of the violence of empire and colonialism. The vernacular thus stands in the place(s) of difference, articulates difference, and indeed actively produces difference. The way in which this production is *seen* is crucial to the status of vernacular discourses, particularly in the case of African-American vernaculars. For as Gates's theory of Signification makes eminently clear, these vernaculars have established themselves from the start as a site of an ongoing, productive troping, a troping which takes the *same* and returns it as *difference*, and their particular social history in the United States has been inexorably bound up in this *production*. Ever since the first sheet music and recordings of an African-American music—indeed ever since the minstrel shows of the mid-nineteenth century—the African-American vernacular has been (re)produced as a cultural spectacle. Sometimes, as with the minstrels, this spectacle

was one of an exaggerated, comic distortion of racial difference; sometimes, as with ragtime and early Jazz, it was received by many of its
white audiences as signifying a frenetic state of happiness and jollity;
sometimes, as with the blues, an endless sorrow. And now, even
though it is black *rage* that has grabbed the mic at what the Goats call
"Uncle Scam's Well Fair and Freak Show," there remains a doubleness
that only Signfyin(g) can represent: an artistic modality whose "trick
of the shade" is to continually exchange the different for the same, the
"unserious" for the "serious."[15]

2. Language in a minor key

> I'm outspoken, my language is broken into a slang
> But it's just a dialect that I select when I hang."
>
> —Special Ed, "I Got It Made"[16]

To return to language: whatever the spectacular politics of hip-
hop, its most significant and continuing incursion is conducted within
language—which is, conversely, the most potent and widely-dispersed
medium of social control for the comfortable classes and their political
sideshows. If there is a field in which hip-hop's revolution will be
fought, it will be first and foremost that of language, a fact which is
underlined by the recurrent metaphoric mixture of rappers' own technologies (microphones, pencils, and tongues) with those of armed
struggle (guns, hand grenades, artillery). Here, also, is a particular
crossroads at which the linguistic and political theories of postmodernism intersect with the theory and practice of hip-hop. Specifically,
given the Signifyin(g) operations which constitute the core of hip-hop
practice, the question must be asked: in what way is this Signifyin(g)
deformation deployed by hip-hop, and what are the specific consequences of this deployment? Can linguistics provide a kind of model for
the tactics and effectivity of the kind of cultural resistance staged by
hip-hop?

One of the underlying problems, as has been evident throughout
this book, is that the handy oppositional terms—"standard" English vs.
"Black English," ghetto vs. suburb, and their corollaries—while
acknowledging the spectacularized politics of race and language, are
much too large and clumsy when it comes to examining the micro-

politics of everyday interaction. For while I have no doubt that, for the mass of young white kids growing up in middle-class suburbs, the ghetto and its languages are thought of as *terra incognita*, I do not believe that these kids are actually as ignorant about it as they appear (or as some of them think themselves). Yes, economic apartheid, radio-airwave apartheid, and even record store apartheid (many stores now stock rap discs behind the counter on the excuse of anxieties about "theft") exist—but like South Africa's apartheid, they never worked and never will. There are numerous contemporary cultural and linguistic interconnections—and also historical junctures and intersections—between "black" and "white" cultures. Whether it is via a friendship formed in school, secondary encounters via mass television, magazines, or music, or simply in the shared use of iconic artefacts, public spaces, or cultural products, the lines of contact are innumerable. Language, that most well-word coin of all, changes hands so often that the image it bears loses all recognition, and yet perhaps it is precisely in this vernacular (re)circulation of words that hip-hop culture, like other African-American artforms before it, has its greatest impact. Anonymous, and yet continually shifting in connotative significance; used again and again but never used up, appropriated, deformed, returned, discarded—language is perhaps the only particle small enough to fit in every crack in the system.

Yet barricades remain, despite the "flow" of language that often renders them useless. It matters not, for instance, that no one in Florida will stop speaking Spanish if the state legislature passes a bill making English the "official language of Florida"; what matters is the spectacular struggle for hegemony in a world that is radically different from what xenophobic Floridians imagine as "theirs," against a large and upwardly mobile Hispanic population that nonetheless shares many of the anxieties about assimilation that trouble African-Americans. In the power struggle over and through language, the *grand moves*, while the least effectual, nonetheless mirror the everyday struggles, anxieties, and questions of intelligibility that are negotiated, one word at a time, in the heteroglossaic space of vernaculars. Despite differences in terms of specific histories, then, there are certain phenomena of linguistic interchange and struggle that can be described in a general fashion, and which offer the requisite subtlety to enter into an analysis of the vast flux of language(s) as they are spoken/written/read/heard.

In their analysis of language in *Kafka: Toward a Minor Literature,* Gilles Deleuze and Félix Guattari develop the concept of a 'minor language' that takes its situation from the texts of Franz Kafka. For Kafka, a Prague Jew for whom writing in German was both impossible and unavoidable, there was no fully 'native' tongue. In the end, he chose not the literary German of Berlin or Vienna, but the German of Prague:

> The impossibility of writing other than in German is for the Prague Jews the feeling of an irreducible distance from their primitive Czech territoriality. And the impossibility of writing in German is the deterritorialization of the German population itself, an oppressive minority that speaks of a language cut off from the masses, like a "paper language" or an artificial language; this is all the more true for the Jews who are simultaneously a part of this minority and excluded from it, like "gypsies who have stolen a German child from its crib." In short, Prague German is a deterritorialized language, appropriate for strange and minor uses. (This can be compared in another context to what blacks in America today are able to do with the English language).[17]

By "deterritorialized," and "minor," Deleuze and Guattari designate the exact opposite of nationalistic "standard" languages (the "King's English," or French as defined by the Académie Française)—language at its heteroglossaic margins, German at its most "un-German," where not only its vocabulary but its syntax have undergone both the greatest alterations (at the hands of other languages, and the passage of time) and also a certain ossification (because isolated from both the "paternal" population of speakers). As a consequence of its position at the 'outer limits' of language, they see the literature of this minor language as a "cramped space which forces each individual intrigue to connect immediately to politics."[18] They also claim that in such a minor literature, "everything takes on a collective value...precisely because talent isn't abundant in a minor literature, there are no possibilities for an individuated enunciation that would belong to this or that "master."[19]

Without doubt, this initial conception of a 'minor' literature is a theorization of potentially significant position for vernacular practice; yet it is equally certain that it is riven with problems. If a 'minor' language is always constructed by its difference from the 'standard,' does not such a conception end up merely reinforcing the standard-

ness of the standard? If its space is "cramped," is this again to be
contrasted with the wonderful spaciousness of a "major" literature, in
which alone the "great" artist can spread his wings without being
weighed down by the merely "political"? Finally, the shortage of
"talent" that Deleuze and Guattari postulate as a causal factor of the
kind of collectivity they would like to applaud is clearly not a cause but
an *effect* of a residual valuation of the "major"; in short, such a valuation partakes of precisely that territorialism, that linguistic nationalism, which Deleuze and Guattari so emphatically denounce. In the
history of hip-hop, as has become clear, "individual talent" is neither
scarce nor anti-collective; indeed rap music has woven collectivities
precisely through the strong and readily identifiable voices of individual rappers and DJs.

By the time they wrote *A Thousand Plateaus*, however, these
"nomadic" authors had come to terms with the extent of their own
imbrication in these various problematics, and it is significant that
their coming to terms is in many ways signalled by a return to and
reconsideration of the historical relations of African-Americans and
English. The supposed "lacks"—of talent or of grammatical structure—in "minor" literature, they acknowledge, are only such in the
terms of the dominant or "standard" language, and in fact these lacks
are no longer symptoms of decline or a limit in space ("cramped"), but
rather of a movement towards deterritorialization. This shift is under-
scored by a reversal of terms; whereas before the minor was implicitly
defined against the major, now it is the minor language which deter-
mines the fortunes of the major, both as its machine of variation and
its creative soul.[20] The apparent lack of a "full" set of grammatical
distinctions (its "syntagmatic" or sequence-ordering shortage) corresponds, for D&G, to an overload of variation (a "paradigmatic" or
lexical excess). All major languages, in fact, are becoming-minor, and
more: becoming-minor, through its production of variation, is the very
machine of becoming itself.

It certainly seems as though Deleuze and Guattari have come full
circle, and have found a way to place the minor, and by extension the
minority, in a place of honor in the Hall of Languages. Yet in many
ways, their revaluation of the "minor" is a still more subtle disguise for
a romanticization of the "minor": how very useful to us, us who teach
at the Université de Paris, that the peasants and immigrants are
keeping "our" language lively! The difference between Deleuze and

Guattari's "minor" and what I would call a *resistance vernacular* is that such a language must take the *further* step of *deploying variance* in order to deform and reposition the rules of "intelligibility" set up by the dominant language. For there is a power struggle at work in all linguistic difference; if the "major" language places such emphasis on the categorical order of things, and if the vernacular stakes its claim on the intensities of variation that deform these categories, this is not because the vernacular is either the origin or the destiny of the "standard," but because the vernacular is, by its very existence, an act of resistance to the "standard."

In this light, it is crucial to note that what Deleuze and Guattari describe as "major" and "minor" are *not* discrete, mutually exclusive, linguistic subsets, but rather two contending and overlapping modes of power, which produce two different structurations of the same linguistic situation. The power of the "major" language is staked on the continual search for and codification of *constants*, via grammar, manuals of usage, the educational apparatus, and the sort of linguistics (such as Chomsky's) that discards variance as a kind of secondary, extra-linguistic phenomenon. The mode of power of the "minor" language, on the other hand, is that of variance, deformation, and appropriation; it is not so much that it refuses or opposes the structural constants sought by the major, as it is that it does not acknowledge the "constant" as a unit of value; on the contrary it values the variant. In so doing, by setting words into a kind of play (such as Signifyin(g)), the "minor" is a kind of anti-structure; its speakers and writers perform an ongoing deconstruction of the major. As a result, as Deleuze and Guattari note, all "major" languages are in a continual state of "becoming-minor."

In the case of black English vernaculars, of course, this is hardly news; the linguistic deterritorialization wrought upon the lineage of "standard" Englishes by black vernaculars is the foremost process whereby what is now called (by "major" linguists) "American" English has been shaped. Again, the politics of race have had a hand in the duration and strength of this incursion; while most European immigrants have, within a generation or two, come under the linguistic and cultural umbrella of "white," African-Americans, generation after generation, have seen equality and opportunity denied; the difference which black vernaculars marked has thus continued as a site of linguistic struggle, which has produced grammatical and lexical alterations as one of its traces. The exception to this in-equation, it should be said, is the black middle class, whose linguistic assimilation has been read as a symptom of a larger loss of identity, and consequently has become a sign of class anxiety on both sides of the fence. From Ice-T's "bourgeois blacks [who] keep on doggin' me" on down to Sir Mix-a-Lot's "Word to the bourgeois: fuck all y'all," the word from the black underclass to the black middle class has been one of accusation.[21] The historical irony here is the inverse relation between class hierarchies and cultural ones; even as the older generation of the black middle class has esconsed itself with a comfortable collection of cultural artifacts (jazz records, Nigerian bronzes, and books of African folktales), many of their daughters and sons have looked more towards the language and consciousness of the ghetto in search for a more authentically *black* identity, to the point where picking up ghetto vernaculars has been seen by many as an empowering way to reclaim blackness.

3. African-American vernaculars and vernacular politics

> To write as a complete Caribbean woman, or man for that matter, demands of us the retracing of the African part of ourselves, reclaiming as our own, and as our subject, a history sunk under the sea...it means finding the art forms of these of our ancestors and speaking in the *patois* forbidden us. It means realizing that our knowledge will always be wanting. It means also, I think, mixing in the forms taught us by the oppressor, undermining his language and co-opting his style, and turning it to our purpose.

> —Michelle Cliff, "A Journey Into Speech"[22]

> The space of the tactic is the space of the other. Thus it must play on and with a certain terrain imposed on it and organized by the law of a foreign power...it is a maneuver...within enemy territory...It must vigilantly make use of the cracks that particular conjunctions open in the surveillance of the proprietary powers. It poaches in them. It creates surprises in them. It can be where it is least expected. It is a guileful ruse.

> —Michel de Certeau, *The Practice of Everyday Life*[23]

The history of African-American language and music has been one of innumerable mixes, cuts, crosses, and influences, unfolding within an increasingly fast-paced dynamic of style and fashion. Two movements have been pivotal, however, in shaping what might otherwise have been a chaotic mix: on the one hand, the recording industry, which, since the early part of this century, has continually sought to appropriate, homogenize, and market African-American musical styles and genres, and on the other, the synthetic diaspora of African music traditions within and against European musical forms. This second movement has gained urgency from a critical consciousness of the dangers of the first, and indeed many of the most revolutionary shifts in African-American music have been shaped via a conscious resistance to such commodification. From the start, this double movement worked by syncope and Signifyin(g), staging itself as *difference*, floating like a butterfly and stinging like a bee. If European rhythm was resolutely 4/4, African-American music drew from West African polyrhythms and produced something new, not pure polyrhythms, but the undercurrent of the offbeat *against* 4/4 time: *syncopation*; the enduring legacy of this move can be heard when the group Mad Kap lays a Scot Joplin sample over a hip-hop drumbeat, and the rhythms *match perfectly*.[24] Again, just when the gentle syncopation of swing seemed destined to predominance in the early '40s, it was rejected on two fronts: on the one hand, via explosion (the boppers with their fondnesss for strange intervals, offbeat accents, and breakneck tempos), and on the other via Signification (the "jump" blues that upped the ante on the "down" beats while at the same time upping the tempo). Of course each break partook of the other, but the riffed/rift lines were clear enough, particularly in a time of continuing radio and music hall apartheid.[25]

Jazz continued its left turn, moving so far away from commercial forms that it in effect Signified itself into highbrow status (the so-called hard bop), a music for those who *knew*, a *fundamentally* difficult music, while "jump" blues took its place as a music of dance and socialization, eventually reaching the point where it shifted the paradigms of pop and compelled the recognition of the music industry. Hip-hop, Signifyin(g) on both these histories, in a sense makes *both* moves—towards a steadfast insularity, which brushes off the unknowing by kickin' slang and dropping mile-a-minute rhymes, yet still with a heavy, bass-laden beat that has had a tremendous and continuing influence on any and all forms of commercial dance music. The difference between the former, "hardcore" school of street rhymes, heavy bass, and gangsta narratives, and the latter, more dance-oriented rap is at times as significant as the difference between legitimacy and illegitimacy, despite artists such as Ice-T who boastingly taunts "How could a brother be so hardcore / And still keep you on the floor like a maniac?"[26] And in fact, many artists who have had considerable crossover success still return to the hardcore beats and rhymes, paying homage to their roots while still seeking radio airplay. At the same time, however, hardcore artists such as Ice Cube continue to defy conventional wisdom by recording albums without a single song aimed at radio, and proceeding to top the charts anyway.

Ultimately, though, the difference between a 'hardcore' rapper, or a rapper who is 'true to the street,' is not so much a matter of musical styles as of *attitude*. Amiri Baraka puts it most succinctly in his book *Black Music*, when he defines Jazz—and by extension, African-American music in general—as first and foremost an *attitude*. That is, not a matter of the scales, beats, or words one is singing, but of their delivery, their attack, their movement from and back into the material life and cultures of African-Americans.[27] In this sense, hip-hop, like its precursors, is a fundamentally *materialist* artform, an artform that stakes its claim to meaning in the material realities of African-American cultures, to the point where its audience has come to regard any movement out of this context as a betrayal, a sell out.[28] It is not simply a matter of race or class, though they are central factors; there remains almost as wide a world of difference between a white rapper with street respect (such as MC Serch) and a black rapper who has lost that respect (e.g., MC Hammer) as if the races were to be reversed. Street respect means beats that can blare out of a jeep, rhymes that drop knowledge that is *relevant* to kids in the hood, and *attitude*. The female gangsta rapper Bo$$ puts this attitude succinctly: "I don't give a fuck, not a single fuck, not a single solitary fuck, motherfucka!"—that is hip-hop attitude in a nutshell.[29]

Nonetheless, despite the seeming ease with which attitude underwrites hip-hop's claim to authenticity, there remains an element of the accidental, the unknown within hip-hop, that situates it as a singularly *vernacular* artform. First, street respect is impossible to capture in a studio; it is not a matter of production but of *consumption*, and even the most respected artist can take a tumble overnight. Secondly, hip-hop's authenticity, like that of jazz, is continually posed *against* that which it is not, and there is a hair's breadth of such difference between

innovation and repetition. Hip-hop, like jazz, is fundamentally impro-
visatory, and must be reinvented from moment to moment, out of a
dynamic mix of re-citation and Signification. As Bennet Schaber has
noted in his pioneering essay "Modernity and the Vernacular,"

> My claim is not that vernacular writing and its social poetics form a
> tradition (whether this word is understood as a relation to time or
> to content) but that it must be construed as a situation, one that
> might be understood as a creation *ex nihilo*, of something that
> might be called social and only belatedly cultural. When Guillaume
> writes a poem *"de dreyt nien,"* out of and about absolutely nothing,
> and when Thelonious Monk "play[s] things I've never heard before,"
> something of the same situation is, I believe, at stake in both cases.
> Both men are interested in the creation of something absolutely
> new; and both ask, explicitly or implicitly, from where it comes and,
> more importantly, for whom it is destined and in what mode it will
> be recognized as such. The medieval poet and the modern jazz
> musician both compose works which are, first and foremost, chal-
> lenges to the ones who read or hear them (just as both challenge
> themselves with the enigmatic nature of their own compositions
> and creations). The Poictevin poet and the African-American pianist
> share a common situation: both struggle to make a vernacular
> culture, which in principle does not yet exist, come to life.[30]

The *situation* of hip-hop as a vernacular artform is similarly unstable,
similarly centered around the impossibility of closure. This could,
admittedly, be said in a sense of any form of popularly disseminated
music, but there is an important difference with African-American
musical forms, since authenticity is staked on an innovation whose
closure is its commodification—that is, at the moment it becomes
identifiable, its modes reproducible, it *dies*. The inbuilt resistance of
hip-hop to such a death lies in its ability to continually reinvent itself;
like the toasters and sound-system deejays of ska and reggae, hip-hop
takes *version* as a verb, not a noun.[31] Thus, even if a certain hip-hop
style gains a commercial quality that is read as its cultural fossilization,
the hip-hop deejays and producers can grind this stone back into sand,
breaking it up and "breaking it on down" until it becomes something
new.

Hip-hop, thus, does not quite create itself *ex nihilo*—and neither,
for that matter, did the Troubadours or the boppers—but out of a reac-

tion with and against existing conventions (including inevitably its own), carried out via a reappropriation of vernacular materials such as samples, machine beats, or the voice itself. Yet to the extent that such vernacular matter, prior to its re-use, is a sort of "nothing," then perhaps Schaber is right; as Chuck D puts it, "That's how rap got started, Brothers made something out of nothing."[32] If there is a certain *modernism* in the aesthetic and attitudinal self-possession of bop, there is a certain *postmodernism* in the continual re-citing of the same as difference in hip-hop (and in fact there is something of each in the other—as with Coltrane's cutting on tunes like "My Favorite Things" or the fourteen-piece jazz ensemble that forms the digable planets' touring backup band). Yet in both cases, there remains a deep commitment to pushing, bending, and even breaking the limits, a commitment which involves both the invention and citation of origins (even though no origin exists, and this knowledge is a condition of such citation) *and* the defiant push towards what KRS-One calls "The Style You Haven't Done Yet." Like the frequently sampled refrain of "I'm Comin'" that flavors the heavy beats of Public Enemy, Ice Cube, and LL Cool J, hip-hop too is a music for the future, a music that lays itself open to its own infinite permutations, building a tradition even as it erases it.[33] Indeed, given their common heritage and modes of development, it is no surprise that the '90s have seen an increasing number of jazz-flavored hip-hop acts, ranging from the digable planets' sampling of Sonny Rollins to Guru's full-fledged hip-hop/jazz fusion on his record *Jazzmatazz*, to US3's hip-hop-bop musical readymades.

Yet even if the hip-hop vernacular *does* produce something from "nothing," the question inevitably arises as to what extent their production is merely reactive or derivative. Certainly, it is a common strategy for the detractors of the "new" or the "revolutionary" to see them as mere reactions *against*, and by implication less authentic, less valid, less empowering. The difference between reaction, reappropriation, and transformation is inevitably central, since it not only frames the discussion from the "dominant" side of the equation, but is central to the act of musical and verbal Signifyin(g); just as certain ideologies of the aesthetic hold nowadays that art must not be merely 'derivative,' vernacular practice insists that all art is already derivative. Indeed, the recycling of materials at hand is a central vernacular practice that exists far beyond the limits of music; when an old tire is converted to a planter, stones are reclaimed from demolished buildings, or an urban garden takes form on a vacant lot, the same kind of operation is at stake. But is it a kind of *production*? A potential site for the refusal of the dominant or hegemonic culture?

Such questions form the crux of the status of the vernacular, and in fact such questions lie at the center of the debate on postmodern culture in general. Modernisms, so the story goes, believe in the power of the individual to create something *new* and are the inheritors of a Romantic individualism that puts the individual in a position of a quasi-deity. This remained true even for high modernists such as Joyce, who were prone to put all kinds of "found" materials—snippets of actual conversations, newspaper clippings, or advertisements—into their "creative" texts, even appropriating whole structural frameworks (e.g., *Ulysses*). Postmodernisms, or so says this tale, are more the offspring of Dadaism and Surrealism than of high modernism; all supposed "creation" is a reshuffling, a collage, and indeed the postmodern text seeks if possible to interrupt and turn aside any desire for the "original" or the "new" by foregrounding the jagged cuts and sutures which hold them "together" (or perhaps, ideally, *do not*). The difference in this narrative is not one of substance (since the "mix" of old and new may in many cases be the same) as much as one of *stance*; the Romantic illusionist has been replaced by a postmodern *dis*illusionist, whose art lies in her/his own erasure and interruption.

Such a tale is no doubt overly simplistic, but it is widely received, and underpins many more complex and crafty arguments about the status of the postmodern. And, tellingly, it underlies the question of *production* itself. Like medieval merchants, whose making of money from exchange alone rather than "labor" as it was then defined aroused widespread resentment, postmodern productions arouse the ire of those who subscribe to the Romantic notion of textual production; to them it seems that postmodern practice is a *failed* attempt to make something out of nothing.[34] In this sense, vernacular practices clearly prefigure and underlie the techniques of postmodernism, from the Dadaists' reappropriation of urinals and pipes to such contemporary works as the infamous "Piss Christ."

Unfortunately for up-and-coming rappers, the copyright laws maintain the status and position of that white Eurocentric Romantic "author," such that their material assault upon the constructions of "originality" faces legal as well as critical opposition. Nonetheless, there can be no question that the vernacular re-use of sonic material deemed to be "property" situates hip-hop on the edge of a practice which questions, in a way all the theoretical eulogies for the "death of the author" have not, the notion of originality and authorship. Recently, most major hip-hop acts have paid or been forced to pay licensing fees, but it has not always been so, and it may not be so in the future. For hip-hop returns again and again to its roots, each time finding new tactics in the old, and already its own sonic trace is so vast that many producers get most of their samples from within hip-hop itself, or even from their own previous work. For hip-hop, postmodernist practice is not merely a fashion, it is a necessary means, and the music *will* go on and on, *by any means necessary*.

In the final analysis of the vernacular, however, one point remains intransigent: how can a speech that founds itself on a relationship to (if not always or only a reaction *against*) a "dominant" or hegemonic dialect effectively *resist* that dialect? Donald B. Gibson puts the point succinctly:

> The vernacular remains by definition vernacular, by virtue of its relation to something that dominates it. Unless one can supplant the dominant language by, for example, taking over the lexicon, assuming control of linguistic utterance (controlling the press and publication), then one in calling for dominance is likely to be merely rhetorical.[35]

Clearly, such a linguistic overturning of the hegemonic tongue is something unreasonable to hope for—or is it? After all, the state, like the capitalist economic system, has yet to be overthrown, and no amount of valorizing the vernacular seems likely to make a dent on the linguistic hegemony exercised via education, mass media, and corporate protocols. What could a few vernacular stone-throws accomplish against such a behemoth?

Frantz Fanon, describing the situation of the colonized who dream of overthrowing the colonizers, perceived a similar "logic" of self-defeat:

> There are some individuals who are convinced of the ineffectiveness of violent methods; for them, there is no doubt about it, every attempt to break colonial oppression by force is a hopeless effort, an attempt at suicide, because in the innermost recesses of their

brains the settler's tanks and airplanes occupy a huge place. When
they are told "Action must be taken," they see bombs raining down
on them, armored cars coming at them on every path, machine-
gunning and police action...and they sit quiet. They are beaten
from the start.[36]

Fanon, however, does not argue for an idealistic vision that would
imagine some way out of this scenario; he argues instead that this
mental scenario of engagement is precisely the one that the colonizing
powers seek to instill. In its place, he argues for *guerilla* tactics, for a
battle of forays and blinds, of strategic strikes that daunt the hegemonic coalition precisely because no one knows where or when they
will come next.[37] There is no way to win with a battalion of tanks when
they are matched against a tactically scattered guerilla force—a lesson
demonstrated most recently in Afghanistan—because it does not
reproduce the very terms (of *dominant* and *subordinate-wanting-to-
dominate*) in which the system thinks.

The vernacular, I would argue, works in precisely this way; it is
not a monolithic battering ram (and indeed, where would one batter?),
but a guerilla incursion; it steals language, steals sounds, steals the
media spotlight, then slips away, regrouping at another unpredictable
cultural site. An engagement with the forces of the hip-hop vernacular,
as Bill Clinton and Dan Quayle discovered in the 1992 campaign, is
foredoomed to the kind of bogged-down defensiveness that besets an
army in guerilla territory. Quayle's criticisms of Ice-T, like Clinton's
attack on Sister Souljah, were meant to use their subjects as media-
ready Willie Hortons, another couple of dangerous verbal criminals.
On the one hand, in terms of "actual" political power, it was easy for
the media to make both attacks appear petty (as indeed they were); in
terms of rhetorical "power," all their attacks accomplished was to
increase the credit of the rappers (particularly Souljah, who went from
relative obscurity to the cover of *Newsweek* in the space of two weeks).
Ice-T, for his part, lost no time stencilling these political silhouettes on
his fuselage; the spring of 1993 found him rapping "Bush, Quayle, and
Clinton got a problem with me—the motherfucking T!"

Sampling, as noted above, is another potential guerilla tactic; it
takes words literally out of the mouths of politicians and media personalities and remixes them in ways that highlight their absurdity.[38] And,
while such Signifying satire may take a while to reach a recording, hip-
hop and other dance clubs provide an almost instant venue for techno-

rebuttal. In Britain, when the remarks of one Minister against the concert-going neo-hip nomads known as the "Travellers" became particularly heated, they became the star attraction at clubs, where words from a diatribe delivered that very afternoon were repeated and mangled by dancefloor deejays.[39] Beyond simple satire, these texts often become part of a new sonic collage which makes its own subversive intertextualities, as when Paris combines newscast voiceovers and Bush speeches in the introduction to his musical assassination "Bush Killa" (I have split the quote into two continuous strands to represent typographically the points of overlap):

> The media have become part of the Bush Administration...... . This is all
>   Of course, national polls do show that
>
> very good, we love what's happening... it would appear, preliminarily, that Americans do overwhelmingly support the war in the Gulf...
>
> the first strike was a success... the right stuff...it is a kind of euphoria
> Yay, America! We can do it! ... This is tremendous! Baghdad is lit up
>
> ... it has been a steady, one-sided parade of propagandists from the con-
> like a Christmas tree!.......We began to feel as if we were living under
>
> servative élite...
> martial law .. *It is a big idea ... A new world order ... A new world*
>
> . . .
> *order...A new world order....* [40]

It is with good reason that Paris calls himself a "Black Guerilla," and he is not the only one. In the aftermath of the Rodney King beating, transcripts from car-to-car radios used by the L.A.P.D. recorded one cop's use of the memorable phrase "It was straight out of *Gorillas in the Mist.*" More than in any other instance, this line, and the deep-seated racism it disclosed, became a site for multiple incursions, each of which Signified on this phrase with a vengeance. Paris recorded a cut, "Guerillas in the Mist," as did Ice Cube's new posse, known as Da Lench Mob, who made it their title track of their debut album, and numerous other raps picked up on the phrase and telegraphed it from coast to coast. The transformative engine set forth by this one homophonic twist provides a paradigmatic instance of guerilla Signifyin(g): the cop used the phrase, no doubt, as a result of his racist equation of African-Americans with gorillas (though exactly what "scene" he had in mind is obscured in the mists of his mind, since it is rare for scientists to attack the subjects of their study with tazers and nightsticks). Nonetheless, the cluster of connotative images—what Roland Barthes calls the "connotative signifieds" of "gorilla" and "black man" clearly overlap in the consciousness of many people, including a large number who would loudly proclaim that they are "not racists." Against this hegemonic metonym, and its deployment in the service of brutally repressive violence, hip-hop shifts the connotative signified along a radical pole suggested and enabled by homonymic indifference. While "gorillas" remain at the level of objects, whether of scientific study or as a means of dehumanizing Africans or African-Americans, "guerillas," as Ice-T puts in in a similar context, are not "runnin' from ya" but "runnin' at cha." An entirely different connotative signified— this time tied up in the history of struggles in Vietnam, Afghanistan, and indeed Africa—takes the place of the L.A.P.D. officer's utterance. In this way, hip-hop undermines the dominant not by opposing it on a large front (even the L.A. uprising was composed of thousands of discrete acts), but via a tactical, vernacular strategy, a guerilla resistance that not only nullifies but transforms hegemonic utterance.

Da Lench Mob Signifies this reversal through a multiplicity of visual and rhetorical strategies. The cover photos on their debut album, *Guerillas in tha Mist*, show the members of the Lench mob wearing black ski masks and carrying automatic rifles (=guerillas), and yet places them in the midst of a dense forest with a heavy undergrowth of ferns (=gorillas); in the title cut, Ice Cube Signifies on the political doubleness this homophonic/visual slippage enacts:

> Fuck Grape Ape and Magilla
> I'm a killa, Magilla Gorilla
> ain't a killa, white boys swiped Godzilla
> from my supa nigga named King Kong
> Played his ass like ping-pong[41]

Here, a pseudo-genealogy of pop-culture gorillas is sliced and diced by Cube's rhetoric; he wants nothing to do with Magilla Gorilla (the Hanna-Barberra cartoon figure) or Grape Ape (a snackfood mascot); instead he'll take King Kong, the "supa nigga" next to whom all lesser monsters (Godzilla) are watered-down "white" appropriations.

The Lench Mob's use of the gorilla trope goes much farther, however, than these topical allusions; the figure of the gorilla, threatening and alien, is a central one in the rhetorical strategy Houston A. Baker calls the "deformation of mastery." The gorilla's territorial assertions, its "monstrous and deformed" hoots, halt the intruder in his tracks. Its noises, however, are only "deformed" to the intruder, the one who is, as Baker suggests, outside the "veil" of the indigenous language.[42] Just so, despite the discrediting of the racist logic (left over from the "eugenics" movement) that blacks were somehow 'closer to the apes,' the image has persisted to the extent that it elicited instant laughs of recognition among the L.A. cops who received the car-to-car transmission. The Lench Mob's strategy, then, is not to directly counter this logic, but to Signify on it, to provide a monstrous mask, complete with guns *and* a jungle setting, with which to cathect and make mockery of the underlying connotative slippage that made such a comparison possible in the first place. As Flavor Flav says, "Joke's on you, Jack"; it looks just like another PBS nature show, but wait! Don't touch that dial 'till the guerillas in tha mist blow ya fuckin' brains out!

The Lench Mob's strategy is itself an act of the "deformation of mastery," and indeed there is considerable overlap between it and Gates's "motivated Signifyin(g)." Difference is not deployed to offer a reverent rendition, like Wynton Marsalis playing on an old Louis Armstrong riff, but to take a pre-existing connotative signified and blow it to kingdom come. The homophonic similarity, in this case, is just the "bait," both in the sense of fishing for a response and egging someone on; "c'mon," it says, "you've heard this one before, I know you have." On a musical level, distorted samples accomplish much the same thing, as when Public Enemy, on their album *Apocalypse 91: The Empire Strikes Black*, mix in painfully distorted but recognizable samples of bluegrass and country music; the out-of-phase banjo invokes not only an image of racist Southern whites, but the minstrel's banjo that was made to enact a seemingly endless jollity. Yet even as these images are brought into view, they fade and waver like funhouse reflections; in a fundamental way, the 'deformation of mastery' calls the very 'mastery' of the connotative field into question.

Chapter 3

The Pulse of the Rhyme Flow:
Hip-hop Signifyin(g) and the Politics of Reception

Is this real, or a fiction? You'll never know
While you're hooked to the pulse of the rhyme flow.

—Ice-T, "Pulse of the Rhyme Flow"[1]

1. Signifyin(g) and Power

Whatever the role played by samples and breakbeats, for much of hip-hop's core audience, it is without question the *rhymes* that come first. Homophony has long posed a particular field of play, whether in the elaborate puns of the troubadour's *trobar clus* or in the "alternative" words to the Pledge of Allegiance that have brought so much comic relief to those at the back of the classroom, and homophony (again, the play of similarity and difference) forms the basis for hip-hop's verbal Signifyin(g) practices. Whether at the level of names (Souljah, Gang Starr, Spinderella), metonymic shifts (Patrick Swayze plays a ghost in the film *Ghost*, so hip-hop lingo shortens "I'm out of here (like a ghost)" to "Swayze!"), or acronymic codes (NWA, BWP, BDP, HWA, LL Cool J[2]), it is this kind of continuous linguistic slippage and play that drives the verbal engines of rap.

This slippage, as Gates was the first to emphasize, lies predominantly at the level of what linguists call the "paradigmatic" or vertical dimension. That is, if the unfolding of language over time is thought of as a horizontal strip, at each syntactical moment a vast range of possi-

81

bilities is vertically "stacked." One can spin the wheel of grammatically and logically possible terms (e.g., 'The cat sat on the: mat, car, tree, grass, chair') and/or the wheel of sounds ('The cat sat on the mat, the rat, the hat, the bat, the gat'); the trick of Signifyin(g) is to do both at once, to find homonymic connections that serve either to undermine, parody, or connect in a surprising way the underlying connotations of language. For instance, Big Daddy Kane:

> The breaker, the taker, money maker, never a faker
> My lyrics are built like Schwarzenegger
> So all my competition gets destroyed
> You need to put your weak rhymes on steroids
> For you ever to press up on the money
> And stand to rippin' a show, and flow
> Provin' the competition can't go
> Because I do all, it's easy for you to fall
> I move on rappers like my name was U-Haul[3]

The initial sequence here (breaker, taker, maker, faker) works directly via homonymic slippage, and is "capped" (surpassed) by the sudden and yet totally fitting connection to Schwarz*enegger* (which itself, indirectly, Signifies on "nigger"), and represents perhaps the oldest rapping strategy.[4] The following lines move from such extended flourishes to a series of metaphoric put-downs, packed with internal rhymes (often involving tricky diphthongs), and concluding with the metonymic "movement" from the act of "moving on" (that is, attacking) to U-Haul, well-known as a lender of *moving* equipment such as trailers. All the characteristic rhetorical strategies of hip-hop Signifyin(g)—metonymy, metaphor, and homophonic slippage—work together here to establish multiple and overlapping streams of association, which everywhere undermine the merely *denotative* with broad and brash de/re-formations of the *connotative*.

Thus, on a *micro* level, Signifyin(g) is a productive agent of difference, an incursion against stability, uniformity, and homogeneity. Yet Signifyin(g) politics also inevitably play on a *macro* level, particularly since Signifyin(g) has from its earliest origins deployed its linguistic "games" in order to frame and mobilize larger questions of power relations. Signifyin(g) is based on the realization that what Euro-American critics (following Gadamer) call the "aesthetics of reception" are in fact relations of *power*. Taking and mis-taking, acts of verbal exchange which are built around the central trope of the Signifyin(g) monkey as trickster figure, are at each turn linked with their material consequences; unlike much of "Western" aesthetics, which presumes the possibility of a "correct" or "accurate" reception, Signifyin(g) accounts for and sets into play the *mis*taking of meaning.

Gates and others have outlined the fundamental figurations of the Signifyin(g) monkey tale, but it is worth repeating them here, if only to set the scene: The monkey and the Lion have a verbal interchange, in which the monkey uses figurative and formulaic language to insinuate that the Elephant (their mutual acquaintance) has been violently attacking the Lion's reputation. The Lion, taking this figurative speech literally, goes to see the Elephant and even the score; the Elephant, after politely informing the Lion that he is mistaken, beats him severely. The Lion, both his pride and his body in shreds, goes back to confront the monkey, who offers a series of additional figurative insults, and (depending on the version) is either beaten by the Lion in turn or escapes through some clever ploy.[5]

As Gates himself has observed, the situation figured in the Signifyin(g) monkey tales is continually re-enacted, particularly when one person (often an adult relative) *signifies* on a young woman or man without the latter being immediately aware of it. This Signifyin(g) is done as a kind of teaching, an initiation into the world of adult black discourse. In a parallel but more volatile way, when many white listeners unfamiliar with the groundrules of the Signifyin(g) game *listen* to a rap track, they too tend to mis-take the figural for the literal. When such listeners hear Ice Cube declare "I'm the kinda nigga that's built to last / You fuck with me, I'll put my foot in yo ass,"[6] they may run to bolt the door and draw the curtains. When they hear Ice-T rap "watch me...don the black ski mask and come to your house / cut off your power, and do you with the lights out"[7] they may feel the urge to reach for the phone and dial 911 (when the operator answers, though, all they'll hear is a recording of Flavor Flav saying "You'd better wake up and smell the *real* flavor / cos 9-1-1 is a fake lifesaver"[8]). Ignorant of black vernaculars and the Signifyin(g) mode, many such listeners have reacted against what seems to them an obscene and violent discourse, and yet in their discomfort what they *also* don't hear is the *real* political polemic which speaks *through* this mode. Or, in a no less problematic manner, other listeners have taken rap as a safety-sealed packet of titillating hostility, its imagery feeding their stereotypes of black culture as intrinsically violent. Thus the first level of mis-taking is when the Lion takes the monkey "seriously" (the Lion has been *signified* upon); the second level is when he *doesn't* take him seriously, failing to realize that the discursive play of Signifyin(g) is also a mode for (among other things) political expression, a "serious" unseriousness.

For similar reasons, the authors of the often-cited book *Signifying Rappers*, for all their canny "insider" posing, misunderstand rap almost as badly as Tipper Gore and her cohorts at the Parents' Music Resource Center. Both take rap lyrics as though they were *actual* threats; while Tipper Gore is morally outraged, Costello and Wallace are titillated. For them rap is "carnivorous," "big and ill-mannered"; they confess to "caucasian contempt for L.L Cool J's and Slick Rick's bantam-cock songs of Themselves."[9] Their publisher, Ecco Press, supplies a back-cover blurb which hails the book as "the first serious consideration of rap" and touts its authors as "white, educated, middle class...at once marginal and crucial to rap's Us and Them equations." *Whose* equations? It is a good thing to have suburban white boys around when you need them—to write a "serious" book, that is. These white boys even confess to being scared, which is to be taken, I suppose, as a sign that rap music has worked its magic on them.

Costello and Wallace also have other axes to grind, however, including a harsh critique of rap's militant black nationalism. They make much ado over Bob Dylan as a proto-rap pioneer, and taunt Public Enemy for being "unable to locate even one pure black source" (begging Chuck D's own question in "Fear of a Black Planet": "Who is Pure? What is pure?"). Sampling, though they pretend to be delighted by it, poses a problem for them, a problem of sources; for them the sampled material remains somehow "stolen." They find it "troubling" that the rappers on the "Stop the Violence" EP "made their names signifying violence"—a statement which would be meaningless if they knew what "signifying" signified. Similarly, in the *Village Voice*, Marshall Berman (otherwise a thoughtful writer on rap) worries aloud about the "romance of violence"; at a PE show he begins to get nervous when the uniformed S1W (Security of the First World) steps onto stage in their "gangsta/fascist chic."[10] Yet the 'violence' these writers locate within hip-hop's acts self-staging is inexorably framed by the Signifyin(g) monkey's verbal reversals; is that Elephant out to get you or not? It is that uncertainty which forms the screen, and the audience that does the *projecting*; literal and figurative violences function not as *essences* but as perceptual gestalts.

2. Hip-Hop and the logic of moral panics

Signifyin(g) violence, whether in Ice-T's gangsta hitman narratives or in the S1W's uniforms (on the cover of *Apocalypse '91*, they look more like ship's captains for some new cruise line), is a highly self-conscious *ploy*, the equivalent of the Monkey telling the Lion "Look out sucker, that Elephant's going to kill you." Yet such a statement belies the *actual* power relations of the Monkey and the Lion; the Monkey is physically the weaker of the two and must rely on a verbal exchange to gain his victory. Just so, while the S1W may look threatening in their concert-wear grey camouflage fatigues, they are not there to attack anyone, but rather to Signify the global history of Black resistance. Nonetheless, they can be *taken* as threatening by audiences who find them so, and like the Signifyin(g) Monkey, hip-hop in a sense *presupposes* such a mis-taking. This would seem to place the politics of reception in a paradoxical position; if Signifyin(g) presupposes a mis-taking, then doesn't such mis-taking become, in a sense, "correct"? And more: if the underlying message of hip-hop Signifyin(g) is a serious unseriousness, a double ploy whose verbal play conceals a linguistic assault, is it not then necessary that there be a degree of actual *force* behind its narratives of violence? To which I would say, yes, there is a violence—or rather, there are *violences*—underlying hip-hop's linguistic militancy, including both the violence of the racist power structure against black communities, the violence within those communities, and the possibility of a revolutionary violence *against* these other forms of violence. KRS-One, both the founder of the "Stop the Violence" movement and the poet behind the seminal gangsta rap "9 mm Goes Bang," Signifies on the mis-taking of rap's representations of violence in his cut "Necessary":

> When some get together and think of rap, they tend to think of violence
> But when they are challenged on some rock group, the result is always silence
> Even before the rock and roll era, violence played a big part in music

It's all according to your meaning of violence and how or in which
   way you use it
No, it's not violent to show in movies the destruction of the human
   body
But yes, of course it's violent to protect yourself at a party
And, oh no, it's not violent when under the christmas tree is a
   look-alike gun
But, yes, of course it's violent to have an album like KRS-One
By all means necessary, it's time to end the hypocrisy
What I call violence, I can't do, but your kind of violence is stop-
   ping me.[11]

KRS-One's Signifyin(g) works first by foregrounding the interpretive
protocols of the Signified listener ("It's all according to your meaning
of violence"), and second by alluding to the many "violent" acts and
representations that society at large already partakes of by virtue of
their "merely" representational status (toy guns, slasher films). All of
that violence, he implies, pales before "what I call violence," even as it
distracts from the actual violence of racism and censorship ("your kind
of violence") which all this ostensible disdain of violence masks. KRS-
One's rhetoric makes the claim that those who attack hip-hop for
"violence" have not yet accounted for the interpretative or cultural
contexts in which they already *consume* violence; behind the moral
panics which deploy the word "violence" to attack rap music is a
culture that already sanctions all kinds of violence.

Frantz Fanon's political theorizations of violence as a means of
resistance to colonial regimes are highly pertinent, not only because
they were so central to movements like the Black Panthers but because
they still inform black nationalism today (Paris, for one, includes an
exhortation to 'follow the path' of Fanon in his rap "The Devil Made Me
Do It").[12] For despite the fact that Fanon was writing about colonial
Africa, the worsening situation of blacks and Hispanics in America's
inner cities has to an increasing degree borne comparison with the
postcolonial situation. Just as in any colonial city, urban African-
Americans have found themselves in a virtual shantytown, only this
time near the center rather than on the periphery of the postmodern
city. Again, just as in colonized nations, black Americans have been
subject to aerial fly-bys, frequent and arbitrary police raids, lengthy
imprisonments, and at times of open revolt (such as the Los Angeles
rebellion) occupying troops. In this context, Fanon's revolutionary

program has taken on a sudden new relevance, as when he describes the colonial landscape:

> The colonial world is a world cut in two. The dividing line, the frontiers are shown by barracks and police stations. In the colonies it is always the policeman and the soldier who are the official, instituted go-betweens, the spokesmen of the settler and his rule of oppression...in the capitalist countries a multitude of moral teachers, counselors, and "bewilderers" separate the exploited from those in power. In the colonial countries, on the contrary, the policeman and the soldier, by their immediate presence and their frequent and direct action maintain contact with the native and advise him by means of rifle butts and napalm not to budge.[13]

The irony that this text, originally published in 1963, now seems to be as relevant to Los Angeles as it is to Capetown, that indeed the landscape Fanon describes as "colonial" is perhaps closer to that of South Central than the "capitalist" situation, has not been lost on the latest generation of rappers. The metaphors for the ghetto—Ice-T's "the killing fields," Ice Cube's "Concrete Vietnam," Public Enemy's "terrordome"—all confirm this shift of landscape.[14]

The attitude towards the police is a telling divider in terms of the reception of hip-hop; in the postcolonial urban landscapes described by KRS-One, Paris or Ice Cube, the police are the agents of an oppressive system, and indeed many urban forces such as the L.A.P.D. have records of racist brutality that go back decades.[15] In the light of numerous recent beatings, which left Rodney King scarred and bruised and Malice Green dead on the streets of Detroit, it is terrifyingly clear that the police function as instruments of oppression. For suburban residents, though, trained from childhood to believe that "the policeman is your friend," and for whom indeed the policeman is their friend, and the friend of their property and privilege, cuts like NWA's "Fuck tha Police" or Ice-T's "Cop Killa" are affronts to a sacred symbol of law and order. As WC and the MAAD Circle put it (in a singsong voiceover on their cut "Behind Closed Doors"):

> The policemen are your friends
> They're here to protect and serve
> But if you're white, then you're alright
> And you won't get kicked to the curb.[16]

Nothing, perhaps, has incited so much negative reaction as hip-hop's anti-police raps, despite the fact that the ongoing brutality and violence perpetrated by the police continues to be a fact of urban life.

In a different but closely related way, gangsta raps also partake of this postcolonial resistance. While rap's narratives (and the gang activities that exist in most large cities regardless of their portrayal on records) are often condemned for glorifying violence, they too bring with them an implicit critique of oppression. As Fanon noted years ago,

> The people make use of certain episodes in the life of the community in order to hold themselves ready and keep alive their revolutionary zeal. For example, the gangster who holds up the police set on to track him down for days on end, or who dies in single combat after having killed four or five policemen...these types light the way for the people, form the blueprints for action and become heroes. Obviously it's a waste of breath to say that such-and-such a hero is a thief, a scoundrel, or a reprobate. If the act for which he is prosecuted by the colonial authorities is an act exclusively directed against a colonialist person or colonialist property, the demarcation line is definite and manifest. The process of identification is automatic.[17]

Such an association should come as no surprise to anyone who has listened to Woody Guthrie's "Pretty Boy Floyd," Dylan's "John Wesley Harding," or any of the hundreds of ballads celebrating the goodness of outlaws, and yet inscribed within the politics of moral panic with which middle-class America has been Willie Hortonized, many listeners (among them no doubt the very people who shouted "Fuck the Pigs" in '69) end up identifying with the police and attacking the rappers. When the outlaw is white, it seems, he is a counterculture hero; when he is black, he is reduced to yet another avatar of the stereotypical violent black male.[18]

Of course, there is always the *other* possibility—that middle- and upper-class listeners, while hitherto trusting mass media's representations of urban criminality, might after listening to such narratives find themselves radicalized. For in much the same way that television coverage of the dogs and firehoses turned on black civil-rights protesters in Birmingham mobilized opposition to racism among white viewers, hip-hop's gangsta revolutionary narratives bear with them a powerful political and emotional punch—provided that one actually gives them a listen. Not surprisingly, alliances have been formed via hip-hop primarily among the younger generation of listeners, who are looking for (sub)cultural modes of identification, and finding them in hip-hop messages and style.

Violence, then, in the context of the debate over hip-hop, is deployed as a mythic *sign*—isolated, considered in the abstract, apart from its motivations or ends—and becomes the keyword of the moral panic that points its finger at rappers. Yet as KRS-One notes, taking his cue from Malcolm X, "We mistake violence for self-defense"; taken outside of the context of the urban war upon the poor, gangsta raps and style may indeed seem 'fascistic."[19] Hip-hop, to the extent that it re-inserts these questions into the material, lived existence of the ghetto, works to counter the discourse of moral panic that surrounds the notion of "violence." The justification of violence may be articulated in many ways—and indeed it is not universal; many rappers, following Martin Luther King Jr., urge only non-violent means of resistance. Yet the point is that hip-hop re-inserts a difference—between *violence* and *self-defense*—that the spectacular media of moral panic erases, and simply by doing that, it works against the reproduction of oppression.

Another frequent accusation levelled against hip-hop is that of misogyny; indeed this accusation is second only to that of violence, to which in fact it is intimately linked. Certainly there is misogyny in rap lyrics, and certainly some rappers, such as Luther Campbell of 2 Live Crew, Too $hort, and Eazy-E, make calling out "bitches" and "ho's" a central part of their lyrical style. Yet the way this misogyny is attacked, as Jon Michael Spenser has remarked, invokes the oldest racist stereotypes in the book:

> A close examination of the reactions rap causes in certain elements of American society reveals a terror that rap may lead to racial insurrection—not the sort of social unrest witnessed during the sixties, but chaotic gang warfare and rampant rape. The frequent juxtaposition of *rap* and *rape* in the media justifies this postulate. Tipper Gore's *Washington Post* editorial, "Hate, Rape, and Rap," is the first instance of this linkage. It occurs again in a *Newsweek* editorial titled "America's Slide into the Sewer," in which journalist George F. Will juxtaposes the rap lyrics of 2 Live Crew and the explicit testimony of legal defendants regarding the attack of a jogger in New York's Central Park in April 1990. In another newspaper article it was reported that during sentencing, one of the

males convicted in the case 'swaggered through a rambling, rap-
styled poem he had composed in jail.'[20]

Again, the same modes of attack that characterize the outcry against
"violence" in rap lyrics are evident: the misogyny of the lyrics is
removed from the original context of their performance, held forth—
in Will's article, by sheer tactical juxtaposition rather than logic—as
signs of *what will happen* if nothing is done about this terrible plague
of rap music, and finally deployed as a synecdoche for black males and
black culture in general. "Those violent blacks," one imagines some
yuppie at breakfast, intoning over espresso and the *New York Times*,
"when will they learn to act responsibly?"

But this is not merely negative press, it is more: the criticism of
"violence" and misogyny in rap lyrics is a tactical move characteristic of
what critics such as Simon Watney (following Stanley Cohen and
Stuart Hall) describe as "moral panics." In a thoroughly spectacular
society, "moral panics" are both the most effective and insidious form
of ideological broadcasting:

> It is the central ideological business of the communications indus-
> try to retail ready-made pictures of "human" identity, and thus
> recruit individual consumers to identify with them in a fantasy of
> collective mutual complementarity. Whole sections of society, how-
> ever, cannot be contained within this project, since they refuse to
> dissolve into the larger mutualities required of them. Hence the
> position, in particular, though in different ways, of both blacks and
> gay men, who are made to stand outside the "general public,"
> inevitably appearing as threats to its internal cohesion. This cohe-
> sion is not "natural," but a result of the media industry's modes of
> address—targetting an imaginary national family unit which is
> both white and heterosexual. All apparent threats to this key object
> of individual identification will be subject to the kids of treatment
> which Cohen and his followers describe as moral panics.[21]

"Moral panics," Watney furthermore demonstrates, are not discrete
and occasional instances of media hype, but rather part of an ongoing
ideological process; indeed the *lack* of something to panic about immediately ups the ante and virtually requires that some cause for alarm be
mobilized, lest the status quo suddenly be called into question. Ultimately, however chimerical or demonstrably inaccurate the symbolic

terrors which are used to incite such panics may be, it hardly makes a difference; what matters is that the system has once again conquered. We who live in a nation that fights a war on the poor in the name of the moral-panic-driven "war on drugs" can hardly afford to laugh at similar ploys abroad, as when Saddam Hussein declares defeat "victory," or the United Nations bombs Somalia in the name of "peace."

3. Who freaked who?

None of the mechanisms of moral panic should obscure the fact that there is misogyny, homophobia, and inter-ethnic hatred in many rap lyrics. Given the conflicting and interrelated discourses of race, gender, sexuality, and class, it could hardly be otherwise; in fact precisely to the extent that hip-hop brings with it an accurate "sample" of everyday events and conflicts in the 'hood, it brings with it the "whole kit and kaboodle" of hatreds, rivalries, and resentments. As Sonja Peterson-Lewis has argued, neither the appeal to "representationalism" nor a gesture (such as Henry Louis Gates's in his op-ed piece on 2 Live Crew) towards the *tradition* of Signifyin(g) and sexual boasting, necessarily render hip-hop misogyny beyond the pale of criticism.[22] The situation, as in other cultural contexts, is more an unresolved struggle than a *fait accompli*; power relationships are at stake in hip-hop, between black and white, male and female, "straight" and "gay," "underclass" and "bourgeoisie," and so forth, but there is no stable dominance.

Specifically, this conflictedness is embedded directly within hip-hop, on account of the *dialectical* structure of Signifyin(g) itself, which is always liable to a rebuttal or "payback." For instance, misogynistic raps have been under attack from the start; the most well-known example being UTFO's diss of a fictional girl by the name of Roxanne in their 1984 cut "Roxanne, Roxanne."[23] This cut spawned no fewer than two dozen response raps, including the recording debut of the Big Mama, Roxanne Shanté. In fact, UTFO cashed in on their own payback by hiring a young girl they named "The *Real* Roxanne" to come into the studio and diss them. Not all of the responses were feminist manifestos, but collectively they demonstrated that an attack on a woman— on *any* woman—in rhyme was going to be answered in rhyme. Notable "paybacks" since then have included MC Choice's "The Big

Payback" (in which she takes the members of NWA down to size,
though via the problematic strategy of questioning their masculinity
with homophobic epithets), and Roxanne Shanté's own version of
"Fatal Attraction," in which she turns the narrative tables and castrates
her faithless Wall Street lover, putting his 'jimmy' in a 'pickle jar.'

Feminist raps, however, have not only been reactive, but *active*,
and despite the reputation of hip-hop as a black male genre, sistas have
been at it from the start. Grandmaster Flash recalls that, 'back in the
day,' there were more female crews than male, though far fewer of
them were able to break into the recording side; pre-1985 women
rappers include Naomi Peterson, the Mercedes Ladies, Sha Rock (the
"+1" of "Funky Four+1"), Sequence, and Big Lady K.[24] Roxanne Shanté
was already well established as a rapper in the mid-'80s, though the
first woman rapper to garner much media attention was the less hardcore (but still lyrically skilled) Queen Latifah. "Ladies First," which she
cut with British rapper Monie Love, is perhaps the best-known femi-
nist-style rap, with a video that showed Latifah planning global strategy
while pictures of Winnie Mandela and Sojurner Truth flashed in the
background; with a voice as boomin' as any man's, Latifah boldly
proclaimed: "A woman can bear you, break you, take you, now it's time
to relate to / a woman dope enough to make you holler and scream."[25]
Shanté offered her own manifesto with "The Year of the Independent
Woman," where she criticizes women who make their identities depen-
dent on men:

> How many runny-nosed kids can you have?
> How many nights can you work on the ave?
> Your so-called man has a car and a *Visa*
> He's livin' large while you're livin' on pizza
> Unemployed while you're waitin' for the perfect mate
> Let's get one thing straight, cause it's gettin' late
> What you're waitin' for, it's never really comin'
> No one hears the sorry tunes that you're hummin'
> I'm here to bring you the news
> That if you're singin' the blues everyday
> It will not change the views that people have of you.[26]

Shanté addresses this rap directly to her homegirls, even as she
Signifies on racist stereotypes, such as the welfare mother with
"runny-nosed kids." Rather than offering condescending advice, she

offers a critique of the sexist double standards which allow men, though "livin' large," to remain uncommitted to the women in their lives. Yet this critique is followed by a call to solidarity: "Lend me your ears, dry up your tears, and let's hear three cheers for the year of the independent woman."[27]

Similar strategies have been followed by many other women rappers, as in Salt-n-Pepa's "Tramp" (quoted in chapter 1), Yo Yo's "Girl, Don't Be No Fool," MC Lyte's "When in Love," and Nikki-D's "18 and Loves to Go."[28] These raps share an interior focus, a kind of home-girl-to-homegirl mode of address, that enables them to be critical yet encouraging; their didacticism is pointed but supportive. Such a mode of address, however, is not the only one women rappers employ; in the past few years, over fifty female MCs have emerged, and their raps run the gamut of hip-hop styles. Most recently, a number of women, such as the Bo$$ and Bigga Sistas, have broken out with a hardcore "gangsta" style as rough or rougher than that of any of their male peers. Following hip-hop's re-appropriation of "nigga," many of these women style themselves "bitches," taking on and seeking to re-define the very epithet with which misogynistic rappers such as Too $hort and Luther Campbell sought to degrade them.

Hardcore women rappers can be further broken down into two overlapping schools, which could be called the "sex" school and the "gangsta" school. The "sex" school, whose leading proponents are HWA ("Hoes wit' Attitude"), BWP (Bytches Wit' Problems) and MC Choice, stake their claim for power on a graphic, woman-in-charge sexuality; they make a mockery of inflated claims of male sexual prowess (BWP's "Two Minute Brother") and demand equal time for oral sex (Choice's "Cat Got Your Tongue" or the Yeastie Girls' "You Suck").[29] Many women of this school like to go toe-to-toe with the male counterparts, as when Nikki-D battles with Apache to see "Who Freaked Who." The sexual antagonism of these raps can get hot and heavy; while Apache insists "I fuckin' freaked you," Nikki-D declares that by the time she's done with Apache he'll "need a tourniquet for [his] nuts."[30] Not all "sex" raps, however, assert a more dominant role for women; some, such as HWA's "Fuck Me Baby" are simply up-front advertisements for sexual services, but despite this, the overall effect of these rappers is to set a new standard of (hetero)sexual assertiveness for women.

The other "gangsta" school of women rappers is relatively new; while Antoinette tried to make it big with "The Gangstress" back in '87,

it wasn't until the early '90s that the "gangsta bitches" broke onto the
streets and into the charts. Bo$$'s 1993 debut, *Born Gangstaz*, charts
new lyrical and musical territory; over heavy, p-funk beats she weaves
narratives of street-smart revenge, coupled by skits, such as "Thelma
and Louise," which show her and her homegirls blowing away at
egotistical men with semi-automatic gunfire over the noise of breaking
glass and squealing tires. Significantly, 1992–93 has seen a number of
women rappers move closer to a gangsta style; both Yo-Yo and MC Lyte
have moved to distance themselves from their softer, more R&B
moments and emphasize a no-nonsense "ruffneck" attitude.

4. Gangsta, Gangsta

Gangsta rap, in general, has expanded its influence in the early
'90s, no doubt in part due to the very criticism that the mass media
have heaped on the genre. While gangsta style has always been part of
the hip-hop mix, its singling out by the machineries of moral panic as a
synecdoche for hip-hop as a whole has made even rappers who gener-
ally eschew the style feel a sense of solidarity and respect. White audi-
ences have surely played a part in this, as the sales records of NWA
emigrés like Dr. Dre and Ice Cube demonstrate, despite the fact that
much of the "message" in gangsta raps is aimed directly at the hood; it
is an irony of hip-hop's reception that the more it turns inward, the
more it addresses itself (as 2PAC says) 'strictly to my niggaz,' the more
certain white listeners want to hear it. The broad appeal of these narra-
tives, increasingly, is the ground where battles of the (il)legitimacy of
hip-hop are fought, since by one criterion, the most "authentic" raps (if
being hardcore 'gangsta' "no radio" produces "authenticity") are
regarded by rap's critics as the greatest signs of its *in*authenticity.

Underlying these reactive and highly volatile demarcations is
what Michael Eric Dyson has aptly dubbed the "anxiety of authentic-
ity," an anxiety framed by the dissonance between the sense that only
those who actually *belong* to a certain race have a right to produce
music identified with that race and the concomitant recognition that
"race" qua race is an inexorably mixed and overdetermined factor in
social identity.[31] This anxiety has been exacerbated by the ways in which
the *loss* of racial identity has historically been the admission ticket to
increased *class* status, recognition of which has led some schools of

Afrocentricity to associate lighter skin with race treachery, the desire to 'pass' for white (or to in any way accede or appeal to aesthetics or standards perceived as 'white'), and eventual assimilation. Within these terms, the presence of a large white audience has alternately been a source of pleasure (as a sign that music offers both amelioration and remuneration of racial inequity) and of suspicion, as when a successful black artist is accused of "selling out" by working too hard to appeal to white audiences. And, within African-American communities, this anxiety has disclosed the growing class rift between the urban black underclass (for whom middle-class status is a distant and foreclosed territory) and the black middle class, which at many junctures has been spectacularly opposed to rappers and their worldview.[32]

Never has this rift been more apparent than during the recent moral panic over so-called gangsta rap. In 1994, the reaction against this particular genre reached a crisis point in the form of congressional hearings instigated by Dr. C. Delores Tucker. Dr. Tucker, a longtime civil-rights activist and former Pennsylvania Secretary of State, took offense to "gangsta rap" lyrics, and organized a series of protests in the Washington, D.C. area. In one, Tucker and other protesters (Dick Gregory notable among them) were arrested for blocking the entrance to a "Nobody Beats the Wiz" record store. Unlike Tipper Gore and her dormant Parents' Music Resource Center, Tucker wanted more than warning labels; she demanded an outright ban on "gangsta" rap records. Yet, like Gore, Tucker (a member of the Democratic National Committee) used her Washington connections to call for congressional hearings—lobbying which bore fruit in February 1994 in the form of separate hearings in both the House of Representatives *and* the Senate.[33] The witness lists at these hearings—Tucker, Dionne Warwick, Sgt. Ron Stallworth (a Utah police officer and "Gang Intelligence Coordinator"), and Robert Phillips (the deputy medical director of the American Psychiatric Association) for the prosecution, along with Yo-Yo, Michael Eric Dyson, and Def Jam's David Harleston for the defense— speak to the contradictory politics and economics of race. Tucker and Warwick, standing in for the old guard of the civil rights movement, express incredulity at the words of rappers and ask that they be banned; the only motive they can imagine is cash. Yo-Yo, a young black female rap artist, and Harleston, a corporate figure from 'the house that LL built,' take pride in their achievements and artistic success, and resent the implicit "sucka" theory of ideology that is Tucker's subtext. Dyson, self-described 'petit-bourgeois Negro intellectual' and in more ways than one the man in the middle, was the wild card. An ordained minister as well as a cultural critic, he broke the implicit dichotomies of the testimony, and offered an unflinching plea (even quoting from Snoop Doggy Dogg) that others hear the message of the rappers. Both hearings concluded without any concrete moves towards censorship, and yet the balance was a fragile one, and despite Dyson's testimony the only part of the message of gangsta rap that Tucker and her allies heard was the "obscene" language, conveniently highlighted on cardboard placards and handed out to attendees.

Not long afterwards, deep in the heart of Texas, another DISS-cussion took place in an equally complex and contradictory space. The *Source* had gathered 'gangsta' rappers at one of the homes of James Smith, president and CEO of Houston's Rap-a-Lot records, home to hardcore gangstas the Geto Boys and hard-talking women rappers like MC Choice. The house, surreally unlived-in and yet thoroughly bourgeois in its outward configurations, was itself a synecdoche for the larger cultural dissonance: the black underclass finds a voice, and with his share of the proceeds a black entrepreneur builds a thoroughly bourged-up house where rappers can sit on the patio and talk about the moral panic running through other, similarly-shaped houses where the parents live in fear of that same black underclass, even as *their* kids pump up the Geto Boys in their Walkman headphones. These ironies weren't lost on those in attendance at this 'gangsta' summit:

> **James Bernard:** How does [rap] challenge the government?
> **James Smith:** Just the power with this rap. It's all about what we do with this shit now. But it is the biggest challenge to the government ever since I can remember. They can't fuck with it because there so many real dominatin' niggas comin' together that —
> **Havoc:** And when you have white America listening to it, they kids who didn't know what's really goin' on in these Black communities now will really hear from a real perspective
> **James Smith:** Their parents hid it from them for so long and now we tellin; 'em what really goin' on, they hardly believe it. They like this shit like they like the movies.[34]

Smith's simile has its own telling resonance; a world where the black underclass and the largely white middle class meet only via the screen of artistic representation—whether it's music, video, or film—has its own, other dangers. Hip-hop may well be "reality rap," but there are few ways for its white listeners to get a 'reality check.' It's a slippery slope, though not the one that C. Delores Tucker is worried about—but at the same time it demonstrates the *fundamental* problem of what Hacker describes as the "two nations" of America, a problem which rappers inhabit, but certainly didn't *create*.

5. Sexuality, Class, and Black Machismo

The racial and class antagonisms inherent in the debates over hip-hop take on a different look, however, when they are examined alongside the homophobic black machismo that forms another facet of the worldview of many rappers. Anti-gay lyrics are commonplace in rap lyrics (e.g., Flavor Flav's "Letter to the New York Post," MC Ren's "Kiss my Black Azz," or Ice Cube's "No Vaseline"), and outright threats, such as Brand Nubian's threat to "shoot a faggot in the back for actin' like that" or Shabba Ranks's suggestion that gays be crucified, form one extreme of this larger hostility. Yet however hateful these lyrics, they must, like Professor Griff's anti-Semitic diatribes, be seen as specific enunciations framed by specific discourses on sexuality, race, and identity; to do less is to embrace the "moral panic" logic, which would have an entire musical tradition held up to scorn on the basis of such lyrics. That this is untenable is further underlined by performers such as Ice-T or the Disposable Heroes of HipHoprisy who have taken a stand *for* gay rights, and by the increasing visibility of gays and lesbians within the hip-hop scene.

The politics of sexuality in hip-hop are as spectacular as those of violence; while assertive, aggressive sexuality is a key ingredient of hip-hop attitude, it has so far almost always been *hetero*sexuality. Yet beneath the posturing of macho males and rough-and-rugged females lie significant anxieties about both their personal sexuality and the mass political mobilizations of gays and lesbians. Women rappers who have taken an aggressive and highly sexualized stance have faced condemnation both as second-rate imitations of men *and* as butchy lesbians, and indeed many of them have taken pains to assert their heterosexual status. Male rappers, while they have been able to make copious claims for their sexual prowess *without* having their heterosexuality called into question, have nonetheless shown considerable hostility over their direct and indirect relations with gay males, who have always been a central part of the dance club scene, and whose increasing industry visibility has led to confrontations such as the one over the editorship of Quincy Jones's pilot hip-hop magazine, *Vibe*.

Vibe was originally a joint venture between Jones and veteran hip-hop super-agent Russell Simmons, but Simmons pulled out of the project, in large part due to disagreements over staffing. Simmons's biggest complaint was that the person hired as editor-in-chief, Jonathan Van Meter, was white *and* gay. "I don't think it makes me homophobic to say that," Simmons was quoted by the *New York Times* as saying. " I just think the most homophobic group invading popular culture in the last fifty years is probably rappers. I would like to see some straight black man involved in the editing of this magazine, someone whose experiences are similar to that of the rappers."[35] Simmons's logic aside (what other prejudices would be needed to make an ideal editor?), he plays identity politics with a vengeance, and he is not alone. In the spectacularized identity politics of race, real (but impersonal) hazards (such as the domination of the hip-hop recording industry by major multinational record conglomerates, which Simmons helped to engineer) often go unexamined, even as personified antagonisms with other minority groups (Koreans, gays, Jews) stir disproportionate anxiety and hostility. Underlying this spectacularization, inevitably, are the mass politics of group identities, in which constituencies have coalesced around cultural positions such as "gay," "Latino," "working class," or "woman"; the economic decline of the late '80s and early '90s has placed these groups in competition for a shrinking pool of political and economic resources which, whatever it has done for the system as a whole, has tended to undermine solidarity between these groups.

A telling historical rift came during the debates over the new "Rainbow" curriculum for New York City schools, which included materials with favorable representations of gay families, along with other ostensibly more multicultural images and histories. In the moral panic that arose against this curriculum—which eventually toppled the Schools Chancellor himself—"black" and "gay" functioned as incommensurable terms, partly on account of the masculinist and patriarchal codes of both white and black working-class communities, but also partly because of the sense by working-class and poor blacks that there were already *enough* groups waiting in line at the dwindling soup kitchen of institutional cultural affirmation. One black heterosexual woman, whose views were typical of many people involved in these debates, framed this view succinctly:

> We've been fighting for multicultural education for all these years and haven't gotten shit, and here come these rich white gay white boys and their friends in the liberal elite, getting what they want while we're still at the back of the bus.[36]

Racism's recurrent blockage of black social and economic progress, continuing long after slavery *per se* but continuing to enforce subaltern status through other means, fuels this rage; while the flood-tide of European immigrants in the late nineteenth and early twentieth century has been absorbed into "white" status and privilege, and some Asian-American communities have enjoyed a rapid rise into the professional classes, the black urban underclass is indeed still "at the back of the bus"—with the black middle-class only a few seats forward. And, while lesbians and gay men have gained powerful political voices by entering into the politics of identity, they have also hopped on to the same overcrowded bus, where thanks to the Reaganomic cutbacks in social programs of all kinds, there is less room than ever before.

Gayness, furthermore, is seen by some African-Americans as a second-order identity, layered on top of middle- or upper-class status. To be a gay boy is to be (or aspire to be) a 'gay rich white boy'; from this set of associations, gayness is constructed as a kind of leisure culture that black boys in their right minds shouldn't give a shit about. Something of this kind must have been in Amiri Baraka's head when he implied to James Baldwin that Baldwin could not know the pain of being black if gayness was a part of his identity. Black gay identity, which is now commonly seen as a *double* oppression, canceled itself out for Baraka: -1 for being black, +1 for being gay = zero. This attitude persists to an extent even in the writings of writers such as bell hooks, who criticized the film *Paris is Burning* on account of the way black gay men's ideal of femininity is essentially "rich" and "white"—a sin of which hooks absolves the film's subjects by blaming the filmmaker (a white lesbian) for underlining it.[37] Yet as Essex Hemphill has pointed out, the problematic linkages of class and sexuality are not the fault of the filmmaker *or* those interviewed, but the product of the intertwined histories and yearnings of gayness and blackness. The drag queens' ultimate standard of excellence—"to be *real*"—is, as Hemphill observes, to 'put on an act'—but the "realness" of the act is intensified, rather than diminished, by the very material inequities within which black culture, and black gay culture, have historically been situated.[38]

In arguments like these, as with the debate over New York's "Rainbow Curriculum," sexuality complicates the race/class dichotomy, ultimately working to blur such categories in direct opposition to old-line black nationalist insistences on race and hetero masculinity as linked essences.[39] It is precisely this linkage, in fact, that has resurfaced in the attitude of some male rappers, whether or not they quote chapter and verse from the historical predecessors. The threads of this ideological stance go back to the earliest manifestations of black nationalism, which linked the fate of the race intrinsically with the authority of the black male.[40] The black male has been, as it were, castrated by the white system of power, "his" women reduced to concubines for the white man. To reclaim his "manhood," so the story goes, the black male must re-assert dominance by reclaiming the black woman, and even (by the lights of Eldridge Cleaver) raping white women to pay back the slaveholders for their collective crimes. Black maleness, then, along with Black male heterosexuality, become in this story the core of black resistance and militancy—whence the politicized misogyny of '60s black nationalists such as Stokely Carmichael, who declared that the only position for women in the Black Power movement was "prone."

This narrative is not often explicitly articulated by rappers, but it is clearly one of the texts that underlies many sexist and homophobic rap lyrics. Ice Cube, in an interview with Angela Davis, was generally in agreement with her on many issues, but on one point he was adamant:

Ice Cube: The black man is down.
Angela Davis: The back woman's down too.
Ice Cube: But the black woman can't look up to the black man until we get up.
Angela Davis: Well why should the black woman look *up* to the black man? Why can't we look at each other as equals?
Ice Cube: If we look at each other as equals, what you're going to have is a divide.[41]

In a related way, Queen Latifah, for all her royal attitude, seems to defer to men when she boasts in "Ladies First" that "We are the ones who give birth to the new generation of prophets"[42]—after all, given a choice, wouldn't it be more empowering to actually *be* a prophet than to give birth to one? Even raps that set themselves up as extolling the virtues of the black woman, such as the Poor Righteous Teachers' "Shakiyla," have a condescending tone, and their praise of women focuses on their physical beauty and childbearing capabilities.[43]

This unequal deployment of power along gender lines is analogous in many ways to the attitudes towards homosexuality expressed in many hip-hop lyrics: a lesbian, by not being available to the supermale black liberator, insults his ego *and* threatens the revolution;[44] a gay man can not perform the "revolutionary" reclamation of hetero "manhood", which makes him a potential traitor to "male" solidarity. And, while rappers such as Ice-T argue that, for better or worse, such a mentality is already hardwired into the unwritten codes of conduct of urban gangs, he elides the possibility of black homosexualty: "The tough guy survives, so you're taught to prey on anything that's weaker. So you can't expect a lot of these hip-hop kids, who have grown up in the projects, to understand being gay."[45] Ice-T assumes here both that there are no (visible) gays in the ghetto, and that gays are necessarily 'weaker'—placing *him* within the very machismo he is setting out to 'explain.' Yet clearly, there have always been black gays and lesbians, and indeed gay black men have Signified on machismo since way "back in the day"—far from being a matter of ignorance, black homophobia is much more often a rivalry between well-acquainted groupings, each with distinct cultural turf to defend.

One immediate site of this friction between blacks and gays lies in the politics of dance halls and clubs. The gay club scene has been crucial in the establishment of the modern dance music industry at least since the early days of disco; indeed, in the late '70s the sentiment "disco sucks" was used as a veiled expression of both homophobia *and* racism. In a similar way, the techno-funk, Euro-disco, and technorave scenes have evolved in large part through their presence in gay dance clubs in the United States and Europe. Hip-hop, taking disco as one of its first sites of incursion, and actively producing trends in dance music such as "electro funk," has moved between solidarity and a kind of tense cohabitation with gay audiences and DJs. For black gay men, the contradiction of an ostensibly "liberatory" music whose lyrics so often celebrate gay-bashing has bitter ironies, and yet paradoxically such music is extremely influential in the club scene. When the Euro-house group Snap! cancelled a Boston gig after they learned the venue was a gay club, there was outrage in the local gay community, heightened by the jarring irony of realizing that a highly popular dance track ("I've Got the Power") which had been heavily played and promoted at gay clubs turned out to have been produced by rabid homophobes.

The situation is changing, however; while Ice-T may be alone among hardcore rappers in actively denouncing homophobia, a number of newer hip-hop groups have taken up the cause of gay rights. Prominent among them has been the Disposable Heroes of HipHoprisy, who released the first anti-gay-bashing rap, "The Language of Violence," in 1992; other bands on the hip-hop/industrial dance fringe, such as Consolidated, have made strong stands for gay rights both on and off the mic. Just as many male rappers, albeit after some heavy lyrical pressure, have worked towards strong and positive "pro-female" raps (Public Enemy's "Revolutionary Generation," Paris's "Asaataa's Song"), it is conceivable that more rappers who have rapped out homophobic rhymes will follow Ice-T's lead. The fight against AIDS, which has disproportionately affected both gay and urban black communities, may serve as a common ground; even Ice Cube has denounced under-funding for AIDS treatment (though only as a tool of genocide against blacks).[46]

6. Black and White: Anxieties of Authenticity

Despite the deep imbrication of hip-hop music within urban black cultures, the fact that so many hip-hop consumers are at a great geographical and cultural *distance* from the cities whence this urban knowledge-dropping emanates means that there will always be those who take hip-hop literally with no attention to its ironies and nuances, and the reaction of these people will *itself* be deployed by the architects and purveyors of moral panic as *evidence* that what they fear is real. Similarly, despite whatever voices "come correct" about issues such as black-on-black crime, sexism, homophobia, the fact that the vast majority of hip-hop does *not* consist of gay-bashing, mindless misogyny, or glorified violence will never prevent raps that *do* from being taken as hip-hop's essence. The system of moral panics requires that the offending parts be taken as a paranoid symptom of the feared *whole*; a case in point is David Samuels' much-hyped piece in the *New Republic*.[47]

The cover photo for the issue featuring Samuels' article depicts a young white male wearing headphones, over which is printed the scandalous banner, "The Real Face of Rap." The accompanying article by David Samuels is itself subheaded "The 'black music' that isn't either." Why isn't it black? Because its industry leaders, like Rick Rubin (one of the founders of Def Jam records) or the editor of the rap magazine *The Source* are white (and, Samuels rather pointedly adds, "Jewish") entrepreneurs, while its most popular artists are themselves not ghetto kids but rather "a tightly knit group of mostly young, middle-class New Yorkers."[48] The fact that the large mass of its audience is white is also problematic for Samuels, though by this token blues and jazz might not qualify either as "black." And why isn't it music? Because its white "mainstream" audience had pressured it into conforming to their stereotypes, making it in the process "like rock'n'roll, a celebration of posturing over rhythm."[49]

Certainly, there is no doubt that many white listeners find the representations of violence provided by N.W.A. and Schoolly-D fit right in with their stereotypes. Whatever the extent to which this violence is taken as Signified and not literal, it is still "safe" in the sense that white listeners can hear it in the comfort and safety of their suburban homes. As PE producer Hank Shocklee, quoted by Samuels, remarks, "It's like going to an amusement park and going on a roller-coaster ride—records are safe, they're controlled fear, and you always have the choice of turning it off. That's why nobody ever takes a train up to 125th street and gets out and starts walking around. Because then you're not in control anymore..."[50] Yet the safe distance of this audience does not *necessarily* preclude the possibility that their hearing Ice-T describe the ghetto as an "economic prison" in "Escape from the Killing Fields" can't raise white listeners' awareness of the fear and desperation experienced by young black kids in South Central Los Angeles.

All this comes round again to the Signifyin(g) problematic, which is that there are no guarantees when it comes to the *reception* of language. Alongside the literal mis-taking of the Signifying Monkey's figurative language, another parable could be formed by the figurative mis-taking of literal language; when the Black Panther slogan "stick-em up motherfucker, we've come for what's ours" is sampled on Paris's album *The Devil Made me Do It*, it no doubt may be received by many listeners not as an empowering reminder of the Panther movement, but merely as another titillating sample of that good old "authentic" black proclivity towards violence. Even if the political messages of rap are taken seriously, there is a further danger that many listeners will do no more than listen, cashing in on the "feel-good" politics of simply *buying* a rap record. As Gates has noted, it can amount to little more than "buying Navajo blankets at a reservation road-stop."[51]

Yet these inescapable problematics hardly need to be taken, as Samuels takes them, as proof that rap is therefore inevitably a "corrupting" re-vending of racist stereotypes.[52] For one, while "gangsta" rap artists continue to provide a large portion of rap's sales volume, they are not representative of an increasingly heterogenous hip-hop culture. Whether in the form of the coolly spiritual, half-sung meditations of P.M. Dawn, the jazz-with-a-hip-hop-attitude of Greg Osby, or the laid-back scattershot play of groups such as De LA Soul or K.M.D., the current spectrum of hip-hop culture cuts across all kinds of racial, ideological, and religious lines. To continue to regard groups like 2 Live Crew as typical representatives of rap (and on that basis to condemn rap in general) is *itself* to perpetuate racist stereotypes.

In addition to the question of rap's homogeneity, Samuels appropriates Gates in order to question the "authenticity" of rap as a cultural medium. Taking up the problematics of reception, he argues that rap's mostly-white audience has "shaped" rap music to its own stereotypes. Rap's authenticity thus is reduced to that of the "Navajo blanket"—it may indeed have "come from" an authentic culture, but only as the commodification of a sort of synecdochal text (hip-hop's gangsta fairytales become to "Blacks" what blankets are to "Indians") whose consumption marks not cultural understanding but rather a studied avoidance of understanding. The "lack of authenticity" comes not only from this exchange, but because Vanilla Ice can be sold at the same roadside stand, much as machine-woven imitations of Navajo blankets are sold at souvenir shops. Yet this ignores the dual ambivalence of any cultural product; in actual practice, many of the "threads" from which rap's blanket are woven come from experiences and words that are certainly "authentic" to those that lived them; others, though "machine-woven" from a miscellany of cultural fragments (black and white), are marked not by their origin (the "author" in authenticity) but pointedly by their *appropriation*. More than perhaps any other musical form, rap problematizes the discourse of authenticity, even as it makes the vexed question of its own reception the pivot of its own Signifyin(g) practice. The rap music that was purchased as entertainment may educate nonetheless; that the two cannot even be separated is implicitly indicated by the title of BDP's album *Edutainment*.

Samuels argues that rap's historical moment "has come and gone," but I would argue that it is still yet to come. Like blues, jazz, or any other full-fledged musical discourse, hip-hop can no longer be characterized merely by citing the products of *some of* its performers. Is rap *male*? Women rappers, present from the start, continue to be a strong presence; Queen Latifah has become not only a successful rapper but a sitcom star and the head of her own label; MC Lyte and Salt-n-Pepa have cut four successful albums apiece—no small feat in a field where a goodly two-thirds never even make it to record number *two*. Is rap exclusively 'a black thing'? From back in the day onto the present, Latino communities on the east and west coasts have been pivotal to hip-hop; Kid Frost, who started his career in the early '80s, is the godfather of Hispanic rappers, and helped form the Los Angeles-based Latin Alliance which includes a large number of DJs and rappers, among them Mellow Man Ace; Latin flavor is also a central part of successful groups such as Cypress Hill and Funkdoobiest. And, despite Vanilla Ice and his Elvisian ambitions, a number of white rappers, such as MC Serch and Prime Minister Pete Nice (both formerly of 3rd Bass) have earned the respect of many hip-hop audiences. The global spread of hip-hop continues in the '90s; as documented on the 1993 Tommy Boy compilation *Planet Rap*, the list includes rappers from Ireland, France, Germany, Denmark, Italy, South Africa, Brazil, Japan, and Canada.[53]

Hip-hop already has a sixteen-year recording history, and its roots go back at least two decades before that. And, while many of the older acts like 2 Live Crew or N.W.A. may be stagnating, new groups are constantly emerging. If there is any parallel, it might be with the status of Rock in, say, 1964—at the end of a decade of sometimes faddish popularity, and (perhaps) at the beginning of a decade of massive popular success. Rock, of course, has been so thoroughly commodified that it is practically a corporate product; already it is seeking refuge in museums and Halls of Fame, whereas hip-hop is threatening precisely because it can't be *contained*. From the start, hip-hop has been a heteroglot science—from the early '80s, when hip-hop crews shared the stage with punks like the Clash at New York Clubs, through rock and metal collaborations such as those between Run-D.M.C. and Aerosmith or Onyx and Biohazard (not to mention the Beastie Boys), on into Teddy Riley's patented "New Jack Swing," and Mary J. Blige's soul-to-hip-hop crossover, the "mix of black and white," stylistically and culturally, has grown so complex that it can no longer be reduced to simple racial dichotomies. Even as the five percenters and Afrocentric rappers push for more "blackness," their own sonic past and future looks to remain interwoven with a tangle of cultural cross-references.

Chapter 4

History—Spectacle—Resistance

We have seen that there is a way in which postmodernism replicates or reproduces—reinforces the logic of consumer capitalism; the more significant question is whether there is also a way in which it resists that logic. But that is a question we must leave open.

—Fredric Jameson,
"Postmodernism and Consumer Society"[1]

Unrecognized producers, poets of their own affairs, trailblazers in the jungles of formalist rationality, consumers produce something...they trace 'indeterminate trajectories' that...do not cohere with the constructed, written, and prefabricated space through which they move... Although they use as their *material* the *vocabularies* of established languages (those of television, newspapers, the supermarket, or city planning)...these "traverses" remain heterogenous to the systems they infiltrate and in which they sketch out the guileful ruses of different interests and desires.

—Michel de Certeau, *The Practice of Everyday Life*[2]

1. Tactics of Resistance

Jameson's question has been the starting point for numerous analyses of the problematics of consumer culture, most of which work from within a theoretical/philosophical network of texts. Only a few of these analyses pay much attention to material culture, and fewer still have founded their arguments on the specific historical experience of African-Americans in contemporary culture.[3] Yet in a crucial sense, I would argue, the history of African-American cultures provides the most astonishing and empowering account of resistance, and of a resistance which from its earliest days has consisted of strategies for forming and sustaining a culture *against* the dominant, using materials at hand. Deprived by the Middle Passage and slavery of a unified cultural identity, African-American cultures have mobilized, via a network of localized sites and nomadic incursions, cultures of the *found*, the *revalued*, the *used*—and cultures moreover which have continually transfigured and transformed objects of *consumption* into sites of *production*.

This remaking, this *revaluation*, is especially evident in hip-hop; through its appropriation of the detritus of "pop" culture and use of the African-American tradition of Signifyin(g), it hollows out a fallout shelter where the ostensible, "official" significance of words and pictures is made shiftable, mutable, unreliable. A television jingle for a breakfast cereal, a drum break from Booker T and the MG's, the William Tell overture, a speech by Huey Newton or Louis Farrakhan— all these are intermingled and layered together in a musical fusion that transforms and transposes, in the process constructing its own internal modes of Signifyin(g). These modes are not only constructed, but endlessly form and repeat an "open," *reconstructable* structure—since the rhythm track, the words, or the mix of Funkadelic may be sampled by digital underground, which in turn will be sampled by Craig G, which in turn will be sampled by.... Hip-hop audiences do not, at any rate, merely *listen*—passive reception is no longer possible. Layer upon layer—one to dance to, one to think on, one to add to the din. Hip-hop itself is not merely *music* (though it is certainly that); it is a cultural recycling center, a social heterolect, a field of contest, even a form of psychological warfare. When a jeep loaded with speakers powered by a bank of car batteries blasts "Gangsta Gangsta" over the lawns of the "vanilla suburbs" of the "chocolate cities" (the phrases are George Clinton's) it is not to sell ice cream.

Of course, hip-hop itself is continually commodified by the music industry, "made safe" (it's only a song) for the masses, recycled yet again into breakfast-cereal ditties and public service announcements. Yet this commodification frequently backfires, transvalued before it even reaches the streets; commercial hip-hop jingles are re-recycled into lyrical and political metaphors, as when the Goats rap,

> I was turning, now I'm done turning other cheeks
> You had ya time to beef, now let Madd like speak
> Ya just a Honey nut, Honey Nut Cheerio
> I pour some rhymes in and now you're soggy, yo![4]

In tropes such as these, Signifyin(g) draws from jingles, newspaper headlines, and slogans in the same way that vernacular discourse for centuries has made use of the locally available (street names, political slogans, folkloric aphorisms)—as texts from and against which to mark a *difference*. However much fire commercial applications—such as Kool-Aid's use of Naughty by Nature's "Hip-Hop Hooray" beat—borrow from the music, the vernacular reservoir is in no danger of drying up.

Such verbal (and necessarily *cultural*) recycling may not, by itself be or be thought of as an act of resistance, of course. When a farmer in a hardscrabble rural economy reclaims parts from one tractor to repair another, or a kindergarten class makes puppets out of discarded milk cartons, these are hardly actions that trouble either the economic base or the ideology of consumer capitalism. Yet this does not at all preclude the mobilization of such acts, their deployment as tactics against the dominant modes of production and consumption. Again, De Certeau:

> A practice of the order constructed by others redistributes its space; it creates at least a certain play in that order, a space for maneuvers of unequal forces...what is there called "wisdom" (*sabedoria*) may be defined as a stratagem...innumerable ways of playing and filing the other's game (jouer/déjouer le jeu d'autre), that is, the space instituted by others, characterize the subtle, stubborn, resistant activity of groups which, since they lack their own space, have to get along with a network of already established forces and representations. People have to make do with what they have. In these combatants' stratagems, there is a certain art of placing one's blows.[5]

While certain of De Certeau's observations are inapplicable here (certainly African-American cultures do not "lack their own space," though the space(s) they do occupy are themselves 'vernacular' in the sense that they are often zones abandoned by white and middle-class residents, and isolated via police curfews, bank and insurance company redlining, and even in many cases physical barricades[6]), I think he is quite right in describing a certain tactical position which many disenfranchised classes, races, genders, and sexualities have occupied (not by choice), and have used to their collective advantage. When, in *Iola Leroy*, a trip to the market turned into an underground news broadcast, when a nineteenth-century quilting bee turned into a Women's Suffrage meeting, when an Oakland block party turned into a Black Panther rally, when a New York City power outage turned into a riot—in all these instances, disenfranchised groups have made use of vernacular spaces and technologies. Hip-hop, armed with electricity (back in the day, pirated from a city light pole), cheap turntables, makeshift amps, and used records, was bricolage with a vengeance, and the fact that this bricolage has in its turn been commodified does not interrupt but in a crucial sense *fuels* its own appropriative resistance, rendering it both more urgent and more richly supplied with 'recyclables.'

The doubleness, the anxiety of authenticity which haunts such acts of bricolage within African-American culture—and indeed, in the wake of the cultural violence of the Middle Passage, almost *everything* has had to be constructed from fragments of both the "African" and the "American"—is in this way intensified to the "breaking" point with hip-hop. Every past commodification—of blues, of rock-n-roll, or jazz, and of hip-hop itself—haunts the musical mix, sometimes in person (a digital sample), sometimes only as a "ghost" or trace (a passing act of Signifyin(g) on some past text). It is hard to think of anything less distinctively "black" than Kraftwerk's "Trans-Europe Express," Queen's "We Will Rock You," or Frank Zappa's "Tiny Umbrellas"—yet each in its turn has been claimed by DJs and used to make distinctive and lasting contributions to hip-hop. At the same time, ample samples of distinctive moments in the history of black musical expression, from Monk to Hendrix to Bootsy Collins, have always been central to the hip-hop aesthetic. It is not what you take, it is the attitude with which you take it (and what you do *with* it) that situates hip-hop within black diasporic traditions.

In any case, hip-hop artists and audiences function in a way that obviates any one-way model of production and consumption, and form instead a high-speed dialectical network, in which producers consume, consumers produce, and today's "anotha level" is tomorrow's old school. To put it another way, hip-hop is not merely a critique of capitalism, it is a counter-formation that takes up capitalism's gaps and contradictions and creates a whole new mode, a whole new economics. It is a mode that, inevitably, exercises a huge attraction on capitalistic machines, since it seems to promise a virtually endless source of new waves on which corporate surfers can try their luck (not to mention an attractive source of income for tracks that record companies already own)—and yet it can also drown them in the tide or leave them caught in some suddenly motionless backwater. And, unlike the days when a Pat Boone cover could clock more sales than a Little Richard original, the lid is off the old musical apartheid; record companies have had no lasting success with Vanilla Ice and his ilk, and have at least been forced to deal with the artists who created the artform. There has been exploitation, to be sure, but the deal is on, and rappers who have learned the ins and outs of the business have been able to gain both financial reward and increased creative control.

This of course ups the ante in some ways, putting the burden on rappers and producers themselves to navigate the sometimes treacherous waters of self-commodification, responsible for creating the product, though far from fully enfranchised in its success. For their part, rappers make few apologies for being 'out to get theirs,' and the status-conferring power of commodities such as jewelry or expensive cars has long been verbal and visual stock-in-trade.[7] Nonetheless, there is a strong ethic against 'selling out,' which for most rappers is not a matter of sales figures but of playing too hard for what Gang Starr calls 'mass appeal.' It is fine if a record sells well, and a large white audience *per se* does nothing to de-authenticate a rap record. "Selling out" is about attitude, about 'hardness,' about a refusal of stasis, predictability, or music that is too easy to listen to. As Chuck D intones in "The Sticka," "Every now and then, I think people wanna hear something from us nice and easy. But there's just one thing, you see, we never ever do nothing nice and easy. We always gotta do it hard, and rough."[8] This hardness is hard in more ways than one—for starters, it is "hard" to define. But it is a central part of the hip-hop aesthetic, this sense of "here's where I'm coming from, take it or leave it." Even rappers who have a fairly R&B-flavored, radio-friendly sound, like Heavy D, still have that attitude; conversely, when rappers who lack attitude try to put on a "hard" exterior—such as MC Hammer—they lose the reciprocal respect of the core audience. This may or may not translate into lower sales—

and for that matter, the same goes for the "hardest" hard attitude—but there is often a remarkable degree of consensus among rap's audiences. This consensus is at times powerful enough to irrevocably damage an artist's reputation, and spell doom for his or her current or future recordings, however well-promoted and bankrolled by the music industry.

The "core" of this hardcore audience, too, may be hard to define—and it is certainly not readily delimited by race. The tremendous commercial success of "gangsta" rap in 1994 showcased all angles of the 'attitude' question, as it demonstrated that the most hardcore sounds often had the broadest audience—with stellar sales for artists such as Dr. Dre, Snoop Doggy Dogg, and Ice Cube—even as the industry hurriedly launched a stream of would-be gangsta rappers, most of whom shot their way straight into the cutout bins. "Can't bury rap like you buried jazz," Ice Cube intones, and yet with his spectacular refusal of commodification, he sells two million records: "I'm platinum, bitch, and I didn't have to sell out."[9] Far from being a mere screen or surface-level add-on, attitude ultimately demonstrates the substance of style. If 'style' were only that, the record industry ought to be able to produce it on demand, but it has not. Added to the ostentatious criticism that the music industry levels against itself in places like the pages of *Billboard* magazine (recently rife with articles denouncing gangsta rap), the industry's frustration at not being able to find its way to the street without a guide Dogg is to a large extent symptomatic of its hypocrisy, and of the economics of the spectacle in general.

It is hardly news, after all, that the same large television, film, and music industries which so readily take up the cry against 'violence' effectively increase the value of the goods they market by doing so. The industry has in fact learned a few new tricks about reverse marketing from hip-hop's *own* strategies; the more vehemently a record is denounced, the more a certain kind of authenticity attaches to it, the more fervently it is desired. Leaving aside the more well-known case of Ice-T (whose controversial *Cop Killer* record, whatever else it was, was *not* a hip-hop album), there are numerous other cases where negative publicity added measurable market value. Paris, a radical political rapper from Oakland, encountered difficulties with Time-Warner (corporate parent of Tommy Boy, to whom Paris was contracted for his second album) over the featured cut "Bush Killa" and the accompanying cover concept (which featured an armed Paris crouching in the shrubbery, ready to assassinate a smiling President Bush). Paris was released from his Tommy Boy contract and took the record to two other labels, both of which rejected it out of fears similar to those expressed by Time-Warner's lawyers (that the song could violate laws against "threats of assault upon federal officials").[10] Finally, Paris released the album himself on his own Scarface Records, and despite the fact that in the course of the delays Bush was voted out of office, advance orders climbed from 75,000 to 200,000 on the strength of the publicity surrounding what was now known as a "banned" record.[11] In the end, Paris's established reputation enabled him to profit from the attempt at censorship (and indeed set an example followed by Ice-T in his break with Time-Warner a few months later).

Of course, however one reads these events—whether one chooses to see them as the rappers *using* the industry or vice versa—there remains a more material threat in terms of what such pressure might mean for less well-established artists. KMD, for one, a group with a widely-respected debut album, saw their sophomore effort summarily dropped by Elektra after an article in *Billboard* criticized the racial politics of its cover artwork. Thanks to the acquisition of several major hip-hop labels by large corporations in the mid-'80s, only two substantial independent labels—Priority and Profile—could offer artists an alternative to corporate ways and means. The music industry's policy of acquiring successful independent labels has led to an economic recolonization of the music, against which rappers continue to struggle; in a strictly economic sense, it is at least as important that Ice Cube's million-selling records are on Priority as that they are militant and uncompromisingly hardcore. If hip-hop wants to make a serious challenge to the forces of commodification, it needs to do more than simply make lyrical resistance; to date, few rappers have acted on this necessity with the degree of awareness of, say, Isaac Hayes or James Brown, both of whom backed their calls for musical and cultural black self-reliance with industry savvy and their own business organizations. Paris's independent release, Ice-T's move to Priority, and the formation of independently managed subsidiaries (such as the new Flavor Unit label), suggest that such awareness is on the rise.

Nonetheless, the large record companies do serve some of the interests of rap artists; as the only entities with sufficently deep pockets to sustain the cost of signing numerous new acts, they bring a lot of new talent into the pool, though admittedly a lot of dross as well.

Veteran rapper Chuck D describes their attitude: "what's goin' on through rap music, is, sign anybody you can find, and throw it up on the wall, and what sticks sticks, and what doesn't will slide off into obscurity."[12] However clumsily, this process offers one route for new rappers to gain access to the market. Small labels, in contrast, can only promote a relatively small pool of artists, and if too many new acts bomb, the solvency of the whole company may be on the line. The narrow pathway to nationwide distribution is one reason why hip-hop acts often have a difficult time getting a good contract, good promotion and distribution, and getting their albums released in a timely manner. While hip-hop is finely tuned to the issues of the moment, the record industry frequently bumps back an album for months at a time in search of a more auspicious set of competing releases, a delay which in some cases reduces the impact of their message or stylistic innovations.

A still deeper difficulty underlying all of the marketing problems with hip-hop is the fact that its central black urban audience has only a fraction of the buying power of predominantly white suburban listeners. Alternatives to purchase, whether listening to the radio, dubbing tapes for friends, or buying lower-priced bootlegs, are a necesary part of rap's urban circulation, but none of them add to sales figures, giving more affluent fans a distortedly high influence on the artists and albums the music industry considers "successful." Partly in response to this, and partly as an alternative to the clogged and crooked pipeline of major-label success, there exists a burgeoning underground hip-hop scene in many major cities, where artists with self-produced tapes are able to get club and radio play sufficient to sustain their artistic and financial needs. Underground success can sometimes lead to label contracts, but even if it does not, it is often worn as a badge of honor. To use Paul Gilroy's "wavelength" metaphor, underground rap is on a very low frequency; its sound may not be heard as widely, but it is heard more intensely, and has a powerful though often unseen influence on hip-hop as a whole.

Hip-hop's loose "posses," families," and "crews" are another counter-hegemonic structure, one that often bridges the major-label, independent, and underground scenes. Rappers and DJs who have enjoyed major-label success frequently do everything they can to nurture new talent, and are among the biggest (and most powerful) fans of the underground scene. Whenever possible, these artists give guest spots to unsigned mentors, and in many cases they have been able to negotiate record contracts for these same mentors. It is a linked chain of community that cleaves close to the black vernacular ethos of friendship; if you are "down with" another artist, you become a link on that chain. Record companies, for their own motives, are receptive to these chains, since often their A&R departments aren't as strong with rap as with other genres of music, and this structure gives them a free connection to other potential successes. At other times, though, the posse ethos takes record labels down a dead-end street; not *everybody's* sister-in-law or second cousin is an unrecognized genius. Whatever its commercial analogues, however, this collective ethos is one of the central and recurrent features of hip-hop, and whatever disses are exchanged on the mic, almost every rap album has a page-long list of shouts and props.

Finally, it is important to note the double valences of hip-hop's overall success in the 1980s. However the process of commodification may have skewed the development of rap, rappers and DJs themselves have generally managed to stay one step ahead, setting new trends which the industry only belatedly apprehends. And, in creating the first generation of hip-hop superstars, the industry has also ended up supporting those artists' work, including their music, live shows, and their own internal industry projects. The answer to the question "who's commodifying whom?" is as dialectically unresolvable as Apache and Nikki D's "Who Freaked Who?" Many rappers see their profits as a payback from a corrupt system; Chuck D has his own model of his ties with Sony Music, saying "I try to do my best to stick 'em. I say, well, they're the ones to stick up more than anybody"—or as Sir Mix-a-Lot puts it, "I'm the pimp, and the ho's the system."[13]

2. History as Resistance

"Music shall tell the history"

—Prince Buster[14]

In his pioneering study of black culture in the United Kingdom, *There Ain't No Black in the Union Jack*, Paul Gilroy sets forth three key themes around which the resistances mobilized by black expressive culture have been deployed: a critique of work, a critique of the state, and

> A passionate belief in the importance of history and the historical
> process. This is presented as an antidote to the suppression of
> historical and temporal perception under late capitalism.[15]

This third point is, I think, crucial; in the increasingly amnesiac world of bourgeois American culture, history itself is, in potential at least, a form of resistance. Much of suburban America presents a landscape singularly devoid of history; everything is new or at least remodeled. The educational process does little to foreground historical consciousness; for the most part, the past is presented as an arbitrary series of dates and events, with little evident relevance to the present. Even and especially when it comes to contemporary events, suburbia retains a thick buffer of reference; the events in the inner cities that replay themselves over television screens are as remote—perhaps more remote— than the Vietnam war. What little use capitalism has for history is by way of connotative associations with isolated historical synecdoches: Crazy Horse Malt Liquor, Ajax detergent, King Arthur flour.

In stark contrast to this de-historicization, this levelling of the past that bourgeois consumers habitually ingest, hip-hop, as rapper Michael T. Miller insists, is "a vehicle for the telling of history," and more: a vehicle for telling the repressed and suppressed histories of African-American culture.[16] The central histories at stake, inevitably are recent—the worsening situation in the cities under Reagan's funding cuts, crime, drugs, police brutality, and U.S. militarism abroad—but they also extend b(l)ackwards through the years of hope and frustration in the '60s and '70s (Paris's "The Days of Old") back to the experience of slavery and the Middle Passage (Public Enemy's "Can't Truss It"). And, unlike high school textbooks that alienate historical events from their cultural contexts, the urban griots of hip-hop offer visceral, first-person histories, complete with sound effects, street dialogue, and samples that re-invoke the affective *presence* of the past. As the "tour guide" voiceover on Ice Cube's "How to Survive in South Central" puts it, "Ain't nothin' like the shit you saw on TV!"

Finally, with all the other histories it re-tales, hip-hop offers its *own* history, whether through didactic raps such as Ice-T's "Body Rock" or Subsonic 2's "Unsung Heroes of Hip Hop" or via the ongoing and infinitely extendable dialectic of "diss" and "payback" tracks (e.g., the battle between Marley Marl's Juice Crew and Boogie Down Productions, which began with "The Bridge" and BDP's "The Bridge is Over" in 1986 and continued through numerous personal paybacks ranging from Roxanne Shanté's "Have a Nice Day" (1987) to MC Lyte's "Steady Fuckin'" (1993). Even in a track not explicitly identified as a "payback" or "answer" rap, the numerous instances of Signifyin(g) on previous rappers' turns of phrase, combined with the verbal "shouts" thrown out to peers and heroes, continue to build a complex historical web of influence, confluence, and effluence; it is not so much that hip-hop *tells* history, it's that it is history; drop the needle anywhere and you will find lyrical vectors to every other site on the hip-hop map.

The points of reference in hip-hop's histories, however, as often musical than verbal, and while the vast bulk of samples date to the '70s, many rappers have reached back to such '60s funk and R&B pioneers as the Meters, Book T. and the MG's, Rufus Thomas, and Otis Redding; the rapper Laquan even reaches back to 1937 to sample the opening line of a blues by the legendary Robert Johnson.[17] The recycling of these samples resituates them in a postmodern milieu even as it invokes the past; many hip-hop DJs pick a sample precisely *because* it is obscure, though others are just as ready to sample a trademark riff (Naughty by Nature's OPP, for instance, which is built around substantial samples from the Jackson Five's "ABC"). In many cases, DJ raids upon the music of previous generations reach back well before their own birthdates, such that their own search for sounds becomes a kind of genealogical *re*search; as a fringe benefit, many older listeners may first be drawn to a rap by the familiarity of the sampled material.

To see just how revolutionary these continuing raids upon the sound archives of black history are, one has only to listen to a few hours of heavily-formatted "oldies" programming on any of the hundreds of stations across the country that support it. On "oldies" radio, James Brown's 1960's (or George Clinton's 1970's) are nowhere to be heard; instead, listeners are inundated with a top-ten "pop" chart wave, over which they can surf safely without wondering what they are missing. Garry and the Pacemakers, the Beatles, the Byrds, the Hollies, the Four Seasons, Crosby, Stills, and Nash, James Taylor, Jefferson Airplane—the "oldies" playlists falsify not only the aural archive of the past they pretend to represent, but even the actual sounds of pop radio in the decades they "recreate"; from the mid-'60s through to the dawn of Album-Oriented Rock in the mid-'70s, AM radio was a multicultural crossroads—at least when compared to '80s and '90s format-driven radio.

In the face of this homogenized, safety-sealed version of history, hip-hop brings back the musical past that many white and middle-class listeners have conveniently forgotten. And, to the soundtrack of this historical incursion, it adds powerful beats and rhymes that draw listeners into the Signified situation, pushing the limits of connotation to make language come undone in a zipless fuck of aural frenzy:

> Step to this, as the derelict re-animates
> No jim hat as my mouth ejaculates
> I states mumbo, I speaks jumbo
> Phonetics are a phonograph of rhyme, ya petro...

> —3rd Bass, "Derelicts of Dialect"[18]

Reanimating "dead" sounds, bringing repressed histories back to vivid life, hip-hop sustains a profound historical consciousness, all of which serves to frame contemporary struggles within a continuum of African-American history.

Look at an inner city hood—South Bronx, South Side of Chicago, South Central L.A.—and you'll see a place marked—*pockmarked*—with history. Vacant warehouses and factories testify to a lost industrial base and the shattered dream of the "great migration" north and west; hole-filled streets testify to a declining tax base accelerated by bank and insurance company redlining. At the same time, liquor stores and convenience stores at every corner testify to yet another generation of immigrants who are enjoying a slice of the American pie that many African-Americans are still denied; in this context, Ice Cube's threat to burn Korean grocery stores "to a cinder" becomes suddenly comprehensible. Overhead, police helicopters flash the streets with searchlights, giving the residents of broken-down bungalows and row houses a free soundtrack to *Apocalypse Now* (minus the Wagner). The underlying logic is clear enough: *history* is a burden to be borne; those who can afford to have already dispensed with theirs.

All this leads up to the question of the contemporary, with which, despite its deep historical roots, hip-hop is most concerned. Again, there exists a kind of media apartheid; black issues, black interests, black perspectives are hard to find on cable TV (outside of BET and a few shows on Fox); the news media pander to white paranoia and present the inner cities as a landscape of criminals, carjackers, and drug fiends, to which the comfortable residents of Simi Valley (or

Westchester county, or any other suburb of a large urban area) respond by voting for more police revenues and stiffer jail sentences (this despite the fact the mandatory prison terms (most for drug-related offenses) have made the United States the most incarcerating nation on the planet, both per capita and in overall numbers). Against this protected bourgeois enclave (one thinks of the "weak middle class" '60s maverick Phil Ochs described nervously sipping their martinis while outside was heard "the ringing of revolution"), hip-hop offers a different drama, one in which the ghetto, like a chaos-ridden post-colonial nation (Somalia, anyone?) is under siege by police that act more like an occupying army than "peace officers," in which life moves at a literally "breakneck" pace ("with cocaine, my success came speedy," raps Ice-T), roaring down the streets in a low rider, equally on the lookout for police and other gangs.

If there's a contemporary analogy, it may well be Northern Ireland. Just as Ulster Protestants and Ulster Catholics, though inhabiting the same "nation," have different histories, different remembered grudges, different holy days, different neighborhoods, and different rationales for their paramilitary forces, inner-city blacks and Latinos inhabit a concrete and psychic territory that is less familiar to many white Americans than the surface of the moon. Hip-hop, at least, offers two revolutionary possibilities: (1) by getting inner-city kids to see the cost of endless gang warfare and black-on-black crime, they can unite them in opposition to the larger power-structures of racism; and (2) insofar as young white listeners come to hip-hop looking for an analog to their own alienation, these listeners will get a dose of "ghetto consciousness" that will give them a far better understanding of the politics of race and class than a Peter Jennings special (or many college educations, for that matter).

"The race that controls the past, controls the living present," declaims a voice (Louis Farrakhan's?) at the beginning of Public Enemy's *Fear of a Black Planet*, and true to this insight, hip-hop fights its battle on both fronts, making insurrections against both the homogenized past and the safety-coated present. Even in tracks that don't contain obvious political references, the recursion of sampled sounds and the linguistic slippage of Signifyin(g) at least *disorient* the listener, forcing her or him to recheck their "bearings," just as the heavy bass and booming drums have the often-underestimated virtue of *irritating* those who don't want to hear the message they carry. And, on hip-hop's home territories, the music gives a soundtrack to the everyday ups and downs of life, even though in the inner cities random killings, police raids, and poverty *are* everyday.

3. The hip-hop continuum: refabricating the prefabricated

Given the continual struggle against commodification that hip-hop has had to fight, how has it managed to endure? One answer, albeit a tentative one, is offered by Hal Foster in his collection, *Recodings: Art, Spectacle, Cultural Politics*. Unlike so many art critics, Foster is well attuned to cultural and political issues, and he departs from other critics of modernism in finding political valences where others have seen only a *flight* from the political. Foster takes a cold hard look at bourgeois culture's tendencies towards appropriation and recuperation of subcultures. Foster knows better than David Samuels the implication of "violent black youth" being transformed from a threat into a commodity; since bourgeois culture craves difference, appropriating subcultural forms and turning them into commodities solves two problems in one blow. For example, as Dick Hebdige has delineated in *Subculture*, while "punk" in the United Kingdom was, for a brief shining moment, a thoroughgoing high-voltage attack on everything respectable (in becoming which, of course, it made appropriations of its own), it was not long before studded leather jackets, dark glasses, and bleached and spiked hair made a miraculous journey across the Atlantic, where, stripped of their cultural significance, they neatly took the place of faded jeans, rock t-Shirts, and ponytails as handy-dandy markers for American youth in search of a quick fix of rebellion.

For Samuels, the popularity of rap is nothing but a rerun of this appropriative commodification—his problem was he never saw the sequel. Foster, along with his awareness of the rapidity with which commodity culture dismantles and re-assembles subcultural signs, sees the flipside of such a move: robbing the mythmakers. Whether performed in the name of "recovering" the "original" context of the commodified sign, or "to break apart the abstracted, mythical sign and...reinscribe it in a countermythical system," such reappropriation emerges as not merely *a*, but *the* tactic of resistance. Hebdige notes the appropriations via which punk invented itself—from glam-rock, the mods, and the more militant West Indian club scenes—and Foster acknowledges the power of subsequent re-reappropriations, such as those via which elements of punk style have resurfaced again and again (even forming a central element in the early Def Jam recordings of artists such as the Beastie Boys and Public Enemy).

Hip-hop recognizes what Samuels does not: there is no "unfabricated" community, no "essential" blackness outside of the continual, *tactical* enactment of blackness. When Chuck D raps about brothers going "under color," he's Signifyin(g) a move *beyond* the merely under*cover*; he's talking about the erasure of identity. Whereas the ideology of bourgeois consumerism takes "black" as a quality that, while always symbolically dislocated (by the spectacular "black underclass") from middle-class status, remains intact despite the (all too rare) achievement of status (e.g., *The Cosby Show*), Chuck D insists that blackness is something that has to be *made*, whose making cannot be negotiated without taking on the ideologies and myths of race. And this is not because there is no authentic "blackness," but rather because within the African-American dialectics of identity that hip-hop moves, authenticity and constructivism are not antagonistic but mutually resonant. Black Americans have always had to *make something out of nothing*, to make use of materials *at hand*; they have not been as heavily influenced by the ideology of the "lone creative genius" for whom "originality" is always such an obsession. A look at the acknowledgments on a typical hip-hop album demonstrates a collectivity that is larger than (and indeed, sustains) the specific agonistic stances of one or another rapper or DJ. In a collective work such as hip-hop, there is in a sense no singular "author," however many instigators of discourse there may be; rather, there is a cast of characters: Flavor Flav and Chuck D, Humpty-Hump and Shock-G, Professor X and Professor Griff. None of these would be substantial without their costumes, without their enactment: Flavor Flav's clocks, Humpty's nose, or Professor X's ankh-emblazoned leather hat. Yet this does not at all prevent these "stagings" from being "serious" (another rather Eurocentric standard); despite the fact that his big nose is plastic, Humpty can still cut a rap ("No Nose Job") about how cosmetic surgery is used to erase blackness:

> They say the whiter, the righter; yeah, well that's tough
> Sometimes I think that I'm not black enough

Hip-hop *stages* the difference of blackness, and its staging is both the Signifyin(g) of its constructedness *and* the site of its production of the *authentic*.

In this staging, hip-hop follows in the tradition of the blues, jazz, and jump blues ("rock-n-roll"), exchanging the unreal "real" for the "real" production of the constructed. From the Red Hot Jazz Babies to Sun Ra's Space Arkestra, from Cab Calloway to George Clinton, this staging has always had its costumes, its lingo, its poses. And, as with these other artforms, the insurrectionary aspect of this "act" has been that it has forced Euro-American culture to take stock of its own costumes, lingo, and poses—that is, to see "whiteness" as a quality; it is not surprising, in this light, that many young white kids in this century have turned to black culture to get culture, to search for identities. The logic of the "same"—of the white, middle-class world as a norm which never has to account for itself—is called violently into question by the Signification of difference, and this Signification has never been played as far to (and beyond) the limit as it has been by hip-hop culture. Indeed, part of the attraction of hip-hop for many white fans is precisely that it brings difference and identity back into play, while for black fans there can be the compensatory sense that blackness is restored to the apex of the cultural pyramid. Critiques of the historical 'errors' or conflation of Afrocentric rappers are beside the point, as the mythic history at stake here is—just as with its Eurocentric counterparts—not an effect of "actual" history (as if such history could be wholly recovered) but an imaginary genealogy whose point is a sense of cultural continuity, unity, and pride.

For, as Paul Gilroy makes compellingly clear, 'whiteness' and 'blackness' have both been *constructed*, though often via polarizing dialectics that have justified injustice and rationalized racism. If people are to recover a sense of identity that is both usable and relevant, they must of course know and understand this bitter history, but they must also gain the license to forge cultural links and empowering narratives. England, after all, had no sound historical evidence upon which to hook its genealogy to Aeneas and the martyred city of Troy, and yet it did so—and gave itself a mythology otherwise lost in the collision of its Saxon and Norman pasts. Inhabitants of black diasporic cultures have repeatedly created mythic pasts and utopian futures, drawing on African, Judaic, Islamic, Christian, and secular histories, and to try to invalidate such creations by an appeal to historical accuracy is wildly hypocritical. At the same time, critics such as Gilroy are right, I believe, in criticizing versions of Pan-African particularism which fall into the same error as the most disreputable Eurocentrism—that of assuming that some 'pure' identity exists which could be assumed *without* taking account of its imbrication within other cultural histories and myths, from which, indeed, so much richness and complexity derives.

The Afrocentrism of hip-hop, in any case, should not be overly generalized; many rappers, even when adopting African names, dress, and icons, are as conscious of the *construction* of this identity as any '70s funk band suiting up in its bell-bottomed 'space cowboy' outfits. Others, while they may joke at times about their dress, are absolutely serious in their call for a separatist black nationalist order. For these Afrocentric rappers, particularly X-Clan, the use of African beats and Egyptian headgear, constructed or not, are signs of a self-conscious 'step blackwards' that picks up where Garveyism and the Nation of Islam left off; "African" consciousness forms the ethical center of these rappers' rhyming practice. Hip-hop reflects the whole range of Afrocentrisms, ranging from the didacticly particularist to the playfully constructivist, and indeed includes rappers whose message partakes of other paradigms altogether, such as KRS-One's tactically-modified humanism or Michael Franti's eschewal of the roped-off models of culture implicit in some strains of identity politics. There is even, in the House of Pain, a historical reclamation of the (no less diasporically conflicted) Irish-American identity as a site of resistance.

Yet if there is no pure blackness, does that mean, as Michel Foucault claimed, that there is 'no *soul* of (or *in*) revolt'? If postmodernity reconfigures identity, is resisting consumption tantamount to shattering images in an infinite house of mirrors? Not necessarily. The vernacular conjunction of forces that enabled the uprisings in L.A., (whether in 1965 or 1992) shattered more than glass, and the cultural "noise" of hip-hop has done more than simply given Tipper Gore an earache. In this 'society of the spectacle,' as Guy Debord has dubbed it, cultural myths rise and fall in an almost operatic struggle upon the electronic stages of television, radio, and compact disks. The myth of the 'concerned' liberal white goes toe-to-toe with hip-hop's carnivalesque mirroring of his/her own stereotypes; the Goats' "Uncle Scam" runs drug cartels, wars, and drive-by shootings like booths at an amusement park. If images of Willie Horton scared middle-class Americans into voting for George Bush, the images and words of Ice

Cube, putting his gat in the mouth of Uncle Sam and shooting "'til his brains hang out'" will scare them more, and this fear in turn will inspire laughter (as when Cube, on *Predator,* samples the voice of a young white girl in a talkshow audience and loops the results "I'm scared...I'm scared...I'm scared").

Exploding myths via exaggeration, hyperbole, and the carnivalesque may not be the strategy of sober-minded politicians, but in the hands of rappers it is a powerful tool; Queen Latifah isn't kidding when she says M.C. stands for "microphone commando." And, in a time of the stagnation and indeed the reversal of civil rights and economic gains won during the struggles of the 1960s, even progressive soberminded political agendas sound like the ditherings of pre-'60s "Uncle Toms," as the rhetoric of Malcolm X is suddenly contemporary again. If white kids, in Ice Cube's phrase, "eavesdrop" on hip-hop, the message they get will not only dramatize this scandalous history (as invisible to many suburban whites as the initial struggles of the SCLC in the deep south), but call on them to declare, as in the old union song, which side they are on. Ice-T, in his caustic prophesy "Race War," predicts that in the coming struggle a lot of white kids will be "down with the Africans," just as many blacks (he implies) will be more loyal to class position than to race ("down with the Republicans").[19]

If consumer capitalism were to succeed in making even these kinds of dire warnings into titillating products on a par with adventure movies (and indeed, the increasing isolation of white and black worlds makes such confusion likely), then indeed the grounds for resistance would seem slight. Yet the African-American experience is rich with occasions where the self-conscious *return* to roots—whether blues tonality, West African rhythms, or the oral tradition of the Dozens, has marked a successful revolt in both stylistic and cultural terms. Indeed, were it not for the success of these revolts (each of which has taken place during a time of social and economic setbacks), there would be no distinct African-American culture alive today. In a symbolic reopening of the old assimilationist/separatist dichotomy, hip-hop demonstrates not only that an insistence on *difference* is both vital and sustainable, but that perhaps the agonistic tension between spectacular subjectivities is precisely the psychic engine needed to create and maintain difference against a hegemonic consumer culture.

There are hazards here—among them the romanticization of underclass status and the all-too-readily-granted *symbolic* "superior-ity" that have again and again marked white responses to African-American culture—but also a recognition. A recognition that in a crucial sense, the old "American dream" of an *undifferentiated* society never was and never will be, that aesthetics never breathed apart from questions of power, that in fact all of us, whoever "we" are, are situated by and within African-American culture—this is the recognition which hip-hop militantly throws back "in your face," and which necessarily works to undermine the strategies with which whites have distanced themselves from the urgent problems of the inner cities. It is no coincidence that in 1991, the song "From a Distance," a pseudo-folkie love anthem, waxed lyrical about how peaceful and harmonious everything looks "from a distance"; what went unsaid was that the distant eye of this song was implicitly *white,* and that the problems that passed before its pathetic gaze were those of urban America, postcolonial Africa, and the Middle East (where a new crusade against the Infidel was fanning nationalist sentiments in the United States).

At that same historical moment, rappers, reflecting urban discontent and a lack of sympathy with Bush's "Desert Storm," took a far more oppositional series of tactics. Public Enemy linked the experience of the Middle Passage to the "holocaust still goin' on" in the cities with "Can't Truss It," and produced a guerilla song and video staging the assassination of Arizona Governor Edward Meecham (an unreformed racist and opponent of the Martin Luther King, Jr. holiday). The Disposable Heroes of Hip-Hoprisy attacked Bush's Gulf war policy with "The Winter of the Long Hot Summer," as well as corporate consumer culture in "Television: Drug of a Nation." Not to be outdone, Ice Cube delivered his sharpest raps against the U.S. government on his album *Death Certificate,* whose cover featured the body of "Uncle Sam" laid out in a morgue with a toe tag, and whose lyrics inveighed against Bush's patriotic rhetoric:

> Now in 91, he wanna tax me
> I remember, the son of a bitch used ta ax me
> And hang me by a rope till my neck snap
> Now the sneaky motherfucka wanna ban rap
> And put me under dirt or concrete
> But I can see through a white sheet
> Cos you the devil in drag;
> You can burn your cross, well I'll burn your flag

> Try to gimme the HIV, so I can stop makin' babies like me
> And you're givin' dope to my people, chump
> Just wait till we get over that hump
> Cos yo ass is grass, cos Imma blas'
> Can't bury rap like you buried jazz
> Cos we stopped bein' whores, stoppped doin' floors
> So bitch you can fight your own wars
>
> So if you see a man in red, white, an' blue
> Bein' chased by the Lench Mob crew
> It's a man who deserves to buckle
> I wanna kill Sam cos he ain't my motherfuckin' uncle...[20]

Not since the heady days of the late '60s and early '70s, when cuts like Edwin Starr's "War," the Last Poet's "White Man's Got a God Complex," and the James Brown's "Funky President" provided the soundtrack for the political trials of the Black Panthers, had such a potent dose of lyrical dynamite been tossed at the feet of the U.S. government. Many African-Americans, indeed, perceived the situation in 1991 as a war on two fronts: against Iraq in the Persian Gulf (and the U.S. attacks on civilian areas in an Islamic country touched a nerve with many inside and outside the 5% nation) and against black youth in the inner cities (the 'Nam-like overtones of the constant sound of helicopters was not lost on a South Central Los Angeles which was home to many black veterans).

Eric B. and Rakim dramatize this sense of the ghetto as a war zone in their 1992 track "Casualties of War":

> Casualties of war, as I approach the barricade
> Where is the enemy, who do I invade?[21]

The scene here could be '65, '68, or '91; the barricade could be in Watts, Saigon, Paris, or Basra. The political dislocation of the African-American, called upon for combat to defend the very freedoms that were eroding at home, was dramatized by the cases of black veterans of Desert Storm, many of whom returned home only to face greater violence than that of the "war," wounded in drive-by shootings, or (in one much publicized case) killed in what at first appeared to be random gunfire.[22]

Shortly after the media-hyped "victory" in the Persian Gulf, the urgencies of race overtook the spectacle of American militarism abroad. The brutal beating of black motorist Rodney King by a number of L.A.P.D. officers had stirred outrage when it was first televised, and King's name had already been added to hip-hop recitations of the victims of racist violence; what distinguished King's case was, as an A.C.L.U. spokesperson remarked, not that it happened, but that it was *taped*. For years, arguably ever since Grandmaster Flash's "The Message" in 1982, hip-hop had spoken of the increasing tensions in the cities, where opportunities were shrinking and the "war on drugs" was in effect a "war" on black youth. There was apprehension as the verdict approached early in 1992, and in the uprising that followed the not guilty verdicts, the old Panther slogan (revived by rappers) once again sounded loud and clear: "we've come for what's ours." The L.A. uprising, in fact, was the first multicultural urban revolt of its kind, as a substantial number of the participants were Latinos—and indeed, west coast rap had for some years reflected the new ethnic mix via the careers of rappers such as Kid Frost (the 'Hispanic Causing Panic') and Mellow Man Ace (the 'brother with two tongues'). This was a revolt foretold by hip-hop, fueled by its rhetoric, and which in its turn fueled the radical agenda and symbolic intensity of the raps that have followed in its wake. From Ice-T and Black Uhuru's "Tip of the Iceberg," which made a groundbreaking alliance between old-school political reggae (as opposed to dancehall) and hip-hop, to Ice Cube's album *The Predator*, which featured dialogue of Ice Cube going door-to-door killing off members of the L.A.P.D. jury along with the officers they acquitted, the hip-hop response has been one of redoubled rage, and the rage is still smoldering; as Ice-T puts it "the fire is out but the coals are still hot."[23]

Could one quantify the degree to which hip-hop has been responsible for a new black radicalism, and the extent to which this radicalism played a role in the L.A. uprising? In this complex and contradictory world of American race relations, there will never be a revolt-o-meter fine-tuned enough, but at the very least, hip-hop has served as a means of *communicating* political solidarity, not only in the United States but in the Caribbean and the United Kingdom as well. As Paul Gilroy has amply documented, the 'underground' dancehall scene in West Indian neighborhoods in England for years served as part of a tripartite sounding-board for the African diaspora; American R&B travelled to West Kingston and became Ska; Ska travelled to England and gave rise to Two Tone, which in turn travelled back to Jamaica and the United States.[24] In these cultural nomadisms, not only the music but the

critique of racism, or colonialism, and (implicitly) of capitalism (especially in the United Kingdom, where pirate radio and blank-label press-
ings created a truly underground scene) made its way through the
diaspora, linking communities whose common interests might otherwise not have come together. Insofar as a perceived common set of
interests is a first step towards a more revolutionary consciousness,
hip-hop has been a crucial factor in shaping the cultural landscape of
resistance.

And yet it has done more: the 1980s were a critical decade in U.S.
race relations, but the worst symptoms of the crisis were hidden from
the view of middle- and upper-class whites. The media, treating drugs
and crime as *causes* rather than *symptoms* of urban blight, combined
with Reagan-Bush rhetoric to recast black (and Hispanic) urban
America as a land of pushers and killers; white television viewers saw
only a parade of such characters (often in arrests every bit as staged as a
Broadway musical—as when L.A.P.D. Chief Gates invited Nancy
Reagan and a cadre of local and national TV cameras over for some
fruit salad and a tour of a "coke house" bust).[25] This spectacle—the
Willie-Hortonizing of black America—brought calls for longer prison
terms, more cops, and a mysterious silence on the part of many white
political activists as to the increasing violations of civil rights. The older
generation of black leaders looked impotent; even as the rights they
fought for were eroded by the Reagan court, the economic ills of their
communities were worsened still more by the sixty percent cutback in
urban aid under Reagan. Of the senior generation, only Jesse Jackson
retained credibility (and never more than among rappers; Melle Mell's
"Jesse!" has a pioneering place among political raps). Yet after Jackson's
rebuff in 1988 from the new Democratic "centrists," it became clear
that the Democrats, too, were joining in the rush to the right. For
young African-Americans and Hispanic Americans living in the
tattered ruins of the inner cities, 1988 was the first of a series of "long
hot summers," and the urgency and militancy of much political rap
increased proportionately at just this time—most notably, 1988 was
the year that a loose agglomeration of Los Angeles hip-hoppers once
known as World Class Wrekin' Cru re-launched their career as N.W.A.
(Niggaz wit' Attitude) and caught the ears of white and blacks alike off
guard with the no-holds-barred militancy of "Fuck tha Police."

In a spectacular society, filled with flower-waving cheerleaders at
Reagan election rallies and syrupy video sunsets that could advertise

the Republican Party as easily as they could "breakfast at McDonald's," hip-hop made spectacular resistances. Its strategy has been that it is just as effective to pump up the volume, to magnify (and distort) the image of white America's fears as it is to displace them with accurate descriptions of urban reality (though these two strategies often work together, and the strategic mix varies widely from artist to artist). Yet the fact that rappers play with these stereotypes in a way that has a certain tactical effect of white listeners and viewers is not evidence that hip-hop has "sold out" to white audiences. Indeed, only a privileged white audience could conceive of the notion that the spectacle was all being done for their benefit. On the contrary, for many rappers the primary function of this spectacularized Signifyin(g) is to reclaim via a combination of collective anger (and laughter) the inheritance of *difference* that lies at the center of African-American self-knowledge. How to know oneself without measuring with the oppressor's ruler? How to maintain dignity and a sense of historical place in the face of the pressures of assimilation? In large part, hip-hop, like jazz and the blues before it, serves this kind of inner function at least as much as it serves to produce an agenda for others. In the funhouse reflections of hip-hop, as through black comedy such as *In Living Color* or the monologues of Paul Mooney, there is compensation for the distortions perpetrated by white stereotypes, and a whole school of rappers— Digital Underground, the Pharcyde, DEL the Funkie Homosapien, and Funkdoobiest—mix funky bass lines with comedy skits, wild rhymes, and "in" jokes to produce a vernacular funk that carries on the tradition started by George Clinton in the early '70s.

This P-Funk (as in Parliament) school, as it is often called, makes some political points, but most of its energy is directed inward; its central locus is in the BASS register, and its wordplay and images make verbal art out of scatological references. After all, "funk" still carries its olfactory connotations, and what can be "funkier" than a "booty"? Similarly, the so-called underground school makes a virtue of its anti-commercialism and seeks to sustain ghetto audiences without any concessions to radio airplay, buppies, or heavy dance beats. On one level, "underground" connotes uncommercial, even as it invokes the underground railway of slavery days. Yet there are also humorous metaphorical linkages: Das EFX raps about hangin' around in "da sewer" and filmed a segment of *Yo! MTV Raps!* from an underground tunnel in New York City; they also broke the first big rap on diarrhea

("Looseys"). The magazine *Rap Pages* recently did a nationwide survey of the "underground," and documented the increasing movement towards an inward-facing, funky, and resolutely hardcore hip-hop scene—a scene that already marks the beginnings of another bop-like turn away from commodification.

The underground sound is certainly one reason why, despite the commercialization of hip-hop, new artists and new sounds continue to evolve completely outside the industry's official A&R proving grounds. Hardcore rap is another; while associated in the popular press with a monolithic "gangsta" outlook, hardcore rappers in fact have laid claim to a wide variety of ground, ranging from Public Enemy's almost didactic political and social raps to Big Daddy Kane's lyrical fantasies of himself as a super-sexed Luther Vandross, to Dr. Dre's threatening yet laid-back paybacks against his former hip-hop allies. Jazz-influenced (and influencing) rap, touted in 1993 with Guru's *Jazzmatazz* and Greg Osby's *3-D Lifestyles*, has in face been around for a while, at least since the Dream Warriors' debut back in 1990, and continues to grow both via live bands (e.g., the Brand New Heavies, or Freestyle Fellowship's in-house "Underground Railway Band") and samples (the digable planets' use of Sonny Rollins). And, all along, rap's broadest influences have been on dance music, not only with "New Jack Swing" but with a new generation of musicians who have crossed over from R&B *into* hip-hop, such as Mary J. Blige. It is no longer possible to take the diverse agglomeration of music that falls under "hip-hop" and make sweeping statements, whether of praise or condemnation.

Chapter 5

"Are You Afraid of the Mix of Black and White?" Hip-hop and the Spectacular Politics of Race

1. Spectacular Tactics, Vernacular Techniques

All (sub)cultures, in a sense, are a part of the vernacular continuum, which in some cases bridges cultural identities and in others intensifies old antagonisms; that one or another subcultural moment is stocked with bits and pieces from other subcultures (past or present, allied or opposed) should hardly be a scandal. Yet it is readily evident from the various discourses that frame and form the boundaries of subcultures—the metaphorical idioms of their coded lexica, the incessant revolving door of who's 'in' and who's 'out,' and the tense interplay between subcultures and their (virtually instant) commodification—that it is not just cultural historians who try to sort out one culture from another in their critical centrifuges. Subcultures themselves, while collectively aware of their appropriative and intermingled roots, are no less anxious to reinscribe the boundaries between "us" and "them," between "those who know" and "those who don't." Such a strategy would seem to work against any coalition of resistance(s), but perhaps it only insists that there is a difference between a *tactical* alliance and the kind of mainstream coalitionism in which activists like Malcolm X and Stokely Carmichael long ago discerned a condescending, "helping" hand.[1] Again, the enactment of difference *precludes* a "coalition" which is based on appeals to the indifference of "humanism"; as Paris raps, "I ain't pro-human 'cause all humans ain't pro-black."[2]

All this suggests the ways in which subcultural political activism threatens not only the established order of the "dominant" classes, but also many of the established structures and institutions of the "official" resistance, such as the N.A.A.C.P. It is not just the class-based antagonism between inner-city kids and the largely middle-class membership of these organizations; it's that the subcultural game—the *trickster* game—moves via tactics that are never and will never be reducible to a political platform or a legislative reform. The "official" resistance must issue calls to come and "reason together," must lobby Congress and trade support on one cause for support on another, must play the power networks of the political web; in order to be accepted within these power structures, it too must take the humanist turn and embrace in-difference. Yet subcultural resistance, never more so than with hip-hop, must continue to *stage* itself as relentlessly uncompromising; its codes and modes of action move in a way that is both vernacular (generated on the most local level of speech, acts, dress, and sound) *and* spectacular (seizing the means of representation in order to interrupt "our regularly scheduled broadcast"). It may be localized, as with dance clubs, pirate radio broadcasts, or parties in the park, or it may form a larger nexus of force, as with the "Stop the Violence" movement; in either case it short circuits the cumbersome "process" of politics in the usual sense, staging itself instead directly via the mythic counter-narratives that conventional politicians more often leave unarticulated. And, while it is true in a sense that, as artists such as Tiger and Chuck D have said, rappers are only 'entertainers' or 'rhymesayers,' it is also true that even "real" leaders such as U.S. senators or the head of the N.A.A.C.P. are often only effective insofar as they adroitly play the spectacular game of mass-media attention, within which 'news' and 'entertainment' are inexorably blurred.

Through its mythic representations, hip-hop offers both a critique and an alternative worldview to the assumed ideological grounds of the dominant, first by making the unarticulated assumptions *evident*, and second by setting these assumptions into play with counter-myths of its own. To take an example, the video for Paris's "The Devil Made Me Do It" opens with a number of scenes that invoke the familiar narratives of urban despair: a young boy running through an abandoned building, a young mother holding a child, and a glassy-eyed addict reaching out for another fix. By themselves, these images could be from one of the Ad Council's series of blurbs for the "Partnership for a Drug-Free America." Yet into this landscape comes a figure from another myth: the outlaw, the prophet, the Black Panther: Paris and his posse walking out of the mists of an urban street. Intercut with this is another scene of young black men—presumably members of the Nation of Islam—in suits and ties, marching in step in the shadow of the Golden Gate Bridge. Over these scenes, Paris directs two messages: one of self-discipline—"build your brain and we'll soon make progress"—and another a critique of the very ideology of pathos that the images of urban despair so often underwrite: "Nigger, please, food stamps and free cheese / can't be the cure for a sick disease."

Stripped of the easy empathy within which they are usually framed, the repeated images of the crack addict, the single mother, and the running boy become suddenly accusatory, especially after the viewer sees who the boy has been running from: Uncle Sam. This Uncle Sam, though, is different; beneath his smile and ready-wave lurk madness, as we see him in the final scenes standing in a barren room, leering and laughing maniacally as the voice-over warns us to "beware the beast man." Uncle Sam as the Great Beast of the Book of Revelation? "Triple-six moved quick but missed me," boasts Paris, who is "swinging the sword of the righteous," a black avenging angel. Yet at the same time, Christianity's pious conventions are forcefully rejected; white culture has given blacks "false gods at odds with Allah / love thy enemy and all that hoopla," intones Paris, as his images fades out, replaced by that of a white policeman grinning malevolently. There is no resting point within this video narrative, only a restless movement through which, by reversal and negation, the very act of passively sym*pathetic* viewing is rendered impossible.

Such a narrative has immediate consequences, as it enters via television into the very same spectacular space as cop shows and the evening news. Rappers are dead serious when they claim to have prophesied the Los Angeles uprising; Paris's video arrived a short while before the video of the Rodney King beating, which it (along with many other hip-hop narrativers) foreshadowed; in a central sequence, Paris declares that you cannot let yourself be "beat down," even as he is pressed up against a squad car by a white policeman, whose baton pounds his back in rhythm with the beat. Putting the two spectacular moments together, I played the Paris video for a mostly white fresh-man class; many were skeptical of its narrative claims, saying that it was an "exaggerated" narrative made just "for effect." At the time, the Rodney King video had just been broadcast, and many students had not seen it; I played it after our discussion of the Paris video, and at once their attitude was reversed. Suddenly, the Paris video seemed tame by comparison, a mere dramatic *sample* of a much larger problem. The reality which they had been unwilling to attribute to the "fictional" video they readily granted in the face of the "real" video.

News video, for better or worse, rarely comes in the form of such raw footage as the King tape; more often it is predigested and elaborately framed. During Reagan's re-election bid, campaign staffers worked with news crews to get the best possible visual angles; the president visited high schools in predominantly white middle-class Republican strongholds, and spoke from a beribboned platform with pom-pom waving cheerleaders lining the bleachers behind him. Meanwhile, protesters were held off-camera, locked out of the staged scene, or dragged off by security guards without ever dimming the glow in Reagan's face.[3] Yet this edited, staged performance was retailed every night as "news," while the no more staged performances of hip-hop artists were relegated to "fictional" status. Paris's video, possibly on account of its "insane" Uncle Sam or a few clips of Bush's State of the Union address, was rejected by MTV as 'too divisive,' even though they had previously approved a rough cut—a move which can be read either as the rejection of too much harsh "reality" or as a tacit compliance with the regime of "official" as opposed to insurrectionary fictions.[4] Either way, MTV (which regularly airs "anti-censorship" spots) continued its hold on the commodification of music videos, of MTV as a 'happy medium' where nothing "divisive" could stop traffic on the one-way-street of consumption.

Such incidents illustrate the difficulty of resistance in the regime of spectacular politics; in order to be seen at all, one must invoke a character in the official narratives, what Michael Franti calls "brand name negroes"; check the boxes: Welfare Mother, Coke Addict, Gang member, impoverished child, bootstraps buppie. Hip-hop's way into the spectacle is also its greatest danger: by picking up these narratives and Signifyin(g) on them, it runs the constant risk of being collapsed and conflated *within* them by those who don't "get" the doubleness of Signifyin(g). Yet these same strategies, because they account for the problematics of reception in the society of the spectacle, are in practice far more effective than naive strategies which assume somehow that their message can get through the media simply on account of its innate justice or truth-value. To be a 'player,' as rappers put it, is to 'play' the media game, to have the audacity to raise the stakes even when your hand may be empty. It is this kind of audacity that takes hip-hop attitude to a higher level, as the spectacle enables what might previously have been only isolated acts and 'blows them up' on the giant screen of media representations.

2. Race Matters

Throughout such engagements with the spectacular, the ideologies of race form a crucial and yet often unarticulated ground, whether you are talking about hip-hop or any other statements by black political and/or intellectual figureheads. Here, the essentialist and constructivist models of racial identity oscillate with blurring rapidity, creating a sort of spectacular sleight-of-hand. Many black nationalist groups, for all their seeming radicalily, are founded upon tremendously conservative notions of racial identity, which are not simply essentialistic (in that they take race as a fundamental and unblurrable category of existence) but linked to a deep-seated patriarchal ideology that matches Rush Limbaugh in its emphasis on the centrality of black male authority for moral redemption. Yet this rhetoric is precisely the same as that turned *against* leaders such as Louis Farrakhan by white "liberals" and "black moderates"—which is that, if "the race" is a symbolic monolith, then every leader has a fundamental duty to represent and be responsible to a common black ethos. The lack of such a common ethos— painfully evident in such gatherings as the summit meeting of black leaders called in June of 1994 by the N.A.A.C.P.—only seems to increase the amplitude of "calls" to adhere to racial unity. Rather than take strength in the complex and often conflicting positions within black communities, a call for unity often means a call to step in line. Ultimately, this can end only better serving the interests of the dominant political hegemony, as all a white politician has to do to undermine the black leadership is to gesture to one of its most extreme members, such as Minister Khallid Muhammad. Then, at a stroke, other black leaders are under immense pressure to line up behind a microphone and issue a "condemnation"; if they do not, they will by imputation be equated with the extreme position.

On the other hand, constructivist positions, as appealing as they are to a wider range of people, labor under the burden of articulating the complexities of race and identity in a society where complex fractions of identity are routinely "rounded off." That is, while it is true that in a sense there is no unitary "black" subject position, that race is a social construction, and that in either biological or cultural terms, America has (and has long had) a profoundly "mixed" culture, it is *also* true that the economic, social, and personal mobility of Americans is increasingly disparate along lines of both race and class. For advocates of race essentialism, as for constructivists who have inherited the DuBoisian idea of the "talented tenth," a black man with a law degree and a lucrative practice is a shining example of race uplifting; yet when this same man is assaulted by police and pulled out of his late-model Mercedes, his is *not* a lawyer, *not* a civic leader—he is a young black male. It becomes increasingly difficult to articulate a position of blackness that is true to the ethos of achievement without being sucked into a bland bourgeois moral order. Music enters into and complicates this problematic; as a medium of cultural exchange, its intermixtures and cross-connections are richly resonant, and its audiences cross almost every social division, particularly race. And yet, playing within this race- and class-polarized society, where economic apartheid has replaced political oppression, the music also is the site of the most insistent and potent articulation of race essentialism, class warfare, and inter-ethnic struggles.

In effect, the dialectic between "essentialist" and "constructivist" turns out, perhaps, to be an unstable formation, though its very instability makes it useful to partisans of different sides. Its shifting definitions of race identity, its changes and *exchanges,* are plastic elements in a spectacular field of media-amplified discourse; within its terms, identity is both the object of desire and a kind of negative chit, a rhetorical hot potato that no one wants to hold for long. Signifyin(g) on both Lacan and Malcolm X, I would like to give identity, within this spectacularized system, the designation "x" (small x). X here can be *both* the unknown, the lost and mythified African identity seen in essentialistic constructions of race as a simple "African" whole, recoverable once one has removed the false patina of "slave identity," and at the same time a mark of a constructivist black identity, an identity gathered up from the fragments left by the wrenching violence of the Middle Passage, slavery, and racism, an "x" as a defiant refusal to be DEF-ined. And, as in algebra, the most astonishing quality of 'x' is its ability to be x-changed and inserted into diverse equations without its value ever being divulged.

Within this frame, "moral panic," as well as the ethos of "unity" just described, are both modes of x-change, modes of differentiation and oscillation, spectacular modes of power. In both, the object-x ends up being traded by others, even when the debate ostensibly takes place entirely within "the" black community as a political entity. Whereas the "moral panic" deploys *fear* of harm to the body (whether politic or personal), the "unity" mode of spectacular x-changing ends up articulating a spectacular divisiveness that only plays into the hands of the political hegemony. Figures like Dr. C. Delores Tucker embody *both* these modes; the discourse of moral panic is launched in order to call black spokespeople—in this case, the current generation of rappers—on the carpet for lowering the race instead of uplifting it. Yet, so played, it can only increase the class and generation gaps that already divide the mythically united black community. Hip-hop, while it cannot help but engage in these spectacular arenas, nonetheless offers a distinct third possibility for the politics of x-change, both through the turned tables of verbal and musical Signifyin(g) and through its transvaluative mode of remaking consumption as production. The object of x-change in hip-hop is music itself, which both returns a prophet/profit on the at times voyeuristic interest of suburban middle-class listeners, and blows bass in the face of moral panic by threatening to invite both white listeners and the children on the black middle class to affiliate along generational lines with the disaffected black underclass, a thing of horror to many members of the black bourgeoisie such as Calvin Butts or Delores Tucker. Butts and Tucker, affiliated with the hegemonic interests of the moral panicists, trade on the fear that middle-class, "talented tenth" achievements may be *degraded*—ignoring the fact that the brass ring whose tarnish they decry is so far out of the reach of the black underclass that it has become an object of derision rather than desire.

This derision is a central part of hardcore and political hip-hop, itself part of a larger cultural formation constructed by the urban black underclass, which can be characterized as the *negative* dialectic of x-change: Object x here radiates a kind of anti-desire, a refusal. Even when commodity objects are evoked, they are as much a parody as an embodiment of bourgeois style: low-rider convertibles painted metallic lime-green (a signifier borrowed—by some lights, stolen—from Chicano culture), Jeeps loaded down with an almost comical number of bass-heavy speakers, fur-covered recliners, gold-plated brass knuckles. Yet again, however, it should not be assumed that this refusal is not itself liable to a kind of table-turning from the black bourgeoisie; Tucker's insistence that rappers are merely paid prostitutes of racist stereotypes, the Steppin Fetchits of the '90s, and Amy Linden's contention that gangsta rap is merely the latest incarnation of minstrelsy, represent an attempt at a rebuttal of rap's most popular (and thus, threatening) edge.[5] The gangsta ethos, based in part on a refusal of bourgeois notions of "work" and "responsibility," is scandalous to the black bourgeoisie, which tends to see this refusal as playing into white hands, while to these rappers, it is the black middle class who has turned traitor. As Sir Mix-a-lot succinctly puts it, the message from hardcore rappers is "word to the bourgeois, fuck all y'all," and the message to rappers from Calvin Butts, riding on a steamroller over rap CDs, is the same in reverse, however much he might be averse to a word like "fuck."[6]

Thus essentialistic conceptualizations of race, however attractive to the black underclass, have had to be modified in order to take this anti-bourgeois resentment into account; after all, if as Shazzy says "Black is a Nation," how come so many sistas and bruthas are selling out? And, conversely, how do black underclass communities have and apply their own ethic against those who betray *their* codes, if in the name of "unity" it is impossible to criticize other members own race or class? Chuck D, the most vocal advocate of a black nationalist position, addresses himself directly to this and other problems within the generally essentialistic conceptual territories of this position. While there is, for Chuck, a black and white "nature," or essentialistic identity, there is *also* an ethic of action. Whites who act in solidarity with blacks have their "nature in check," and blacks who betray their race "act devil" while "under color" of race. By Signifyin(g) on under cover/under color, Chuck signals a more complex model of racial identity, one with (at least) an interior (of being) and an exterior (of actions), which can at times be in dissonance.[7]

Nonetheless, just as there are figures such as Khallid Muhammad, there are rappers who prefer the strictly demarcated logic of race separatism; Ice Cube, for one, with his frequent references to whites as "devils," and tracks like 1993' s "Cave Bitch" (an extended and particularly nasty diss against white women), as well as his patriarchal rhetoric of black women "looking up to" black men, is a more or less unreconstructed N.O.I. nationalist, whether or not he actually considers himself a member (and his testimony here is vague). Modified nationalists like Chuck D account for a more complex model, though still frequently echoing N.O.I. rhetoric. At the other end of the identity spectrum, rappers such as Michael Franti of the Disposable Heroes of Hip-Hoprisy, and white rappers such as the Beastie Boys' Mike D, speak to and within a profoundly mixed landscape of identity, within which both "black" and "white" as essentialistic markers are rejected. It reaches the point with Mike D when he can loudly reject and claim not to understand "white" cultural codes, even though he himself is "white."[8] For, while few critics are willing to analyze "white" as a cultural category, it is clearly a dialectical construction with a history running in common with "black," as Paul Gilroy decisively demonstrates in *The Black Atlantic*. It is a singular act of cultural amnesia that journalists and critics in the 1990s can talk about "white" in a completely unproblematic way, never so much as alluding to the multiple racialized and prejudicial conceptions which a generation ago were coin of the realm in the print media: the drunken Irishman with the face of an ape, the greasy Italian automatically assumed to belong to the Mafia, or the mentally-deficient Polish who was the cue for all kinds of jokes hinging on mistaken logic. The history of how these and numerous other racialized ethnicities became blurred into the larger supracategory of "white" is largely unwritten, but bears as heavily on the racial politics of expression and reception as the histories of "black." Indeed, it is a signal development that one site where these pre-"white" ethnicities emerge is in hip-hop, where Irish rappers such as House of Pain make much of their barroom bravado.

So what does it mean when, within Dyson's "anxiety of authenticity," a "black" rapper's music is widely enjoyed by "white" listeners? For ethnic absolutists, it is a crisis, whether they are hardcore rappers such as Ice Cube (who says he prefers to think of white listeners as merely "eavesdropping") or critics of rap such as David Samuels, who regard such reception as de-authenticating the music itself. Similarly, what does it mean when, as in the 1994 anti-gangsta rap congressional hearings, the old guard of civil rights *and* music faces off against the new black generation and those who sympathize with its message: C. Delores Tucker, Dick Gregory, and Dionne Warwick versus Yo-Yo, Nelson George, and Michael Eric Dyson? Even as hip-hop is often taken as the synecdoche and seal of authenticity of blackness, it is eminently clear that for many middle-class black Americans, it is just the opposite: a generational regression along both race and class lines, a *betrayal.* And, at the same time, hip-hop's political moves have taken up (and been taken up by) other oppressed groups, moving the x-change of history still further.

The specific tensions between blacks and Korean-Americans in Los Angeles and New York move within a similar dynamic, exacerbated by the lack of educational opportunity, insurance company and bank redlining, and lack of local funding that made small shops available to Koreans in neighborhoods where blacks were unable to get loans to open their own businesses. The resentment of blacks, watching yet another group climb the class ladder at their expense, combined with the Koreans' lack of familiarity with the folkways and ethos of the communities in which they did business, has proved a caustic and sometimes deadly admixture, leading to boycotts and (in one instance) the shooting of a young black girl by a Korean shop owner.[9] Calls for everyone to "just get along," whether voiced by Rodney King or liberal whites, have a hollow echo given these histories.[10] The politics of pluralism have reached a kind of limit-zone in the nineties; the myth that society can, with a little cajoling, function as one big happy diverse family has done far more harm than a more realistic assessment of the multiple lines of conflict along boundaries of race, ethnicity, class, sexuality, and gender. Hip-hop has issued its own (multiple) takes on this crisis, ranging from Ice Cube's threats to burning Korean stores "to a cinder" before they can turn the ghetto into "Black Korea," to Ice-T's impassioned historical message in "Race War" that "Orientals were slaves, too / Word! to this fucking red white and blue"—on the basis of which, Ice-T argues, *all* subaltern ethnicities must be seen as "black" in order to effectively resist the logic of the racist hegemony, as divisions between them can only serve the racist worldview.[11]

Yet however powerful hip-hop's messages about race relations, they too have to enter into that cultural heteroglossia where tensions *between* socially-produced identities fan the coals of resentment, over which liberal middle-class politicians then gingerly dance over like a gaggle of new-age firewalkers. And, on the larger stage of culture as spectacle, the symbolic claims and genealogies of identity politics replay this dance, pitting oppression against oppression in an age when all interests (except those of large corporations and the wealthy olig-archy of those that control them) are "special" interests, all competing for space in education, cultural and arts funding, social programs, and other national agendas. Even beyond competition for resources and recognition, there is competition among specific histories of oppression, which compete on a symbolic level. For instance, a measured insistence on the incommensurability of histories of oppression has long been articulated by many Jews, who object to appropriations of the word "holocaust" to situations such as Chuck D's calling black experience in America the "holocaust still goin' on."[12] What is at stake in such instances is the *singularity* of oppression, a move against the appropriation and/or metaphorization of acts of oppression. Yet this move belies the fact that almost all mass movements against oppression have drawn from the historical reservoir of the experiences of other groups; the American revolution (to take only one example) was still resonating in the mind of Ho Chi Minh when he wrote his well-known letters to President Truman asking for U.S. aid in throwing off the yoke of French colonialism.[13] However much a group would like to *own* its histories, they are inevitably going to have unexpected lines of influence; if the Jewish captivity in Egypt becomes a metaphor for slaves in the United States, why shouldn't the alienation of young urban blacks strike a chord in the minds of other alienated groups or individuals? If no lines of commensurability can be established, the possibility of alliance is destroyed; an absolute insistence on historical difference, in the end, is potentially as counter-revolutionary as an insistence on uncritical assimilation into a homogenous mass. It is a mark of postmodernity that, even as the full "ownership" of one's own oppression becomes impossible, its appropriation becomes a site of struggle.

The Jews, whose experiences of diaspora, oppression, ghettoization, genocide, anxiety over assimilation, and the dream of a promised land are in each case the paradigmatic instance of such events, in many ways prepared the symbolic ground which other groups have followed.[14] The civil rights movement of the late '50s and early '60s, in which many Jews fought against racism alongside blacks, took up many of these discourses, which certainly resonated with the black historical experience; the roots of this resonance go back over two centuries via the Spirituals' metaphors of "Let My People Go" (and calling the Ohio River the "River Jordan"). The campus anti-war movement of the mid- to late-'60s, the women's liberation movement of the early '70s, and the post-Stonewall gay rights movement all took their cues from the struggle for black liberation, which in turn borrowed many of its political strategies from Jews, Marxists, Ghandi, Fanon, and other critics of colonialism. Translated and reflected via the multiple tangents of the black Atlantic, it is irrevocably heteroglot: you end up with Desmond Dekker singing about the "Israelites" (who are black and whose messiah arrives from Ethiopia for a Kingston motorcade), MC Solaar rewriting spaghetti Westerns as anti-colonial struggles, and Afrika Bambaataa making black anthems based on German techno-rock in the name of a "Zulu" nation he was inspired to create after watching a British film. It's not that the torch can't be passed, it's that there are more torches and more hands to pass them by the minute…

3. Hip-Hop and the black diaspora

Given these transnational and mobile cultural movements and appropriations, it is vital that hip-hop itself not be read simply within the context of African-American cultures. Hip-hop, like earlier black artforms, is triangulated along multiple lines, lines which retrace the bitter triangle of the slave trade. Tricia Rose, for instance, offers a compelling and thoroughly material account of why hip-hop culture arose in places like the South Bronx at the particular historical moment they did, and there is no question that without events such as the construction of the South Bronx Expressway and the 'urban renewal' it was purported to bring, the social pressure-cooker might not have gotten hot enough to produce the specific energies necessary for hip-hop to emerge when it did. And yet, at the same time, Rose's account only peripherally addresses the role of the Caribbean connec-tion, and then only in terms of Kool DJ Herc and his sound-system ethos. Herc, however, was only one of thousands of people who came to New York from the Caribbean, and who brought with them elements of black style and culture that were distinctly different from those of New York City. "Yes, a de yardman start it," Herc proclaims on 1994's *Super Bad*, and a quick listen to the messages of reggae DJs like U Roy, who started recording the early '70s, confirms this genealogy. Indeed, while political messages came relatively late within Jamaican music, they were there from the earliest days in the lyrics of Calypso carnival songs, such as the Lion's "Boo Boo La La" (recorded in 1937). The Lion's call to "Burn down the London Theatre / Burn Down the Big Empire!" pre-dates PE's "Burn Hollywood Burn" by more than five decades, and suggests that the Caribbean connection brought much more than merely the technologies of sound-systems and talkover, however important those were.

The tremendous influence of the '90s wave of dancehall-inflected hip-hop owes much to these already-established lines of descent, and groups such as the Fugees, the Fu-Schnickens, and Mad Kap have formulated a sound that moves with ease between dancehall style, hip-hop rhymes, and (with the Jamericans) lovers' rock. Any rapper worth his or her salt (or pepa) has *got* to drop a few lines in the Jamaican patois, or bring on a dancehall toaster to introduce their tracks. More recently, groups such as Born Jamericans and Worl-a-Girl inhabit a still more syncretic musical space, drawing in the full range of black Atlantic musics and producing songs that cannot be deterministally located as "dancehall," "rap," or "R&B," however richly they partake of all these forms (and others besides). Such syncretisms are also emerging at other points within the black Atlantic; in the United Kingdom, both United States and Caribbean influences converge, and mingle further with East Indian musics, particularly Punjabi 'bhangra' music, whose polyrhythmic tabla beats link up with hip-hop syncopations like pieces of a jigsaw puzzle; rapper Apache Indian could boast that he was "#1 on the Bombay charts" at the same time he was scaling similar charts in the United Kingdom and United States.

And, just as there are global elements missing from many accounts of hip-hop, so are some it its *local* histories. Latinos on both east and west coasts have been a part of hip-hop culture from its earliest days, and a source of both solidarity and competition. The earliest hip-hop beats were influenced heavily by New York's Puerto Rican youth, whose own dance subculture gave breaking many of its first moves and styles; as Juan Flores observes, Puerto Rican and black cultures in the city have had a "long and intricate" interrelation, within which it would be inaccurate to identify many particular elements as exclusively the cultural property of one or the other group.[15] Similarly, on the west coast, Chicano culture—dropping *Calo*, cruising in low-riders, and sampling scraps of bass-heavy Latin groups such as WAR—all became central to West Coast hip-hop style.[16] Hip-hop's Latin connection has been the source of some tension, but also a tremendous amount of creative collaboration, and in fact many of the most successful rap groups of the early '90s, such as Cypress Hill, are distinctly shaped by this collaborative fusion.

As hip-hop has traveled to other parts of the globe, it has found ripe points for intercultural influence in many parts of Latin America; Chuck D recalls young kids in South America who were trying to learn English so they could cop a few hip-hop rhymes, and groups such as Salvador Astral mix rap-style vocals with traditional Latin drumming styles—themselves a cultural hybrid of African, Spanish, and indigenous rhythms.[17] From all the outposts of the old colonial order, rap music shouts out the rhymes and rhythms of revolution.

In the 1993 film *In the Name of the Father*, Gerry Conlon (played by Daniel Day-Lewis), newly arrived in a British prison, notices a jigsaw puzzle of the British Empire in the prison's rec room with a number of pieces missing. "Where's all the missin' pieces?" inquires Conlon, at which the others in the rec room break into laughter, and a dredlocked inmate explains:

> My 'oman ... have it dipped in liquid acid. LSD, mon. We been dropppin' the British Empire for de last six month, now.

A perfect ploy, it might be added, for sneaking drugs into a British prison. In a similar way, the apparently disconnected fragments of the black diaspora, as well as other communities both fragmented and interlinked by the experience of colonialism, are "missing" from the official maps of culture—but not to those who know how to "drop" them. The deformation of mastery, to use Houston A. Baker Jr.'s term, implicit in such acts against the maps and modalities of Empire is both the driving engine of musical and verbal production as well as the reason why so many who have been the beneficiaries of colonialism and racism find it so hard to look into what seems to them a distorting mirror.

The outposts of Empire and the black diaspora have always had underground channels of communication, but the technology of sound recording, particularly in its digital form, has enabled these channels to carry musical and cultural data at an ever-increasing rate. With the sheer volume of this data, new cultural syntheses and developments have been made possible, and hip-hop is the first as well as the most important product of this new possibility. Whatever the material histories of the South Bronx, hip-hop drew deeply on the Caribbean connection to prime its pump, and once primed traveled along well-established black Atlantic vectors in translating its influence into the United Kingdom, just as it did in spreading from New York to Chicago, from Houston to Los Angeles. And, in the mid-'90s, the influence is continuing to spread, producing both new outposts, such as Paris—where Sénégalese rapper MC Solaar drops rhymes in French about Gary Cooper and Smith & Wesson—and new hybrids, such as Worl-a-Girl's fusion of dancehall, ska, and R&B with silky En-Vogue style vocals. Worl-a-Girl not only draws from but literally embodies the black Atlantic, as its four members hail from Brooklyn, London, Jamaica, and Trinidad respectively.

The new digital technology makes these intermixtures even more readily available, as an album can now be recorded in several locations, even mastered in more than one studio, and still be spliced together seamlessly in a single 5 1/4-inch diskette. Taking hip-hop's heteroglot mix to a still further level, producers such as Bill Laswell (who produced the seminal meeting of hip-hop and jazz, Herbie Hancock's "Rockit") now assembles recordings on his own Axiom label in which artists such as Bootsy Collins, Foday Musa Susa, Ziggy Modeliste (longtime Meters drummer), Shabba Ranks, The Jungle Brothers, Nicky Skopelitis, Buckethead, and Zakir Hussain get down for an intercontinental ballistic jam session. Similarly, Peter Gabriel's Real World label, besides bringing individual artists such as Nusrat Fateh Ali Khan or Ayub Ogada to the attention of United States listeners, sponsors projects such as the *Jam Nation* CD, which brought United States and United Kingdom performers together with musicians from South Africa, Zaire, and China.

It would be foolish, however, to hail all transcultural or multicultural recordings or cross-influences, since the whole point of vernacular artforms is that they come from a particular place at a particular time, and are sites not only of invention and creativity, but of history and resistance. I would agree with Paul Gilroy that, those who hail the metalesque "ska" band Bad Brains as the ultimate turn in cultural hybridity clearly end up on the side of recuperation and indifference, a kind of fuzzy plurality that loses sight of the histories still at stake in specific cultural identities. Yet I would also be very wary of any cultural litmus test, since to an extent what is 'vernacular' can never be delimited, however precisely it can be described. Afrika Bambaataa made techno-funk a 'black' thing, and audiences (black and white) *did* understand—an act of cultural appropriation and at the same time of continuance and tradition. The route for engagement with black Atlantic artforms that Gilroy sketches is a kind of tightrope, bounded on one side by a move towards particularism and on the other by the humanistic hodgepodge of happy pluralism. It is a tightrope that has been walked before and will be walked again, strung as it is between historical suffering and utopian aspirations, but it is also a tremendously strong c(h)ord, with many different fibers in its weave.

Hip-hop itself forms many of these fibers, and represents a complex weave of black Atlantic style and African-American homespun. As it gains audiences around the world, there is always the danger that it will be appropriated in such a way that its histories are obscured, and its message replaced with others, just as there is also the possibility that it will intermix with other artforms and produce new and unexpected connections. At the same time, even as it remains a global music, it is firmly rooted in the local and the temporal; it is music about "where I'm from," and as such proposes a new kind of universality based not on indifference but on an assemblage of local and intercommunicating nodes. Thus, hip-hop, along with other vernacular media, needs to be seen as part of a new structural order which is both local *and* global at the same time. In this it is unlike, say, cable television or fast-food chains, with their one-way roads from production to consumption—but very much like the Internet, with its multiple, multiway gateways, each passing the rhetorical stuff from node to node, routing around obstructions and resisting any central attempts at censorship or monitoring.

4. Hip-Hop's Futures

Hip-hop in the mid-'90s faces all kinds of new challenges and contradictions; no longer new, though still refusing to become old. Not that only young artforms—or artists—bring major innovations; after all, the Jazz that Bop stood upside its head was already geriatric, and appeared caught in a squeeze between the commercialized 'big band' sounds and the conservative bias of most white Jazz critics. Bop's revolution, for being unexpected, was only more profound, in that it demanded not only a whole new kind of musicianship, but a whole new kind of audience, and it managed to produce both. And yet there is an uneasiness about seniority; even as many old school rappers and DJs try to jump-start second careers, those not quite as old (*middle* school?) have had to struggle to keep up with the times. KRS-One reclaimed his crown with 1993's *Return of the Boom-Bap* and a little help from GangStarr's DJ Premier, and yet veteran artists such as L.L. Cool J. or Big Daddy Kane have produced albums that have generated very mixed reviews. The *Source* even joined *Rolling Stone* in criticizing Public Enemy's 1994 album, *Muse Sick in Hour Mess Age*, even making fun of Chuck D's age (34)—safe for the *Source*, maybe, but hardly for a magazine whose namesake band will soon be hitting their sixties. Hip-hop's senior statesmen (and women—Roxanne Shanté keeps coming back for more) are fighting for their lives, just as it seems a flurry of rappers from the under-fourteen set (ABC, Kriss-Kross, Shyheim, and others) are determined to grab the mic. Women rappers have come into their own, but, with less to prove, their younger sistas tend either to eschew womanist politics for that "f'all y'all" good feeling, or to walk around with a hoodie and a gat proving they can out-gangsta their male counterparts. The major record labels, at the same time, are shying away from more political rappers, preferring instead to trot out a stream of posturing mediocrities who have all the moves but little of the message. Old school anthologies are coming out in droves, but no one is quite sure where the new school is coming from.

It is a vulnerable time, reminiscent of rock-n-roll during its late-seventies lull, before it gave convulsive birth to punk, and then retreated to "oldies" and "soft rock" channels. The Rock-n-Roll Hall of Fame is nearing completion on the shores of Lake Erie, and let rappers beware: there is more danger in a museum than in all the congressional committees you can imagine. The 'junk heap' of esteemed yet embalmed culture that Amiri Baraka warned against is ready for more: "come on down!" Finding the higher level, the next plateau where hip-hop can reinvent itself, becomes harder at each step. Nonetheless, there are many hopeful signs, among them the increasing presence on American airwaves of Jamaican and United Kingdom black music, as well as the increasing awareness of black musical history that has found its torchbearers in artists such as The Sounds of Blackness (who traverse it all, from spirituals to rap), Gil Scott-Heron (one of the few seminal influences on rap who has the authority to bring a "Message to the Messengers"), or Greg Osby, who brings hard-bopping live saxophone to bear upon hip-hop beats and verbal loops.

Ironically, it is at just this time that academic interest in hip-hop is suddenly blossoming, as new books seem to appear every few months explaining the context or significance of hip-hop culture. Some of these follow the old pattern of the bluffers' guide, including alphabetic listings of artists and handy lists of hip-hop words and phrases, and are geared to a general readership; others approach hip-hop from the perspectives of cultural history, black studies, or musicology. The interest, as well-intentioned as it is, raises many of the same questions about the ossification of art that Baraka laid forth thirty years ago, and that I have developed in my own arguments. And now it is time for the serpent to bite its own tail, in that I would not exempt this book from this kind of advisory sticker: The contents of this volume—or any other—do not and cannot represent the full range of hip-hop culture; at best they are snapshots of a movement. That is not to say that some snapshots aren't more useful than others—they are—but only that, until books become as fully multi-media as the culture(s) they discuss, they are always going to be substantially incomplete. The turnaround time for an academic book, in any case, is often a year or more, such that the most current issues that (for example) I can discuss here may already be fading from the scene by the time these words are read.

But the dangers suggested by the juxtaposition of hip-hop's restive pause and the flurry of academic interest are substantial; returning to the passage from DeCerteau quoted in the introduction, it must be asked whether cultural studies really come to praise insurrectionary arts or to *bury* them. This is of particular concern with hip-hop culture, since the central styles and attitudes which motivate and structure its expressions are all about lack of distance, in-your-face immediacy, and shoot-from-the-hip history—all values that academic discourse abhors. The tensions at work can be seen vividly in an interview conducted with KRS-One by Michael Lipscomb, which appeared in the Afro-diasporic journal *Transition*.[18] Tellingly entitled "Can the Teacher be Taught?," it represents not an alliance with but an attack on hip-hop knowledge; it suggests that KRS-One, a.k.a. "The Teacha," somehow *needs* to be taught, and that Lipscomb the intellectual is going to do the teaching. The interview is headed by a quote from P.M. Dawn's Prince Be—"KRS-One is a teacher, but a teacher of what?"—which implicitly questions the value of KRS-One's teachings (a strategy likely to backfire on fans of hip-hop, who know that Prince Be is about as much of an authority on hip-hop as Casey Casem is on death metal).

Generous soul that he is, Lipscomb is willing to grant that "KRS-One *is* ...a philosopher," but he criticizes KRS for his inconsistencies, suggesting that "perhaps the Teacher has had too many teachers."[19] Lipscomb steps in time and again to "correct" KRS, as in the following exchange:

> **ML:** …you have complex cultural formations, such as jazz, which is not African music…
> **KRS:** Jazz is African music.
> **ML:** It has African elements, like polyrhythms…
> **KRS:** Anything created by black man is African. People divide things up differently because of the way we've been taught. We've been killed, mentally. If a cat had kittens in the oven, would you call them muffins?
> **ML:** I think that dealing with Africa, and with people, is always going to be a little more complicated than that. After all, Africa is a deeply heterogeneous assemblage of cultures and ethnic groups…[20]

Lipscomb, in the manner of academics everywhere, insists on taking terms such as "Africa" literally, sketching in the complex referentialities and insisting that KRS is over-simplifying them. KRS, for his part, is not *denying* these references, but is speaking, as he does in his raps, on a far more mythic level; his Africa is an act of political imagination, a characteristically black diasporic utopian past. To say "the African past (or present) was/is not utopia" is true as far as it goes, but does not acknowledge KRS's *own* complex tropological constructions, nor does it apprehend the vital historical links between KRS's gesture and the mythography of African-American yearnings, let alone the black diaspora as a whole. Lipscomb is not naive, of course, about the two different models of what counts as "knowledge" that are at stake here, but he is unwilling to locate points of communication, or shift his own modes in order to have a full dialogue.

One reason for Lipscomb's reluctance to accept KRS's epistemology becomes clear later in the interview; Lipscomb is taken aback by KRS's claim that "America doesn't exist," and goes into a long litany over the constitution, the Emancipation Proclamation, and how extraordinary it was for Lincoln to end slavery. This raises KRS's ire:

> **KRS:** Why do you say that the Civil War marked the end of slavery? Why not the birth of world slavery? Knowing the vicious system which we're under, when you're making a million dollars a year off these Africans working for free, you wonder how much more

money can you make by enslaving everyone. So, in other words, it's not that they freed the slaves or even wanted to. I'm saying they wanted to enslave the world. The birth of capitalism is the birth of wage slavery.

ML: But you see, almost everyone in America, including blacks, wants to be capitalist...

KRS: We've never been given anything else.

Lipscomb's bourgeois liberalism is drawn out of hiding by KRS's rhetoric and discloses the multiple gaps of class, generation, and expectation that still divide blacks in the United States. Lipscomb holds out the silver lining, speaking of black achievements and how central blacks are what it means to be "American"; KRS, speaking from and for the black underclass, sees the hollowness of such achievements in the light of the continuing racism and classism of "America," a territory he refuses to take seriously. For KRS, the politics have remained much the same since plantation times, only the plantation is now the ghetto; in a powerful moment in his 1993 track "Sound of da Police," KRS offers a subversive etymology for "[police] officer," reeling off a rapid-fire verbal morph:

Overseer, overseer overseer, overseer
Offa-seer, offa-ser, offa-ser, officer
Yeah, officer, from overseer
Ya need a little clarity? Check tha similarity![21]

It is at points such as the Lipscomb/KRS-One interview that it is easy to despair of any fruitful communication or collaboration between academic fields such as black studies or cultural studies and vernacular knowledges as embodied in artforms such as rap music. Houston A. Baker Jr.'s 1993 book(let), *Black Studies, Rap, and the Academy*, is similarly disappointing, as Baker's attempts to praise rap music are framed at each turn by a sort of hands-off-the-exhibit spectatorship; he declines even to have the title of NWA's "Fuck tha Police" printed in full. That Baker, as he boasts in this book, could somehow make a huge contribution to a group of young students in the United Kingdom by getting them to see Henry V as a rapper, a 'def con man,' not only erases rap's intrinsic oppositional stance, but assumes that Baker as a black American scholar must of necessity have some proprietary connection to rap—another wonderful United States commodity these

United Kingdom kids wanted, their desire affirmed by their after-class clamor for scholarships to accompany Baker back to the States. Baker's patriarchal pride in this desire assumes that somehow the music has not *already* traveled back and forth millions of times via the high-speed data lines of the black Atlantic—god help United Kingdom youths who have to wait for American professors to bring them the latest "fresh" and "happening" music—and furthermore that the United States is inexorably the center of black culture.[22] It is little wonder that, at chapter's close, Baker dismisses "hip-house" and "rap reggae" as mere spinoffs, whereas "rap is now classical black sound."[23]

Other academics have come closer to a full engagement with hip-hop culture, though inevitably they tend to take from it chiefly what is of interest to their own work. Richard Shusterman, for instance, whose essay "The Fine Art of Rap" was among the first to take hip-hop aesthetics seriously, is interested in how hip-hop can serve as an exemplary case for the pragmatist aesthetics of which he is a major theorist. My own book is hardly free from this problematic, as it may be read by some as merely a convenient grafting-on of hip-hop to certain postmodernist formulations. Such, however, are the risks of setting up shop at a crossroads where, as the Lipscomb/KRS-One interview demonstrates, the traffic signals recognized by one set of drivers differ significantly from those recognized by another set. Shusterman's work at the very least takes hip-hop *seriously*, and on its own terms, rather than simply tacking it on to pre-existing formulations.

The best book to emerge so far from the intersection of academics and hip-hop culture is without question Tricia Rose's *Black Noise*. Rose founds her account of hip-hop firmly in the lived material circumstances of its originators, and while her book does not engage with a fuller account of hip-hop's place in the black Atlantic continuum, its account of hip-hop's local and tactical resistances in post-industrial America is without equal, and ought to become required reading for all drive-by critics of hip-hop such as Calvin Butts, C. Delores Tucker, or David Samuels. She also engages, both through appreciative critical readings and direct interviews, with hip-hop artists and videos, grounding her assessments of rap's representations in the hands-on conditions of its production. Yet despite its considerable successes, Rose's book leaves a number of threads dangling; in her desire to fill in the local (in terms of history *and* geography) contexts of hip-hop's emergence and rise to popularity, there is little time to relate rap music to previous African-American or Afro-diasporic forms. This connection, fortunately, has been powerfully articulated by Paul Gilroy in his book *The Black Atlantic*, which I have cited and quoted from at many points in my previous chapters. Hopefully, future analyses of hip-hop will follow Rose's *and* Gilroy's lead, and expand upon the potent resonances rap music has generated in the full historical and geographical continuum of the black Atlantic.

To this work, I hope this book has made a modest contribution. And yet I am acutely aware the extent to which I have only been able to sketch in the 'tip of the iceberg,' of how much is left out, as well as how quickly the scenarios shift. It is the ultimate point of my work to insist that academic knowledge and hip-hop knowledge need at least to be on speaking terms, and that such a dialogue depends upon academics seeing that rappers have their own protocols, their own epistemologies, which cannot simply be read according to an academic laundry list of theoretical questions. Those who are going to write intelligently about this music will have to do more than listen to a few stanzas of 2 Live Crew, or offer knee-jerk condemnations of vaguely-defined proclivities towards violence. They must also recognize that hip-hop has its own ethos, and is more than capable of self-criticism—indeed, in the agonistic world of rap, criticism has always been stock in trade. The battle over the future of hip-hop is being fought even now, and not only between industry insiders and the young rappers and producers who make the music. Public Enemy has already thrown down one gauntlet, as its 1994 single "Give It Up" takes gangsta rappers, 40-ounce beers, and blunts to task for destroying black communities. In the video for this single, Chuck D, commanding a spaceship that looks like a cross between a cruise missile and the starship Enterprise, fires his knowledge-ray down to earth, where it zaps drug dealers and converts guns into—*books! (what* books, one wonders?). "No gangster lyin', I'd rather diss presidents," declares Chuck, as he pulls a claymation Clinton out from a dollar bill papier-mâché Capitol building and flings him over his shoulder. At the same time, despite the stereotypical view of 'gangsta' rappers as posturing nihilists, some potent social critique continues to emerge from the speakers of Jeeps and low-riders. As the group OutKast—whose infectious funk-laden grooves are booming as I write these words in the summer of '94—puts it:

> Operatin' under the crooked American system too long…OutKast, pronounced outkast, adjective meaning homeless or unaccepted in

society. But let's look deeper than that. Are you an outkast? If you understand and feel the basic principles and fundamental truths contained within this music, you probably are. If you think it's all about pimpin' hoes and slammin' Cadillac do's, you probably a cracker, or a nigga that think he a cracker, or maybe just don't understand. An outkast is someone who is not considered to be part of the normal world. He's looked at differently. He's not accepted because of his clothes, his hair, his occupation, his beliefs, or his skin color. Now look at yourself! Are you an outkast? I know I am. As a matter of fact, fuck being anything else. There's only so much time left in this crazy world. Wake up, niggas, and realize what's goin' on all around you...[24]

As this credo clearly embodies, hip-hop is about a fundamental opposi-tional stance, one which is not looking for redemption from *anybody* ("fuck being anything else"). The race or gender of the listener is not the determining factor; it's *attitude* that separates "crackers" from "niggaz." And yet, *pace* the "free play" of ludic postmodernisms, that doesn't mean that "it don't matter if you're black or white," but rather that race is not the *only* thing that matters. What "matters" from an oppositional standpoint, in any case, is very different from what might "matter" to the system; OutKast proposes a counter-hegemonic value system, enacted through music, lyrics, and style. It's local—OutKast spends plenty of time sending shouts out to their Atlanta neighbor-hood—and yet it's global, connecting with other black diasporic struc-tures and orienting itself against the erasure of difference, against the paranoiac discourses of moral panic that try to silence young black voices, a sentiment perfectly in key with Chuck D, however he might come off on OutKast's gangsta stance—"mad rhymes for mad times, that's what's up."[25]

Postmodernist theory, at the same time, has been having an iden-tity crisis of its own; under attack from the right as well as by liberal and ostensibly more 'egalitarian' intellectuals, it continues to flourish most fully in the hothouses of graduate programs and large universi-ties. Whatever its claims for attention on intellectual grounds—and I think that they remain strong and compelling—postmodernism must also watch out for its own fully material ass. The caricature of post-modernism as sloppy relativism sliding towards nihilism is indeed inaccurate, but if academics don't pull out of their trance and start articulating *why* this is so to a broader audience, they too may find

their work more heavily targeted than ever before by the moral panicists who raise a hue and cry over "tenured radicals" or professors who
produce unreadable gobbledygook. It is at the level of the politics of
reception—ironically, an area of study to which postmodernist theorists have made central and lasting contributions—that we must direct
ourselves. Here, perhaps, is the best place to frame the collision
between artforms that announce themselves as 'vernacular' and postmodern critique, which seems at times to exist via a discourse that
speaks *about* quotidian cultural expressions without ever seeing itself
as one.

For vernaculars, too, watch their discursive boundaries, and trade
in deliberate (and elaborate) ambiguities; that which is most intimate
is also that which is most coded. Hip-hop as a vernacular discourse
draws ever in towards the center, from the city to the hood to the home
to the homeboys and homegirls, reaching its terminus in artists such
as Flavor Flav, whose idiolect at times seems herme(neu)tically sealed.
So, too, postmodern theories turn inwards—moved by their theoretical perceptions to create discourses which, taking language as the only
lens, seek to remake it via formal plays of difference—and again, the
ultimate, the highest value at times seems the least scrutable. The
common ground, perhaps, in spectacular terms is that nobody likes to
hear things they don't understand and that seem threatening, whether
it's Snoop and Dre rapping about "the day the niggaz took over," or an
academic at a conference talking seriously about the Los Angeles rebellion, and such resentment against the unknown is gasoline for the fires
of the religious right. In more material terms, perhaps its time for a
twofold movement: first, academic postmodernists need to take seriously their *own* claims about the relevance of their theories to everyday
life, need to demonstrate that postmodern values are more than simply
the critique of all values; secondly, rappers, as Gil Scott-Heron urges,
ought to learn more about the histories and issues they are rapping
about. Postmodern theorists, all too often, have forgotten how to shoot
from the hip, while some rappers *only* know how to shoot verbal
barrages first and think later. Pretending that even the best academic
theories—or the most hardcore raps—can, in and of themselves,
change society would be naive, but if there can be a full-fledged alliance
and interchange between vernacular cultural expressions and academics committed to expanding our understanding the contemporary

moment (and the postmodern turn(s) it is taking), then perhaps some real ground would be gained. But it needs to happen soon, 'cos

time

is

running

OUT

Notes

Introduction

1. *Postmodern Culture*, vol. 1, no. 1 (September 1990).

2. Sun Ra, "It's After the End of the World," available on *Soundtrack to the Film* Space is the Place, Evidence Records ECD 22070–2.

3. Theresa Ebert, "Writing the Political: Resistance (Post)modernism," address delivered at a conference on "Rewriting the Postmodern: (Post)Colonialism/Feminism/Late Capitalism," University of Utah, Salt Lake City, March 30, 1990, discussed in Donald Morton and Mas'ud Zavarzadeh, "Theory Pedagogy Politics: The Crisis of 'The Subject' in the Humanities," in Morton and Zavarzadeh, *Theory/Pedagogy/Politics: Texts for Change* (Urbana: University of Illinois Press, 1991), 29–30 n.1.; see also Mas'ud Zavarzadeh and Donald Morton, *Theory, (Post)Modernity, Opposition* (Washington, D.C.: Maisonneuve Press, 1991), 106–130.

4. This point by itself is not new; it has been developed most significantly by Linda Hutcheon, in her lucid book *The Politics of Postmodernism* (New York: Routledge, 1989), particularly in chapter 4, "The politics of parody."

5. Bill Readings and Bennet Schaber, *Postmodernism Across the Ages* (New York: Syracuse University Press, 1993, 6.

6. Paul Gilroy, *The Black Atlantic: Modernity and Double Consciousness* (Cambridge, Mass.: Harvard University Press, 1993).

7. Gilroy, *The Black Atlantic*, p. 36.

8. Cornel West, "Black Culture and Postmodernism," in Barbara Kruger and Phil Mariani, eds., *Remaking History* (Seattle: Bay Press, 1989), pp. 87–88.

9. West, "Black Culture and Postmodernism," p. 96.

10. The Last Poets, "Run, Nigger," on *The Last Poets*, Celluloid CEL 6101. As Tricia Rose observes, "What time is it?" is the first part of the Nation of Islam's well-know call-and-response, to which the answer is "Nation Time." Yet it is the *first* part of this exchange, with its air of "if you have to ask, you don't know," that has become part of the hip-hop's central tropology, circulating far beyond NOI circles.

11. Run DMC, "It's Like That," from *Greatest Hits*, 1983–1991 Profile PCD–1419.

12. Guy Debord, *Society of the Spectacle* (Detroit: Red & Black, n.d.), sections 34, 42.

13. It should be underlined at this juncture that hip-hop was from the start a product of *multiple* cultures, even though its primary producers and audiences were black. Many of the first posses of rappers, break-dancers, and graf writers were Puerto Ricans; as Juan Flores points out, the scene for the emergence of hip-hop in New York in the late '70s was almost as much Puerto Rican as African-American, despite some tensions between these groups (see Juan Flores, "Puerto Rican and Proud, Boyee!: Rap Roots and Amnesia," in Andrew Rossi & Tricia Rose, *Microphone Fiends: Youth Music and Youth Culture* (New York: Routledge, 1994)). There were also several early collaborations between white punkers and black and Latino rappers, such as those between Futura 2000 and the Clash, or Afrika Bambaataa and John Lydon (a.k.a. Johnny Rotten and the Sex Pistols); see the Celluloid sampler *Roots of Rap: The 12-inch singles* (CELD–6205).

14. Chuck D, lecture at Colby College, Waterville, Maine, September 1993.

15. Gilroy, *The Black Atlantic*.

16. Whether or not materialist theories of ideology mark an end to aesthetics remains a hotly contested issue, but my point here is that it is no longer possible to construct an aesthetic without at least taking ideology into account. See Terry Eagleton, *The Ideology of the Aesthetic* (Oxford: Basil Blackwell, 1990), or for a pragmatist turn, see Richard Shusterman, *Pragmatist Aesthetics: Living Beauty, Rethinking Art* (Oxford: Basil Blackwell, 1992), which has a suggestive chapter on rap music.

17. Steven Connor, *Postmodernist Culture*, pp. 9–10.

18. Zora Neale Hurston, excerpt from *Mules and Men*, reprinted in *I Love Myself When I am Laughing . . . And Then Again When I am Looking Mean and Impressive* (Old Westbury, NY: The Feminist Press, 1979), p. 82.

19. Gang Starr, "Tons-o-Guns," on *Hard to Earn* (CD 7243 8 28435 2 8).

20. The Coup, "Not Yet Free," from *Kill My Landlord*, Wild Pitch CD 07777–89047–25.

21. Ice Cube describes the U.S. war against Iraq ("Desert Storm") as Uncle Sam trying to "fuck a brother up the ass," and later refers to Uncle Sam as "the devil in drag" ("I Wanna Kill Sam," on *Death Certificate*, Priority Records CDL 57155, ©1991 Priority Records Inc.): MC Ren tells women he sees in concert that "I'm gonna call you a bitch, or a dirty-ass ho" in "Straight Outta Compton," from *Straight Outta Compton*, Ruthless/ Priority CDL 57102, ©1988 Priority Records Inc.

22. Clearly, rappers make this critique against the ideology of the white power structure because the concept of 'purity' has historically been most frequently invoked when a dominant group wishes to oppose itself to (or purge itself of) an oppressed group. Yet the opposing notion of black 'authenticity' has its own ideology of purity, which some have attacked, as when the authors of *Signifying Rappers* taunt Chuck D for being "unable to locate even one pure black source" (*Signifying Rappers*, p. 89). My own position, as I will elaborate in the chapters that follow, is that hip-hop has always been heteroglot, and has *known* it, whereas the white middle-class hegemony, while no less heteroglot, has *denied* it. For even the most Afrocentric rappers, those most concerned with creating and sustaining an 'authentic' culture, have done so precisely by appropriating artifacts from mass culture, as when Afrika Bambaataa took the "Zulu Nation" name from an the British film *Zulu* (see Toop, *Rap Attack 2*, 57), or when groups such as X-Clan, Lakim Shabazz, or Kwamé appropriate hieroglyphics, "Egyptian" dance moves, and names (e.g., "Isis"). What is "authentic," in these instances, is clearly *produced*, even though it may well form the core of a dialectic of "authentic" vs. "sell-out" or "phony."

23. "Black is Black / White is White / That's all right / No need to fight, Yo! / Much respect if your nature's in check a little / If not expect me to cock-a-doodle-do a riddle," from "Hit da Road Jack" (C. Ridonhour/K. Shocklee/Gary G-Wiz, ©1992 Def American Songs) from the album *Greatest Misses* (Def Jam/Chaos OK 53014), 1992; Humpty-Hump's line is from "The Humpty Dance" (G. Jacobs, E. Humphrey; © 1990 Tommy Boy Music Inc.), from the album *Sex Packets*, Tommy Body TBCD 1026 (1990).

24. "On one level rap is *descriptive* of a certain fluid everydayness (*all-taglich*): tales of concrete situations (reminiscent of folklore); distinctive styles of dress; shared plights; shared socio-historical realities; shared

unconscious associations, etc. On another level, however, rap is *prescriptive* (as anyone knows who has listened to Public Enemy, Poor Righteous Teachers, et al.). But rap as a modality of prescriptive didacticism and socio-political discontent is nevertheless coughed in a mode of linguisticality intrinsic to a sociality of shared experience. In short, whether viewed as a form of description or prescription, rap presupposes the contention that discourse is fundamentally a form of praxis." George Yancy, quoted in James G. Spady, "Password: Nation Conscious Rap," in Joseph D. Eure and James G. Spady, *Nation Conscious Rap: The Hip-Hop Vision* (Brooklyn: PC International Press, 1991), p. 414; Ice-T's lines "[hip-hop] is not some fad / created overnight / it is a cultural movement / that's bred by city life" are from "Body Rock," © 1984 Electrobeat Records.

25. This preference is certainly understandable, given that, in the reductive crucible of the society of the spectacle, there is often room for only *one* cultural synecdoche (e.g. Italians = pizza, Poles = sausage, Muslims = terrorists). Henry Louis Gates Jr., for one, has expressed caution about seeing rap as "the *fons et origio* of contemporary blackness," or over hailing militant rappers such as Chuck D as Gramscian 'organic intellectuals.' (Henry Louis Gates Jr., letter to the author, 12 December 1991). In the place of Chuck D, Gates expressed a preference for the Disposable Heroes of Hip-Hoprisy's Michael Franti, or other rappers who "have a message you don't have to apologize for" (Gates, same letter). I would certainly agree to the extent that I don't think that Chuck D or any individual rapper ought to be regarded as the one authentic black revolutionary spokesperson—but disagree in that I think that Chuck's messages—in part *because* they come out of a more problematic and contradictory nexus of black nationalism, Islam, and the contemporary rhetoric of race, class, and gender—deserve as or more urgent consideration as more "P.C." rappers such as Franti. To invoke the 'organic intellectual' only to decline his or her message because it doesn't pass a litmus test devised by *academic* intellectuals seems some-what hypocritical. See the section "Homeboys Meet Gramsci" in Jeffrey Louis Decker's "The State of Rap," in Tricia Rose and Andrew Ross, eds. *Microphone Fiends: Youth Music and Youth Culture* (New York: Routledge, 1994), p. 101–2.

26. Henry Louis Gates, *The Signifying Monkey: A Theory of African-American Literary Criticism* (New York: Oxford University Press, 1988), p. xxii.

27. This point is made compellingly by Donald B. Gibson in his response to Gates's paper "Canon-Formation and the Afro-American Tradition," in which Gibson states: "[For Frederick Douglass] there was no

value in the stock of the vernacular; nothing to be achieved by claiming it as valuable in the mid-nineteenth century. One may claim its value now, but only from a very high station. One who has proved his mastery of the master's discourse may then claim the value of the vernacular, for no one doubts the claimant's credentials. Woe be the claimant who is not firmly in control of the language of the dominant culture, for he will not have earned the right to deal in such black-market currency. He will be silenced, not heard." Gibson, "Response" to Gates, from Houston A. Baker, Jr., and Patricia Redmond, eds., *Afro-American Literary Study in the 1990's* (Chicago: University of Chicago Press, 1989).

28. I owe this latter point to Karen Carr, who in our discussion and debates on the question of "the" vernacular always insisted that there could be no "the," no historically transcendent vernacular somehow 'outside' of the dominant discourse.

29. "The chronotope is an optic for reading texts as x-rays of the forces at work in the culture from which they spring." M. M. Bakhtin, *The Dialogic Imagination*, ed. and trans. Michael Holmquist (Austin: University of Texas Press, 1981), p. 426; see also Gilroy, *The Black Atlantic*, 4–5, and 225 n. 2.

30. Much of this criticism has focused around Paul DeMan, the deconstructionist critic who, it was discovered, had written anti-Semitic articles in Belgium during the Nazi occupation. Even if one takes DeMan's earlier writings as an indictment of his later views, DeMan's value as an anti-intellectual poster boy to the political right has been far in excess of any complicity between racism and post-structuralist theorists, who in point of fact have at every turn critiqued and worked to oppose racist ideologies.

31. From the title track to H.E.A.L. (Human Education Against Lies).

32. Michel de Certeau, *Heterologies: Discourse on the Other* (Minneapolis: University of Minnesota Press, 1986), p. 129.

33. De Certeau, p. 129.

34. Amiri Baraka (LeRoi Jones), *Black Music* (New York: William Morrow, 1967), p. 18.

35. Jon Michael Spencer, preface to *The Emergency of Black and the Emergence of Rap* (*Black Sacred Music*, Vol. 5, No. 1), p. iii.

36. From "The Hate that Hate Produced," on *360 Degrees of Power*, EPIC EK 48713 (1992).

37. See the excellent accounting and analysis of the politics of hip-hop concerts and "violence" in Tricia Rose's *Black Noise: Rap Music and Black*

Culture in Contemporary America (Hanover: University Press of New England/Wesleyan University Press, 1994), pp. 130–137.

38. See the article "Real Rap Radio," by Roni Sarig and Bobbito (*VIBE*, March 1994, p. 26). The list of radio stations included with this article shows both the commitment of college radio to rap music and the limited visibility of rap on commercial radio (typically, commercial stations program only three or four hours of rap *a week*, and it is often aired between 11 p.m. and 2 a.m.). As another indicator of the hip-hop college connection, at least two radio shows—Professor Jeff Foss of Hofstra University's "Post-Punk Progressive Pop Party" on WRHU FM in New York, and my own "Roots-n-Rap" shown on WMHB in Waterville, Maine, are hosted by college professors.

Chapter 1

1. From Boogie Down Productions, *Ghetto Music: The Blueprint of Hip-Hop* (New York: Jive/RCA, 1989; Issue # 1187-2-J); © 1989 Zomba Productions.

2. Ice-T, Ice M.F. T," on *Home Invasion*, Rhyme Syndicate/Priority Records P2 53858; © 1993 Rhyme Syndicate Records; Bob Dylan, "Ballad of a Thin Man," in *Lyrics, 1962–1985* (New York: Alfred A. Knopf, 1985), 198; lyrics © 1965 Warner Bros. Inc. As a sidenote, it is worth noting that "Ballad of a Thin Man" was said to be Black Panther founder Huey P. Newton's favorite song during his time in prison.

3. Henry Louis Gates Jr., *The Signifyin(g) Monkey: A Theory of African-American Literary Criticism* (New York: Oxford University Press, 1988), esp. pp. 63–64 and 104–105.

4. Blind Willie McTell (as "Georgia Bill"), "Georgia Rag," Okeh 8924, recorded Oct. 31, 1931; available on *Blind Willie McTell: The Complete Recorded Works in Chronological Order*, Document Records DOCD–5007. McTell is Signifyin(g) on Chicago bluesman Blind Blake's "Wabash Rag" of several years earlier; at one point he even slips up and sings "Wa . . Georgia Rag."

5. Baraka, Amiri (LeRoi Jones), *Black Music* (New York: William Morrow, 1967).

6. Ice Cube, "The Nigga ya love ta hate," on *Amerikkka's Most Wanted*, Priority Records CDL 57120.

7. Gates's distinction is worth repeating at length: "[Ishmael] Reed's use of parody would seem to be fittingly described as motivated Signifyin(g),

in which the text Signifies upon other black texts, in the manner of the vernacular ritual of "close reading." [Alice] Walker's use of pastiche, on the other hand, corresponds to an unmotivated Signifyin(g), by which I mean to suggest not the absence of a profound intention but the absence of a negative critique. The relationship between parody and pastiche is that between motivated and unmotivated Signifyin(g)" (Gates, *Signifying Monkey*, xxvi–xxvii.) This distinction is often difficult to keep discrete, however, as will become apparent shortly.

8. Presenting any kind of 'unified' history is indeed a difficult task, as David Toop, author of the best book ever written on hip hop, *Rap Attack!* discovered; his chapters continually recover the same few years of hip-hop history, each time making different narratives and offering different genealogies—which, whether intentional or accidental, turns out to be the best way to (re)tell the history of hip-hop.

9. Mary Katherine Aldin, liner notes to *Soul Shots Vol. 4: Urban Blues*, Rhino Records R2 75758 (which includes a digitally remastered copy of Fulsom's original version).

10. Their version actually out-charted Fulsom's, reaching number 2 on the R&B charts and number 26 on the Pop charts. The record was released on April 7, 1967 as Volt 147; it is available in a digitally remastered version on *The Complete Stax/Volt Singles, 1959–1968*, Atlantic 7 82218–2, Vol. 7 (the recording and chart data are drawn from the book accompanying this set).

11. Lonnie Johnson and Clara Smith (as Violet Green), "You Had Too Much," recorded Friday, 31 October, 1930; released as OKeh OK 8839; available in a digitally remastered version on *Roots-n-Blues: The Retrospective, 1925–1950*, Columbia-Legacy C4K 47911.

12. Rob Bowman, in the booklet accompanying *The Complete Stax/Volt Singles, 1959–1968*, p. 27, states that Fulsom "felt the Memphis duo's recording made fun of his composition."

13. Lyrics transcribed from the digital re-release of Fulsom's "Tramp" (Fulsom-McCracklin) on *Soul Shots Vol. 4: Urban Blues*, Rhino Records R2 75758; lyrics © 1966 Powerforce Music and Budget Music, all rights reserved; used by permission.

14. Transcribed from the digital re-release of Otis Redding & Carla Thomas's version of "Tramp" (Fulsom-McCracklin) on *The Complete Stax/Volt Singles, 1959–1968*, vol. 7; originally Stax 216. Lyrics © 1967 Powerforce Music and Budget Music, all rights reserved; used by permission

(in a quirk of copyright law, Otis & Carla's revamping of Fulsom's "Tramp" is considered merely a *performance*, and thus falls under the same copyright).

15. Again, this undercutting has ample precedent in other African-American musical traditions; for examples one might listen to any of the recordings in which Thomas "Fats" Waller sang a standard along with a female vocalist (Waller constantly Signified on the female vocalists' lines), or to Signifying duets such as Big Maybelle's 1952 "Gabbin' Blues," recently re-issued on Big Maybelle: The Complete OKeh Sessions, Columbia/Legacy CD EK 53417 (1994).

16. Transcribed from Salt 'n' Pepa, "Tramp (remix)," on *Hot, Cool, and Vicious*, © 1988, Next Plateau Records; I use italics here to indicate the sample of Thomas/Redding version, which recurs at various points in the verses and many times in the chorus.

17. See Roxanne Shanté's "Knockin' Hiney," on *Bad Sister*, Cold Chillin CD 9 25809–2 (1989), and BWP's "Two Minute Brother," on *The Bytches*, No Face/Rush CD CK 47068.

18. Houston A. Baker, "Hybridity, the Rap Race, and Pedagogy for the 1990's," in Constance Penley and Andrew Ross, *Technoculture* (Minneapolis: University of Minnesota Press, 1991).

19. Dick Hebdige, *Cut 'n' Mix: Culture, Identity, and Caribbean Music*. New York: Commedia (Methuen), 1987; Daisann McLane, "The Forgotten Caribbean Connection," *The New York Times*, Aug. 23, 1992, sec. 2: 22.

20. Prince Buster, "Earthquake," (c. 1966), available on the Sequel Records compilation *Prince Buster FABulous Hits*, NEX CD 253. Quoted in Hebdige, Cut 'n' Mix, 66.

21. One of the earliest conjunctions between the R&B and Rasta sounds took place at Buster's first recording session in 1960, when he brought Ossie together with the Folkes Brothers and recorded "Oh Carolina." This track is available on the compilation *Tougher Than Tough: The Story of Jamaican Music* (Mango/Island Records 162–539 935–2).

22. Linton Kwesi Johnson describes this progression succinctly: "Rock steady represented the music of the first generation of post-independence youth. It shed all of its U.S. influences and became totally Jamaican...now the social themes came in, protest records; even "Israelites" by Desmond Dekker is a lament about poverty. That's a defining characteristic of reggae music—it's a social music, like calypso, concerned with topicality" (from the Introduction to the liner notes for *Tougher Than Tough* (see n. 21 above).

23. Prince Buster, "Judge Dread," "The Appeal," "Judge Dread Dance," from *Prince Buster*, Skank Records SKA BBLP–4 (originally Blue Beat/Melo Disk BBLP 809). "Judge Dread" is also available on the Sequel Records compilation (see n. 20 above).

24. Quoted in Hebdige, *Cut 'n' Mix*, 66; it is suggestive to note that both Scarface and Capone (as in Pretty Tone Capone) have re-surfaced as monikers for 'gangsta'-style rappers. "Al Capone," recorded in 1965, can also be heard on the *Tougher Than Tough* compilation.

25. Pigmeat Markham, for one, parlayed his "Heah Come da Judge" routine into a number of records between the '30s and the '60s, and has been cited by rappers such as Mike C. (The Fearless Four) as the "first" rapper (Toop, *Rap Attack 2*, 40).

26. While Herc has at times seemed ambivalent about hip-hop's Jamaican roots, in his raps on Terminator X's 1994 *Super Bad* album, he is emphatic:

New York City
The place where it all came from
And also part of the West Indies
Roots! Yes, de Yardman start it
Yes! It came from the roots, the Island...

(From "Make Room for Thunder" (N. Rogers, ©1994 Xtra Slammin' Music/ Shocklee Music), on *Super Bad*, RAL CD 314 523 343–2). As Steven Hager describes it, all of Herc's practices—his emphasis on having the most powerful amplification, his calling out of other DJs such as Flash, his practice of washing the labels of the obscure records he cut up to keep his sources secret from the competition—are virtually identical to those of the early "sound system" ska deejays described by Hebdige. See Hager, *Hip-Hop*, 45–46, Toop, *Rap Attack 2*, 104, and Hebdige, *Cut 'n' Mix*, 64–70 and 136–148.

27. For good examples of the hip-hop and dancehall cross-influences, see Fu-Schnickens, "Ring the Alarm," on *F.U. Don't Take It Personal* (Jive CD J2 1472); Fugees (Tranzlator Crew), "Boof Baf," on *Blunted on Reality* (Columbia CD CK 57462); Mad Kap, "Phuck What Ya Heard," on *Look Ma Duke, No Hands!* (RCA 07863); Shabba Ranks (with KRS-One), "The Jam," on *As Raw As Ever* (ET 47310); Tiger (with Q-Tip), "Who Planned It?" on *Claws of the Cat* (Chaos CD OK 52898); and Worl-a-Girl, "No Gun Shot: and "Ten Commandments," on *Worl-a-Girl* (Chaos CD OK 57549). Worl-a-Girl was not, as it happens, the first group to cut an answer record to Buster's "Ten Commandments"; there were three that came out in 1967 immediately

after it was released—including "Eve's Ten Commandments" (Blue Beat single BB 341), "Ten Commandments of Woman" (Dice single CC 26), and "Ten Commandments From Woman to Man" (King single 45–690, produced by Buster himself!).

28. Toop, *Rap Attack 2*, 66.

29. James Brown, "Funky Drummer," King Single K6290, released July 1970; available on the *Star Time* four-CD compilation, Polydor 849 111–2; personnel and release data from the booklet accompanying this set.

30. These beats are from an ad on page 23 of the Summer 1992 catalog from Brooklyn's Upstairs Records, for a breakbeat compilation called *Stretch Breaks Volume 1*, produced by Simon Harris. "Stretched President" is a speeded-up version of the beat in James Brown's "Funky President"; the stretching process accelerates it from 104 to 121 beats per minute.

31. Toop, *Rap Attack 2*, pp. 113–114.

32. This tradition continued in gospel recordings well into the 1960s; David Toop cities the Rev. J.D. Montgomery, the Rev. Willie T. Sneed, Dorothy Norwood, and Edna Gallman Cooke as examples (Toop, *Rap Attack 2*), pp. 47–48.

33. This was the chorus to Big Bill Broonzy's "Pussycat Blues" (Broonzy was an on-and-off member of one of at least two groups that called themselves the "Hokum Boys" in the late '20s and early '30s).

34. "Terrible Operation Blues" and "Pussycat Blues" can both be found on the Yazoo Records LP *Do That Guitar Rag: Big Bill Broonzy, 1927–1930* (Yazoo Records). Two examples of 'guest' appearances can be found in Harris & Harris's "Teasin' Brown" and "This Is Not the Stove to Brown Your Bread" (both recorded in 1929), on which song & dialog are framed by Blind Willie McTell's guitar; both are available on *Blind Willie McTell: Complete Recorded Works in Chronological Order*, Document DOCD–5006).

35. Toop, *Rap Attack 2*, pp. 47–53.

36. See Michael Small, *Break It Down: The Inside Story from the New Leaders of Rap* (New York: Citadel Press, 1992), 218; this cut appeared in December of 1982 as Tommy Boy TB 831 (12"), and is available on the compilation *Tommy Boy: Greatest Beats*, TBC 1005.

37. Malcolm X, with music by Keith LeBlanc, "No Sell Out," released in November 1983 as Tommy Boy TB 840 (12"); also available on the compilation *Tommy Boy: Greatest Beats*.

38. See Toop, Rap Attack 2, 124–5: "Paul Winley, who had once released speeches by both Martin Luther King Jr. and Malcolm X, had this to say: "It's just like taking one of your idols, one of your heroes and boogie-ing behind 'em. It's just like taking the Pope's speech and putting some disco music behind it—here's John Paul, baby!" Despite Winley's reservations, the overall attitude toward such samples has grown increasingly positive. Some on the initial resistance may have been due to the fact that LeBlanc was white.

39. The industrial-dance band Greater Than One mixed King's "I Have A Dream" speech with powerful beats in their track "Now Is The Time"; among other hip-hop tracks to include such samples are Public Enemy's "Revolutionary Generation" (1990, on *Fear of a Black Planet*) and "Party for Your Right to Fight—Black Wax Metromixx" (1993, on *Greatest Misses*); BDP's "Ya Strugglin'" on the *Edutainment* CD features remarks by Kwame' Ture' (formerly Stokely Carmichael).

40. From the cut, "Our Leader," on Consolidated's *friendly fa$cism*, Nettwerk CD X2–13089 (1991).

41. See Laquan's cut "Presidential Suite/Presidential Suite & Sour/Imprison the President," on his debut, *Notes of a Native Son*, 4th&B'Way CD 444029–2. On "The Days of Old," Paris inserts his *own* voice for the word "poor," adding distortion to mask the substitution. Such sonic mangling was not new, however; way back in the mid-'80s the German industrial band KMFDM had cut up JFK's "Ich bin ein Berliner" speech into such gems as "we would prefer to see Europe weak and divided."

42. Shazzy, "Intro," from *Attitude: A Hip-Hop **Rapsody***, Elektra CD 9 60937–2 (1990).

43. The reference is apparently to L.A. mayor Tom Bradley; the cut is "Guerrillas in the Mist," on *Play More Music* by the group Consolidated (Nettwerk Records X2-0777-7-13171-25; © 1992 Nettwerk Productions. The confusion over just exactly what a Tech 9, more recently simply "nine" *is*, has been Signified on by the Flavor Unit MC's in their video for "Roll wit tha Flava" (1993), in which rappers are shown carrying around large Sesame Street-style number 9's.

44. Samples from the track "I'm Scared," from Ice Cube's *The Predator*, Priority Records P2-57185, © 1992 Priority Records.

45. As Grandmaster Flash himself described it, "The Sugarhill who? The Sugarhill Gang. They don't know me and I don't know them. Who are these people? They got a record on the radio and that shit was haunting me

because I felt we should have been the first to do it. We were the first *group* to really do this—someone took our shot. Every night I would hear this fucking record on the radio, 92KTU, 98, BLS, rock stations. I was hearing this shit in my dreams." (Toop, *Rap Attack 2*, 76).

46. See Walter Benjamin, "The Work of Art in the Age of Mechanical Reproduction," in *Illuminations*, ed. Hannna Arendt (New York: Schocken Books), 220–221.

47. See Toop, *Rap Attack 2*, 105–6.

48. See Toop, *Rap Attack 2*, 106–7.

49. "Planet Rock" can be found on the *Tommy Boy: Greatest Beats* collection, and also on the two-CD Rhino set of "Electric Funk," which showcases other early groups, like Newcleus, Hashim, and Cybotron, which drew on Bambaataa's sounds. The eventual descendants of electro-funk are Detroit Techno, rave, "acid jazz," and "industrial" dance, all of which have risen in popularity in the early '90s.

50. See Mike Davis, *City of Quartz: Excavating the Future in Los Angeles*. New York: Vintage Books, 1992.

51. A sample from the track list of the wide-ranging Rhino compilation *West Coast Rap*, vols. 1–3 gives an idea of the early ethos: "Gigolo Rapp," "Rappin' Partee Goove," "Dial-a-Freak," "Sexy Baby," "NBA Rap," "Freak-a-Holic," and "Big Butt" are typical titles.

52. "Bad Times (I Can't Stand It)," Saturn #2003, 1983; available on *West Coast Rap* Vol. 1, Excello/Rhino R2 70590, 1992.

53. Mike Davis, *City of Quartz*, 275–6.

54. The Future MC's, "Beverly Hills Cop," Flash #002, 1985; Kid Frost, "Terminator," Electrobeat #005, 1985; both available on *West Coast Rap* Vol. 3, Excello/Rhino R2 70592, 1992.

55. Ice-T, "Six in the Morning," Techno Hop #13, 1986, © 1986 Grandma's Hands Music (BMI); available on *West Coast Rap* Vol. 3, Excello/Rhino R2 70592, 1992.

56. This track, "Advance," can be found on the (now out-of-print) "collector's" tape *BDP: The Man And His Music*, B-Boy Records #CA1–2000, © 1988 B-Boy/Rock Candy Records.

57. From "Advance," on *BDP: The Man and His Music*.

58. "Ghetto Music," from *Ghetto Music: The Blueprint of Hip Hop*, Zomba/Jive CD 1187-2-J, © 1989 Zomba Recording Corp.

59. Ice Cube, "I Wanna Kill Sam," from *Death Certificate*, Priority Records CDL 57155; © 1991 Priority Records.

60. Ice-T, "I'm Your Pusher," on *Rhyme Pays*.

Chapter 2

1. From Robert S. Haller, ed. and tr., *Literary Criticism of Dante Alighieri* (Lincoln: University of Nebraska Press, 1977), p. 65.

2. Houston A. Baker, *Blues, Ideology, and Afro-American Literature* (Chicago: University of Chicago Press, 1984), p. 2.

3. The specific historical situations of all these poetic languages need to be recalled; in the wake of the Albigensian crusade, Provençal poets and their *vers* were scattered over Europe, the height of their influence occurring perversely at the very moment of their political destruction; Dante's Italian, though it had a "home" in a sense, still lacked one in that the various city-states were still at odds with each other, and Dante himself wrote in exile from his native Florence; the early bluesmen and women were recorded at the height of the "Great Migration" from the rural South to the urban North and West that marked a quest for the economic enfranchisement promised but not delivered by the Emancipation Proclamation; and Saddat X, finally, as a member of the 5% Nation, a movement within African-American communities towards a "shadow" nation within which Islamic law and faith prevails, but a "Nation" constructed both within and against a structural and political nation (the United States) with its institutionalized racism.

4. Marlene Nourbese Philip, *She Tries Her Tongue, Her Silence Softly Breaks* (Charlottetown: Ragweed Press, 1989), pp. 15–16.

5. Quoted in Gates, "Canon-Formation and the Afro-American Tradition," in Houston A. Baker and Patricia Redmond, eds., *Afro-American Literary Study in the 1990's* (Chicago: University of Chicago Press, 1992), p. 19.

6. Zora Neale Hurston, "How it Feels to Be Colored Me" in Alice Walker, ed., *I Love Myself When I Am Laughing...And Then Again When I Am Looking Mean and Impressive: A Zora Neale Hurston Reader* (Old Westbury, NY: The Feminist Press, 1979), p. 153.

7. In this, the minstrel shows took their ideological cue from the oldest dicta of European comedy, which can be traced ultimately to Aristotle, who linked the laughter of comedy to the use of "inferior persons."

8. See Booker T. Washington, *Up From Slavery* (New York: Penguin Books, 1986), 174–175. While Washington does not directly address the issue of black vernaculars in his autobiography, he wrote his life's story in a very formal English; the one or two instances where he employs these vernaculars is as the punchline of a didactic joke, e.g. on page 128 of this same edition.

9. Malcolm X (with Alex Haley), *The Autobiography of Malcolm X* (New York: Grove Press, 1966, p. 56). As this passage goes on to argue, Malcolm associated the "hip" slang of black urban vernaculars with zoot suits, conked hair, liquor, and cigarettes—as "ghetto adornments" that were to be eschewed as signs of the oppressed status of blacks in the United States.

10. Despite this recurrent polarization—which is primarily a matter of the politics of reception—I do not mean to suggest that there are only *two* choices for African-American writers. As Marlene Nourbese Philip has written in *She Tries Her Tongue*, "to say that the experience can only be expressed in Standard English (if there is any such thing) or only in the Caribbean demotic (there *is* such a thing) is, in fact, to limit the experience for the African artist working in the Caribbean demotic. It is *in the continuum of expression* from standard English to Caribbean English that the veracity of the experience lies" (p. 18). Philip's stress on the continuum applies equally well, I think, to the situation of the African-American writer; both critics and upholders of BVE tend to forget the fact that the majority of BVE speakers also know and use RSE.

11. This subsuming of racial difference within a humanist frame is still prevalent today in many critical circles, despite the critiques that have been made against it by materialist theorists; a typical instance is the statement in the introduction to Booker T. Washington's autobiography by his biographer Louis R. Harlan: "The reason why *Up from Slavery* has never been out of print since its first publication almost a century ago is its appeal to universal human yearnings. Washington seemed implicitly to promise that virtue, upward striving, and divine Providence would bring to anyone success and personal fulfillment." *Up From Slavery*, p. xliii.

12. This same dichotomy, not surprisingly, has been used by anti-rap critics such as David Samuels and C. Delores Tucker. Even within the hip-hop community; some political rappers, such as the Disposable Heroes of HipHoprisy explicitly engage with this crux in cuts such as "Famous and Dandy" (like Amos 'n' Andy), which opens with an extended sample from *Amos 'n' Andy*. Yet the central question here—staged *for whom* and *at whose expense*, is in a sense unanswerable outside of specific instances of consumption, as even the most pathetic racialized fantasy can be potentially

recuperated via a Signifyin(g) turn, as with KMD's "No Sambo" graphic logo.

13. Without radically oversimplifying the permeable and historically shifting demarcations between the 'realistic' and the 'fantastic,' it should be noted that, while until the past two decades surveys of the literature of the period of the Harlem Renaissance tended to foreground the relatively "realist" styles of (predominantly male) writers such as Richard Wright, there were at the same time a number of African-American writers who located themselves within a commitment to the vernacular that could speak both within a realistic mode (Hurston) and also as an element in the *exoticization* of blackness, as with the work of Claude McKay. There were many other choices between these, of course, but it is hardly coincidental that Hurston's work was criticized at the time, most emphatically by Wright, as a pandering to white tastes for stereotypical Negroes. Wright himself, as fate would have it, would be criticized in his later years for moving away from the perceived gut-level realism of his early works, though his movement was in the direction of philosophical novels that worked to situate the crises of race in broader historical and geographical contexts (see Paul Gilroy's fascinating chapter on Wright in *The Black Atlantic*).

14. The radio deejay was Vernon Winslow, a.k.a. Dr. Daddy-O; Winslow originated one of the more influential 'jive' radio personalities of the late '40s and early '50s, Poppa Stoppa, but was forced to train a white announcer to read his scripts. When he read one of his own scripts over the air, he was summarily fired; for details on his career see Toop, *Rap Attack 2*, 38–39.

15. The Goats' debut CD on Columbia/Ruff House records, "Tricks of the Shade," is a concept album with skits between many of the songs that take listeners on a tour of "Uncle Scam's Well Fair and Freak Show," with attractions such as the Columbus Boat Ride (featuring the Nina, the Pinta, and the Sent ta Enslave Ya), Noriega's Coke Stand, and the Drive-by Shooting Bumper Cars (*Tricks of the Shade*, Ruff House/Columbia CK 53027, 1992). The title signifies both on race (as "shade") but also on the gay dance hall term for Signifying, "casting shade" (see the film *Paris is Burning* for a humorous explanation of "casting shade" along with its cousins "reading" and "vogueing").

16. Special Ed, "I Got It Made," from *Youngest in Charge*, Profile Records PCT–1280, © 1989 Profile Records Inc.

17. Deleuze and Guattari, *Kafka: Toward a Minor Literature*, tr. Dana Polan. Minneapolis: University of Minnesota Press, 1986, 16–17.

18. *Kafka*, 17.

19. *Kafka*, 17.

20. Gilles Deleuze and Félix Guattari, *A Thousand Plateaus: Capitalism and Schizophrenia*, tr. Brian Massumi (Minneapolis: University of Minnesota Press, 1987), 106.

21. Ice-T, "This One's for Me," on *The Iceberg/Freedom of Speech... Just Watch What You Say*; Sir Mix-a-Lot, "I Check My Bank," on *Music from the Motion Picture: Trespass*.

22. Michelle Cliff, "A Journey Into Speech," in Rick Simpson and Scott Walker, eds., *The Graywolf Annual Five: Multi-Cultural Literacy* (St. Paul: Graywolf Press), 1988.

23. Michel de Certeau, tr. Steven Rendall, *The Practice of Everyday Life*. Berkeley: University of California Press, 1984, p. 37.

24. See the track "Phuck What Ya Heard," on Mad Kap's debut CD, *Look Ma Duke, No Hands*, Loud/RCA 07863 66161–2 (1993).

25. Amiri Baraka offers one riff on this rift: "The separations, artificial oppositions in Black Music resolved, are the ditty strong classic (Ditty bop). That is, the New Black Music and R&B are the same family looking at different things. Or looking at things differently. The collection of wills is a simple unity like on the street...the Rhythm and Blues mind blowing evolution of James-Ra and Sun-Brown. That growth to include all the resources, all the rhythms, all the yells and cries, all that information about the world, the Black ommmmmmmmmmmmm, opening and entering (*Black Music*, p. 211).

26. Despite Ice-T's claim here, he has in recent years been more prone to dissing crossover artists who leave the 'hardcore' style, as he does on the cut "Question and Answer" on his *Home Invasion* album.

27. Baraka, *Black Music*, p. 14–15.

28. This link with the material is equally central to other forms of African-American music, and indeed forms the strongest undelying link between them; as Gang Starr's GURU remarks on his dedication to his pioneering jazz-hip-hop fusion CD *Jazzmatazz*, Jazz and Hip-Hop are both "real"—that is, they are founded on the actual, historical African-American experience—and in their realness is a rationale for their fusion, the claim that they have something to say to each other. See *Jazzmatazz: An Experimental Fusion of Hip-Hop and Jazz*, Chrysalis CD 0946–3–21998 2 9 (1993).

29. From Bo$$, "I don't give a Fuck," on *Born Gangstaz*, Chaos/DJ West OK 52903 (1993). The double valences of this attitude are fore-

grounded on the album itself, where the rapper's father (real or fictional, it hardly seems to matter here) leaves a message condemning her use of profanity, but ending with "by the way...thanks for the Rolex, baby."

30. Bennet Schaber, "Modernity and the Vernacular." *Surfaces*, p. 31.

31. See Dick Hebdige, *Cut 'n' Mix: Culture, Identity, and Caribbean Music*. New York: Commedia (Methuen), 1987.

32. Chuck D, in *Nation Conscious Rap*, 380. Kool DJ Herc also describes this process memorably: "Just like back in the days, when the massas throw away the chicken back, and also the pig feet, we pick it up and make something out of it. That's what I did with the record; the ones they throw away, I bought, pick it up, turn it into something..." (from "Make Room for Thunder" (© 1994 Xtra Slammin' Music/Shocklee Music), on Terminator X's *Super Bad*, RAL CD 314 523 343–2.

33. The ultimate source of this refrain is Bobby Byrd's "Hot Pants—I'm Coming, Coming, I'm Coming," available on *James Brown's Funky People* (part 2).

34. Richard Shusterman articulates this connection in his essay "The Fine Art of Rap" (*New Literary History* 22 (1991): 613–532).

35. Gibson, response to Gates, Baker & Redmond, p. 48.

36. Frantz Fanon, *The Wretched of the Earth*, tr. by Constance Farrington (New York: Grove Weidenfeld, 1991 [1968]), p. 63.

37. I do not mean to erase here the significant and complex differences between the postcolonial situation in Africa and the historical transit of Africans in America, but clearly all these points in this passage are readily translated into American terms (a fact not lost on groups such as the Black Panthers, who read and frequently cited Fanon). One has only to look at the video of National Guard troops patrolling the streets of L.A. to experience a sudden sense of historical déja-vu.

38. Even when not deployed in an overtly political track, sampling—at least before the recent rash of lawsuits that reinstituted permissions requirements—was what deCerteau might call a form of "poaching."

39. The despised minister was Lord Ferrers, the Home Office minister in charge of the police; see *The Economist*, 15–21 August 1992, 47. While the speed of the rebuttal was new, the practice was not; as far back as 1983, an anonymous artist known only as the "Phantom" cut up a dance single with a tape loop of Margaret Thatcher, producing the "Thatcher Rap" (see Paul Gilroy, *There Ain't No Black in the Union Jack* (London: Hutchinson, 1987), p. 186.

40. From "Bush Killa," on Paris's album *Sleeping With the Enemy* (© 1992 Scarface Records); lines in italics are those of George Bush.

41. "Guerillas in tha Mist" (Ice Cube, W. Hutchinson, G. Clinton, W. Collins, B. Worrell, Mr. Woody; Gangsta Boogie Music, adm. by Warner Bros. Music Inc. [ASCAP]), from *Guerillas in the Mist*, Street Knowledge Records 7 92296–2, © 1992 Atlantic Recording Corp.

42. Houston A. Baker, *Modernism and the Harlem Renaissance* (Chicago: University of Chicago Press, 1987), pp. 50–51.

Chapter 3

1. Ice-T, "Pulse of the Rhyme Flow," © 1991 Rhyme Syndicate Music; on *O.G. Original Gangsta*, Sire/Warner Bros. CD 9 26492–2.

2. The initials of Niggas With Attitude, Bytches With Problems, Boogie Down Productions, Hoes With Attitude, and Ladies Love Cool James.

3. From the cut "Here Comes Kane, Scoob, Scrap" on Kane's 1993 album, *Looks Like A Job For...* (Cold Chillin'/Warner Bros. CD 9 45128–2).

4. Such sequences were most memorably associated with H. "Rap" Brown, one of whose famous boasting/toasting raps began:

Man, you must don't know who I am
I'm sweet peeter jeeter the womb beater
The baby maker the cradle shaker
The deerslayer the buckbinder the women finder
Known from the Gold Coast to the rocky shores of Maine
Rap is my name and love is my game
(Quoted in Gates, *Signifying Monkey*, 72–3).

5. For an explicit hip-hop version of this narrative, see Schoolly-D, "Signifying Rapper," on *Smoke Some Kill* (Jive/RCA 1101–4–J).

6. From "Straight Outta Compton," on NWA's pivotal album *Straight Outta Compton*, Priority Records CDL 57102.

7. From "Pulse of the Rhyme Flow," on *O.G.: Original Gangster*, © 1991 Rhyme Syndicate Music.

8. From "911 is a Joke," on Public Enemy's *Fear of A Black Planet*, Columbia CK 45413 (1990).

9. *Signifying Rappers*, 86, 30.

10. *Village Voice*, Oct. 16–22, 1991, p. 78.

11. "Necessary," from Boogie Down Productions, *By All Means Necessary* (Zomba/Jive CD 1097-2-J).

12. Paris, "The Devil Made Me Do It," on *The Devil Made Me Do It* (Tommy Boy Records TBCD 1030, © 1990 Tommy Boy Music Inc.).

13. Fanon, *The Wretched of the Earth*.

14. Ice-T, "Escape from the Killing Fields" (on *O.G.: Original Gangster*, Sire/Warner Bros. CD 9 26492-2); Public Enemy, "Welcome to the Terror-dome" (on *Fear of a Black Planet*, Def Jam/Columbia CD CK 45413); Ice Cube, "How to Survive in South Central" (on *Music from the Movie Boyz-n-the-Hood*, Qwest/Warner Bros. CD 9 26643-2.

15. See Mike Davis, *City of Quartz*, passim, but especially pp. 271–284.

16. "Behind Closed Doors," © 1991 Base Pipe Music/337 Music (ASCAP); on WC and the M.A.A.D. Circle, *Ain't a Damn Thang Changed*, Priority Records CDL 57156. WC's lyrics hark back to Josh White's old stan-dard "Get Back Brother," whose chorus was "If you're white you're alright / If you're brown, well, stick around / but if you're black, whoa brother—get back get back get back."

17. *The Wretched of the Earth*, 69.

18. This stereotype itself has been satirized and Signified upon in tracks such as Ice-T's "Straight Up Nigga" and "The Stereotype." For a pithy account of the way this same stereotype is deployed to delegitimize hip-hop, see Jon Michael Spenser, "Introduction" to *The Emergency of Black and the Emergence of Rap* (Black Sacred Music, vol. 5, no. 1 [Spring 1991]), 1–2.

19. KRS-One, lecture delivered at Temple University in Philadelphia; reprinted in Nation Conscious Rap: The Hip-Hop Vision, ed. Joseph D. Eure & James G. Spady (New York: PC International Press, 1991), 180.

20. Jon Michael Spenser, "Introduction" to *The Emergency of Black and the Emergence of Rap* (Black Sacred Music, vol. 5, no. 1 (Spring 1991), 12; the articles references are Tipper Gore, "Hate, Rape, and Rap, *Washington Post*, Jan. 8, 1990, 15A; George F. Will, "America's Slide into the Sewer," *Newsweek*, July 30, 1990, 64; "NYC Crime: 3 Teens Get Prison for Assault of Jogger," *USA Today*, Sept. 12, 1990, 2A.

21. Simon Watney, *Policing Desire: Pornography, AIDS, and the Media*. Second Edition (Minneapolis: University of Minnesota Press, 1989), pp. 42–43.

22. Sonja Peterson-Lewis, "A Feminist Analysis of the Defenses of Obscene Rap Lyrics," in *The Emergency of Black and the Emergence of Rap* (*Black Sacred Music*, vol. 5, no. 1 (Spring 1991), 68–79.

23. "Roxanne, Roxanne" (Full Force/UTFO), Select Records # 62254, © 1984 Select Records; available on *Hip-Hop From the Top* (Rhino), which also includes the "Real" Roxanne's payback.

24. Toop, *Rap Attack 2*, pp. 93–95.

25. Queen Latifah and Monie Love, "Ladies First," © 1989 Tommy Boy Music.

26. Roxanne Shanté, "Year of the Independent Woman," © 1989 Cold Chillin/WB Music.

27. Roxanne Shanté, "Year of the Independent Woman," © 1989 Cold Chillin/WB Music.

28. Yo-Yo, "Girl Don't Be No Fool," on *Make Way For the Motherlode*, East West CD 7 91605–2; MC Lyte, "When in Love," on *Act Like You Know*, First Priority CD 7 91731–2; Nikki D, "18 and Loves to Go," on *Daddy's Little Girl*, Def Jam/Columbia CD CK 44031.

29. BWP, "Two Minute Brother," on *The Bytches*, No Face CD CK 47068; Choice, "Cat Got Your Tongue," on *The Big Payback*, Rap-a-Lot CD 105–2; The Yeastie Girls, "You Suck," on Consolidated's *Play More Music*, Nettwerk CD X2–0777–7–13171–25.

30. "Who Freaked Who," © 1992 Tommy Boy Music, on *Apache Ain't Shit*, Tommy Boy TBCD 1068.

31. See Michael Eric Dyson, "Black or White? Labels Don't Always Fit," in *The New York Times*, Feb. 13, 1994, sec. 2, p. H30, col. 5.

32. See Salim Muwakkil, "The rap gap: class divisions divide the black community." *Utne Reader* no. 37 (Jan.-Feb. 1990) p. 52, and Michael Eric Dyson, "Bum Rap," *The New York Times*, February 3, 1994, p. A21, col. 2.

33. The Senate hearing was ostensibly about "offensive" lyrics in all forms of music, but as the witness list made clear, rap music was in fact the sole target of these hearings as well.

34. Rob Marriott, James Bernard, and Allen S. Gordon, "Reality Check." *The SOURCE*, June 1994, p. 70.

35. *The New York Times*, Sept. 20, 1992, national edition; section 9, pp. 1, 8.

36. See N'Tanya Lee, Don Murphy, and Juliet Ucelli. "Whose Kids? Sexuality and the Right in New York City's Curriculum Battles. *Radical America*, vol. 25, n. 1, pp. 9–21.

37. bell hooks, "Is Paris Burning?" In *Black Looks: Race and Representation* (Boston: South End Press, 1992).

38. "In *Paris is Burning*, power remains almost exclusively defined in materialistic, Caucasian, and consumer terms. May long to be rich and famous. Some long to be white and female...they want *things* in a world that has caused more than a few of them not to want themselves. The danger in illusion is that it doesn't remove the facts of racism, sexism, and homophobia, and economic injustice"; and yet again, "The erasure or silencing of identity through the use of illusion might be considered simply an act of entertainment in the context of the balls if it weren't such a willful act of survival and affirmation exercised in a state of increasing desperation." Essex Hemphill, "To Be Real," in *Ceremonies: Prose and Poetry* (New York: Plume, 1992), pp. 116, 121. Hemphill also makes a suggestive comparison between the posturings of gangsta rap and the ball scene (p. 116), which forms one (unacknowledged) basis for Andrew Ross's essay "Poverty Meets Performance: The Gangsta and the Diva." *The Nation*, vol. 259, #6 (August 22/29, 1994), 191–194.

39. One of the most vitriolic and persistent proponents of this linkage is Dr. Frances Cress Welsing, whose "The Politics Behind Black Male Passivity, Effeminization, Bisexuality, and Homosexuality" has been widely disseminated in black nationalist circles. See Essex Hemphill, "If Freud had been a Neurotic Colored Woman: Reading Dr. Frances Cress Welsing," in *Ceremonies*.

40. Paul Gilroy finds some of the earliest threads of this mode of nationalism in the writings of the nineteenth-century black writer Martin Delany, who as Gilroy puts it, argues that "the integrity of the race is the integrity of its male heads of household" and that "women were to be educated only for motherhood" (Gilroy, *The Black Atlantic*, pp. 25–26).

41. "Nappy Happy: A Conversation with Ice Cube and Angela Davis," *Transition* 58 (1992), 182.

42. "Ladies First," on *All Hail The Queen*, Tommy Boy TBCD 1022.

43. Poor Righteous Teachers, "Shakiyla," on *Holy Intellect*, Profile PCD 1289.

44. For one particularly telling rap, see the predictably super-macho Egyptian Lover's double-entendre "Alezby Inn," on *West Coast Rap, vol. 3*.

45. "Talking with…Ice-T, *People* Magazine, April 19, 1993, p. 23.

46. See "I Wanna Kill Sam," quoted in chapter 4 below.

47. The degree to which the *New Republic* has been able to capitalize on this article is suggested by the fact that in three separate mass mailings in the past year, I have been solicited with an envelope that proclaims that if I subscribe I will find out 'why rap music is really white.'

48. Samuels, p. 25.

49. Samuels, p. 26.

50. Quoted in Samuels, p. 29.

51. Quoted in Samuels, p. 29.

52. Samuels, p. 29.

53. *Planet Rap*, TBCD 1076 (1993).

Chapter 4

1. Frederick Jameson, "Postmodernism and Consumer Society," in Hal Foster, ed., *The Anti-Aesthetic: Essays on Postmodern Culture* (Port Townsend, WA: Bay Press, 1983), p. 111.

2. De Certeau, *The Practice of Everyday Life*, p. 34.

3. Tricia Rose's *Black Noise* is perhaps the best general study to engage with these questions, though she focuses primarily on the history of the South Bronx; for the west coast rap scene, Brian Cross also offers a strong, historically-informed analyses of resistance in *It's Not About a Salary…Rap, Race and Resistance in Los Angeles* (New York & London: Verso, 1993).

4. The Goats, "Wrong Pot 2 Piss In" (J. D'Angelo,-M. Stoyanoff-Williams-P. Shupe-W. Braverman), ©1992 Songs of PolyGram International Inc./Oatie Kato Tunes (BMI)

5. *The Practice of Everyday Life*, p. 18.

6. For a graphic example of one such barricade in Los Angeles, see the photography by Robert Morrow entitled "No Outlet," which shows a double blinking-light barrier with the ominous notice "Narcotics Enforcement Area: Open to Residents Only" (in Mike Davis, *City of Quartz: Excavating the Future in Los Angeles* (New York: Vintage, 1992), p. 279.

7. And they are not the first: rappers' boasts about their cars, jewelry, and other possessions have numerous antecedents; Josephine Baker walked

with a panther long before LL Cool J, and Robert Johnson cruised around in his Terraplane fifty years before Chuck D fueled up his '98; anyone acquainted with the history of jazz and blues could readily pick out dozens of further examples.

8. "The Sticka," by C. Ryder-T. Marrow-L. Moorer-O. Jackson-N. Rogers, © 1994 Shocklee Music/Xtra Slammin' Music (BMI)/Top Billin/Gangsta Boogie/Warner Chappell Music (ASCAP), on Terimantor X's album *Super Bad* (P.R.O. Division/RAL CD 314 523 343–2). Chuck's lines here also situate hip-hop's difference within black traditions, Signifyin(g) on Tina Turner's intro to "Proud Mary"; while Turner is gonna start out 'easy' and finish 'rough,' Chuck is gonna be 'rough' and 'hard' from start to finish. See Turner's recording of "Proud Mary" on the soundtrack to *What's Love Got to Do With It?* (Virgin/EMI Records CD 0777–7–88189–2–2).

9. From "The Wrong Nigga to Fuck With," on *Death Certificate*, Priority Records CDL 57155, ©1991 Priority Records. While it is true that Ice Cube, partly because of Priority Records' independent status, has never faced the kind of pressures similar artists with major-label contracts (such as Ice-T), there is certainly something revolutionary about his three solo albums, each of which has gone platinum with virtually no radio airplay whatsoever—something that would have been impossible a few short years ago. The association of radio play with format-oriented "urban contemporary" radio has made many hardcore rappers such as Ice Cube, Ice-T, and EPMD ("No Crossover") to associate radio appeal with "selling out."

10. Such was the explanation offered to me in a letter dated September 22, 1992 from Fred Wistow, Senior VP for Business and Legal Affairs of the Warner Music Group. A similar rationale was evidently used by Island Records, who also passed on the project; Rick Rubin's "Sex Records" label got as far as issuing radio station promo cassettes for the album's lead single, but that deal, too, was cancelled.

11. See David Browne, "Gangsta Wars: 'Bush Killa' sets off new salvos on the rapper front." *Entertainment Weekly*, Dec. 18, 1992, p. 6.

12. Author interview with Chuck D, September 1993.

13. Chuck D, author interview, September 1993; Sir Mix-a-Lot, "I Check My Bank" (© 1992 Songs of PolyGram International/Sir Mix-a-Lot Publishing/MCA Music, Inc.); from the soundtrack to the film *Trespass*, Sire/Warner CD 9 26978–2.

14. Prince Buster, vocal from The Selecter's 1993 remake of Buster's "Madness" (© 1993 Prince Buster Music), on *Madness*, Triple X CD XXX–51171–2.

15. Gilroy, *Ain't No Black*, p. 199.

16. Michael T. Miller, a.k.a. Da P.O.E.T., electronic notesboard posting, Colby College, November 1991.

17. Laquan's "Swing Blue, Sweat Black" (on *Notes of a Native Son*), samples Johnson's "If I Had Possession on the Judgement Day"—originally recorded in November of 1936; ironically, it was not released at the time, and only became available as a reissue in the '60s; see liner notes to *Robert Johnson: The Complete Recordings*, Columbia C2K 46222.

18. 3rd Bass, "Derelicts of Dialect," from *Derelicts of Dialect* (Def Jam/Columbia CK 47369, 1991), © 1991 Rhyming is fundamental/Def Jam Music (ASCAP)/Prince Paul Music/ATV Music.

19. From "Race War," on *Home Invasion*, Rhyme Syndicate/Priority P2 53858, © 1993 Rhyme Syndicate.

20. Ice Cube, "I Wanna Kill Sam" (Gangsta Boogie Music, ASCAP), from *Death Certificate*, Priority CDL 57155, © 1991 Priority Records.

21. Eric B. & Rakim, "Casualties of War" (© 1992 MCA Records Inc.), on *Don't Sweat the Technique*, MCA CD MCAD–10594.

22. The assailant in this case was later found to be a gunman hired by the victim's wife; but whatever the "actual" circumstances, the shooting dramatized a reality of the inner cities, and (if only briefly) woke viewers up to the concept that an American city might be more dangerous than a battle zone.

23. "Race War," on *Home Invasion*.

24. Paul Gilroy, *There Ain't No Black in the Union Jack*, chapter 5: "Diaspora, utopia, and the critique of capitalism" (pp. 153–219).

25. Mike Davis, *City of Quartz: Excavating the Future in Los Angeles* (New York: Vintage, 1992), p. 267.

Chapter 5

1. "They [white liberals] admonish, 'You can't get anywhere without coalitions,' when there is in fact no group at present with whom to form a coalition in which blacks will not be absorbed and betrayed." Stokely Carmichael, "What We Want" [1966]; reprinted in *The Annals of America* (Chicago: Encyclopaedia Britannica, 1976), Volume 18, 377.

2. Paris, "The Days of Old," on *Sleeping With The Enemy*, Scarface CD SCR007–100–2 (1993).

3. An excellent account of the way the White house "handled" visual media during the Reagan era is offered by Carol Squiers in "Picturing Scandal: Iranscam, the Reagan White House, and the Photo Opportunity," in Carol Squiers, *The Critical Image: Essays on Contemporary Photography* (Seattle: Bay Press, 1990), pp. 121–138.

4. Phone conversations with the video's director, Robert Caruso. Nonetheless, Paris's video *was* seen on Black Entertainment Television and Video Jukebox ("The Box"), the latter a 900-number-driven enterprise where, for a fee, callers can request any video of their choosing. As the sole venue for many of the more hard-hitting rap videos, The Box has become one of the keystones of the marketing of rap music in the 1990s.

5. See Kierna Mayo Dawsey, "Caught up in the (Gangsta) Rapture: Dr. C. Delores Tucker's Crusade against "Gangsta Rap." *The Source*, June 1994, pp. 58–62, and Amy Linden, *Niggas with Beatitude: A Conversation with Run DMC*, in *Transition* 62 (1994), p. 183.

6. Sir Mix-a-Lot, "I Check My Bank," on *Music from the motion picture* TRESPASS, Sire?Warner Bros. CD 9 26978–2 (1992); © 1992 Sounds of Polygram International/Mix-a-Lot Publishing/MCA Music Inc.

7. See "Hit the Road, Jack," lines cited in Introduction, n. 13.

8. "I just don't understand white people. White people like stuff that is so overtly wack: Soul Asylum, Rush, *Sports Illustrated*." (Mike D, quoted in US, July 1994, p. 96).

9. I refer here of course to the case of Latasha Harlins, shot and killed by Korean shopkeeper Soo Ja Du in April of 1991; for an excellent commentary on this incident, see Wanda Coleman, "Blacks, Immigrants, and America," in *The Nation*, vol. 256 (1993), pp. 187–191.

10. Rapper Willie D was so incensed by King's platitudes that he cut a rap called "Fuck Rodney King."

11. Ice-T, "Race War," on *Home Invasion*, Rhyme Syndicate/Priority Records P2 53858, © 1994 Warner Brothers Music/Rhyme Syndicate Music.

12. From "Can't Truss It," on *Apocalypse '91: The Empire Strikes Back*, Def Jam/Columbia CK 47374.

13. Ho Chi Minh modeled his own Vietnamese declaration of independence on that of the United States, and in 1945 wrote a series of letters to President Truman and his Secretary of State, speaking of America's "noble

ideals" and urging both cultural exchange and military support. Unfortunately, he had not counted on the virulent anti-communism that possessed the U.S. government in the postwar years; his letters were not even given the courtesy of an answer. See Gareth Porter, ed., *Vietnam: The Definitive Documentation of Human Decisions* (Stanfordville, NY: Earl M. Coleman Enterprises, 1979), vol. I: pp. 83–96, p. 95.

14. Paul Gilroy offers a pioneering and lucid account of this cultural conjunction in his section on "Children of Israel or Children of the Pharaohs?" in *The Black Atlantic* (pp. 205–212).

15. Juan Flores, "Puerto Rican and Proud, Boyee!: Rap Roots and Amnesia." In Andrew Ross & Tricia Rose, *Microphone Fiends: Youth Music and Youth Culture*. New York: Routledge, 1994.

16. See Raegan Kelly, "Hiphop Chicano: A Separate but Parallel Story," in Brian Cross, *It's Not About a Salary: Rap, Race and Resistance in Los Angeles* (New York & London: Verso, 1993), pp. 65–76.

17. Chuck D, author interview, September 1994; published in a modified form in the electronic 'zine *HardC.O.R.E.*, volume 2.5 (1994).

18. Lipscomb, Michael, and KRS-One. "Can the Teacher be Taught?" *Transition* 57 (1992), pp. 168–189.

19. "Can the Teacher be Taught?," pp. 169, 172.

20. "Can the Teacher be Taught?," p. 173.

21. KRS-One (L. Parker), "Sound of da Police," © 1993 Zomba Enterprises Inc./BDP Music, from *Return of the Boom-Bap*, Jive/RCA 01241–41517–2.

22. I deliberately use the dated expressions "fresh" and "happening" to suggest the unlikelihood of such an exchange really producing anything these kids have not heard long before.

23. Baker, p. 100. It is particularly distressing, in the light of Baraka's salient point about the 'junk heap' of culture, that Baker would claim hip-hop as "classical"—without, evidently, much attention to the connotations of this term.

24. From the cut "True Dat" (© 1994 OutKast Music/Organized Noise Music/Stiff Shirt Music), on OutKast's debut CD, *Southernplayalisticadillacmuzik*, La Face CD 73008–26010–2.

25. From Public Enemy, "Give It Up," Def Jam CD 853 317–2 (1994).

Selected Bibliography

Background/General

Beadle, Jeremy J., *Will Pop Eat Itself? Pop Music in the Soundbite Era*. London: Faber & Faber, 1993.

Collins, Jim. *Uncommon Cultures: Popular Culture and Post-Modernism*. New York: Routledge, 1989.

Connor, Steven. *Postmodernist Culture: An Introduction to Theories of the Contemporary*. New York: Basil Blackwell, 1989.

Davis, Mike. *City of Quartz: Excavating the Future in Los Angeles*. New York: Vintage, 1992.

Debord, Guy. *Society of the Spectacle*. Detroit: Black and Red, 1981.

Foster, Hal. *Recodings: Art, Spectacle, and Cultural Politics*. Seattle: Bay Press, 1985.

George, Nelson. *Buppies, B-Boys, Baps, and Bohos: Notes on Post-Soul Black Culture*. New York: HarperCollins, 1992.

———. *The Death of Rhythm & Blues*. New York: Pantheon Books, 1988.

Gilroy, Paul. *Small Acts: Thoughts on the Politics of Black Culture*. London and New York: Serpent's Tail, 1993.

———. *The Black Atlantic: Modernity and Double Consciousness*. Cambridge, MA: Harvard University Press, 1993.

———. *There Ain't No Black in the Union Jack*. Hutchinson Press, 1988.

Haydon, Geoffrey, and Dennis Marks. *Repercussions: A Celebration of African-American Music*. London: Century, 1985.

Jones, LeRoi (Amiri Baraka). *Black Music*. New York: William Morrow, 1967.

Lee, N'Tanya, Don Murphy, and Juliet Ucelli. "Whose Kids? Sexuality and the Right in New York City's Curriculum Battles. *Radical America*, vol. 25, n. 1, pp. 9–21.

Shaw, Arnold. *Black Popular Music in America: From the Spirituals, Minstrels, and Ragtime to Soul, Disco, and Hip-Hop*. New York: Schirmer Books, 1986.

Sidran, Ben. *Black Talk*. New York: Da Capo Press, 1981.

Smith, Winston. "Let's Call This: Race, Writing, and Difference in Jazz."

Spencer, Jon Michael. *Protest and Praise: Sacred Music of Black Religion*. Minneapolis: Fortress Press, 1990.

West, Cornell. "Black Culture and Postmodernism." In B. Kruger and P. Mariani, eds., *Re-Making History*. Seattle: Bay Press, 1989.

Zavarzadeh, Mas'ud, and Donald Morton. *Theory, (Post)Modernity, Opposition: An "Other" Introduction to Literary and Cultural Theory*. Washington, D.C.: Maisonneuve Press, 1991.

Hip-Hop

Allen, Harry. "The political proclamations of hip-hop music." *The Black Collegian*, vol. 20, no. 4, (March/April 1990), p. 21.

Baker, Houston A., Jr., *Black Studies, Rap, and the Academy*. Chicago: University of Chicago Press, 1993.

————."You Cain't Truss It: Experts Witnessing in the Case of Rap. In Gina Dent (with Michele Wallace), Black Popular Culture (Seattle: Bay Press, 1992), 132–138.

————. "Hybridity, the Rap Race, and Pedagogy for the 1990's," in Constance Penley and Andrew Ross, eds., *Technoculture*. Minneapolis: University of Minnesota Press, 1991.

————. "Handling 'Crisis': Great Books, Rap Music, and the End of Western Homogeneity (Reflections on the Humanities in America). *Callaloo* 13:2 (Spring 1990), 173–194.

Berman, Marshall. "Close to the Edge: Reflections on Rap Music." *Tikkun*, vol. 8, no. 2 (March/April 1993), 13–18, 75–78.

————. "Bass in Your Face" (on Public Enemy). *Village Voice*, Oct. 22, 1991: 77–79.

Bernard, James. "A Newcomer Abroad, Rap Speaks Up" (on the global spread of hip-hop). *New York Times*, Aug. 23, 1992, sec. 2:1, 22.

Cary, Lorene. "As Plain as Black and White" (on Sister Souljah and related issues). *Newsweek*, June 29, 1992: 53.

Chambers, Gordon, and Joan Morgan. "Droppin' Knowledge: A Rap Round-table" (discussion with MC Lyte, Queen Latifah, Chuck D, Q-Tip, Heavy D, and KRS-One). *Essence* 23:5 (Sept. 1992), 83–85, 116–120.

Christagu, Robert, and Greg Tate. "Public Enemy #1: Chuck D on Hiphop, homosexuality, and self-determination" [interview]. *Village Voice*, Oct. 22, 1991: 12–18.

Cocks, Jay. "Rap Around the World." *TIME*, October 19, 1992: 70–71.

Cross, Brian. *It's not about a salary...Rap, Race and Resistance in Los Angeles*. London and New York: Verso, 1993.

Davis, Angela, and Ice Cube. "Nappy Happy" [conversation]. *Transition* 58 (1992), 174–192.

Dawsey, Kierna Mayo. "Caught up in the (Gangsta) Rapture: Dr. C. Delores Tucker's Crusade against "Gangsta Rap." *The Source*, June 1994, pp. 58–62.

Decker, Jeffrey Louis. "The State of Rap: Time and Place in Hip-Hop Nationalism." In Tricia Rose and Andrew Ross, eds. *Microphone Fiends: Youth Music and Youth Culture*. New York: Routledge, 1994.

De Silva, Earlston E., "The Theology of Black Power and Black Song: James Brown." *Black Sacred Music: A Journal of Theomusicology* 3 (Fall 1989): 57–67.

DiPrima, Dominique. "Beat the rap" (feminist women in rap music). *Mother Jones*, vol. 15, no. 6 (Sept.-Oct. 1990), p. 32.

Dixon, Wheeler Winston. "Urban Black American Music in the Late 1980's: The 'Word' as Cultural Signifier." *Midwest Quarterly*, 30:2 (Winter 1989), 229–241.

Dyson, Michael Eric. "Black or White? Labels Don't Always Fit." *New York Times*, February 13, 1994, Section 2, p. H30, col. 5.

———. "Bum Rap." *New York Times*, Feb. 3, 1994, p. A21, col. 2.

———. "Rap Culture, the Church, and American Society." *Black Sacred Music* 6:1 (1992), 269–273.

————. "Rights and Responsibilities: 2 Live Crew and Rap's Moral Vision." *Black Sacred Music* 6:1 (1992), 274–281.

————. "Performance, Protest, and Prophecy in the Culture of Hip-Hop." In *The Emergency of Black and the Emergence of Rap*. Special Issue of *Black Sacred Music: A Journal of Theomusicology* 5:1 (Spring 1991): 12–24.

————. "2 Live Crew's rap: sex, race and class." *The Christian Century*, Jan. 2, 1991 (vol. 108, no. 1), p. 7.

————. "Rap, Race, and Reality: Run-D.M.C." *Black Sacred Music: A Journal of Theomusicology* 3 (Fall 1989): 142–45.

Erlanger, Steven (Russia), Nichlas Kristof (China), Edward Gargan (India), Kenneth B. Noble (West Africa), Burton Bollag (Eastern Europe), Steven R. Weisman (Japan), Simon Reynolds (Britain), John Rockwell (France), William Schomberg (Mexico): "The Many Accents of Rap Around the World." *New York Times*, Aug. 23, 1992, sec. 2:22–23.

Eure, Joseph, and James G. Spady, eds. *Nation Conscious Rap: The Hip-Hop Vision*. Brooklyn: PC International Press, 1991.

Fab 5 Freddy. *Fresh Fly Flavor: Words and Phrases of the Hip-Hop Nation*. New York: Longmeadow Press, 1991.

Fernando, S.H. *The New Beats: Exploring the Music, Culture, and Attitudes of Hip-Hop*. New York: Anchor Books, 1994.

Flores, Juan. "Puerto Rican and Proud, Boyee!: Rap Roots and Amnesia." In Andrew Ross & Tricia Rose, *Microphone Fiends: Youth Music and Youth Culture*. New York: Routledge, 1994.

————. "Rappin', Writin', and Breakin'." *Dissent* 34 (Fall 1987): 580–84.

George, Nelson. "In Defense of Rap—Gangsta or Not." *The Washington Post*, Feb. 20, 1994, section G, p. 3, col. 1.

————. "Chocolate City Freeze-Out." *Village Voice*, February 22, 1994, p. 76.

————. *Fresh, hip-hop don't stop*. New York: Random House, 1985.

Goldman, Vivien. "Black Noise, Black Heat" (interview with Chuck D and Hank Shocklee of Public Enemy). *Spin*, Oct. 1992, 45–48, 123.

Goodwin, Andrew. "Sample and Hold: Pop Music in the Age of Digital Reproduction." In Simon Frith and Andrew Goodwin, eds., *On The Record: Rock, Pop, and the Written Word*.

Hager, Stephen. *Hip-Hop: The Illustrated History of Break Dancing, Rap Music, and Graffiti*. New York: St. Martin's Press, 1984.

Hebdige, Dick. *Cut 'n' Mix: Culture, Identity, and Caribbean Music*. New York: Commedia (Methuen), 1987.

Hilburn, Robert. "KRS-One: Hard Raps from a Teacher in the Street." *Los Angeles Times*, April 18, 1992, sec. F:1.

hooks, bell, and Ice Cube. "Ice Cube's rap on sistahs is rough. bell hooks is a radical feminist scholar. Their deepest connection is a passion for speaking the truth." *Spin*, vol. 9, no. 1 (April 1993), 79–82.

James, Darius, "Gangstaphobia" [On the congressional hearings on "gangsta" rap]. *SPIN*, May 1994, pp. 64–66.

Jennings, Nicholas. "The big rap attack: a black form conquers the mainstream." *Maclean's*, vol. 103, no. 46 (Nov. 12, 1990), p. 74.

Kaplan, E. Ann. "The Significance of MTV and Rap Music in Popular Culture." *New York Times*, Dec. 29, 1991, sec. LI: 2.

Kelley, Robin D.G. "Straight from the Underground." *The Nation*, vol. 254 (1992), 793–796.

Kerrigan, Chuck. *Rap Beats on the Drum Set*. Fullerton, CA: Centerstream Publishing, 1991.

Keyes, Cheryl L. "Verbal Art Performance in Rap Music: The Conversation of the '80s." *Folklore Forum* 17 (Fall 1984): 143–52.

Knight, Robert. "Antihero" (on rapper Sister Souljah). *Spin*, Oct. 1992, 96–99.

Kot, Greg. "New Black Voices Send a Loud, Clear Message: Rap Offers a Soundtrack of Afro-American Experience." *Chicago Tribune*, Feb. 16, 1992, sec. 13: 5.

Leland, John. "Armageddon in Effect." *Spin* (October 1988): 46–49, 76.

———. "Rap and Race: Beyond Sister Souljah—The New Politics of Pop Music." *Newsweek*, June 29, 1992: 47–52.

Lester, Sheena. "Diggin' Deep: Rap Pages Talks to the Ladies" [interview with Sister Souljah, Dee Barnes, and the Poetess]. *Rap Pages* 1:7 (Oct. 1992):31–35.

Light, Alan. "Wisdom from the Street" (profile of KRS-One). *Rolling Stone* 605 (May 30, 1991), 41–42.

Linden, Amy. *Niggas with Beatitude: A Conversation with Run DMC*, *Transition* 62 (1994), pp. 176–187.

Lipscomb, Michael, and KRS-One. "Can the Teacher be Taught?" *Transition* 57 (1992), 168–189.

McLane, Daisann. "The Forgotten Caribbean Connection" (on hip-hop's roots in calypso and reggae 'toasts.') *New York Times*, Aug. 23, 1992, sec. 2: 22.

Marriott, Michel. "Hip-Hop's Hostile Takeover" (on controversies surrounding the debut of Quincy Jones's new hip-hop magazine, Vibe). *New York Times*, Sep. 20, 1992, sec. 9, p. 1, 8.

Marriott, Rob, James Bernard, and Allen S. Gordon, eds. "Reality Check" (a roundtable discussion on the attack on "Gangsta" rap including Scarface, MC Eiht, and Spice-1). *The Source*, June 1994, pp. 64–75.

Maxwell, William. "Sampling Authenticity: Rap Music, Postmodernism, and the Ideology of Black Crime." *Studies in Popular Culture*, 14:1 (1991), 1–15.

Muwakkil, Salim. "The rap gap: class divisions divide the black community." Utne Reader no. 37 (Jan.-Feb. 1990), p. 52.

Nelson, Angela Spense. "Theology in the Hip-Hop of Public Enemy and Kool Moe Dee." In *The Emergency of Black and the Emergence of Rap*. Special Issue of *Black Sacred Music: A Journal of Theomusicology* 5:1 (Spring 1991): 51–59.

Nelson, Havelock. "Music and violence: does crime pay?" *Billboard*, vol. 105, no. 46 (Nov. 13, 1993), p. 1.

Pareles, Jon. "Rap and Violence: Perception vs. Reality." *New York Times*, Sept. 13, 1988, 13, 17.

———. "Female Rappers Strut Their Stuff in a Male Domain." *New York Times*, Nov. 5, 1989, sec. 2:29.

———. "On Rap, Symbolism, and Fear." *New York Times*, Feb. 2, 1992, sec. 2: 1.

———. "Hip-hop makes a sharp turn back to melody." *New York Times*, May 31, 1992, sec. 2: 24.

Perkins, Eric. "Nation of Islam Ideology in the Rap of Public Enemy." In *The Emergency of Black and the Emergence of Rap*. Special Issue of *Black Sacred Music: A Journal of Theomusicology* 5:1 (Spring 1991): 41–50.

Peterson-Lewis, Sonja. "A Feminist Analysis of the Defenses of Obscene Rap Lyrics." In *The Emergency of Black and the Emergence of Rap*. Special Issue of *Black Sacred Music: A Journal of Theomusicology* 5:1 (Spring 1991): 68–79.

Potter, Russell. "Black Modernisms/Black Postmodernisms" (Review essay covering Rose, *Black Noise*, and Gilroy, *The Black Atlantic*). *Postmodern Culture*, September 1994.

Reed, Ishmael, and Michael Franti. "Hip-Hoprisy" (conversation). *Transition* 56 (1991).

Roberts, Robin. "Music Videos, Performance, and Resistance: Feminist Rappers." *Journal of Popular Culture*, 25.2: 141–52.

Rose, Tricia. *Black Noise: Rap Music and Black Culture in Contemporary America*. Hanover, N.H.: University Press of New England / Wesleyan University Press, 1994.

———. "Contracting Rap: An Interview with Carmen Ashhurst-Watson." In Tricia Rose and Andrew Ross, eds., *Microphone Fiends: Youth Music and Youth Culture*. New York: Routledge, 1994.

———. "Black Texts/Black Culture," in Gina Dent (with Michele Wallace), *Black Popular Culture*. Seattle: Bay Press, 1992, 223–227.

———, and Elizabeth Alexander. "Call and Response." *Voice Literary Supplement* 109 (October 1992): 11–12.

———. "Orality and Technology: Rap Music and Afro-American Cultural Resistance." *Popular Music and Society* 13 (Winter 1989): 35–44.

Ross, Andrew. "Poverty Meets Performance: The Gangsta and the Diva." *The Nation*, vol. 259, no. 6 (August 22/29, 1994), 191–194.

Royster, Philip M., "The Rapper as Shaman for a Band of Dancers of the Spirit: 'U Can't Touch This.'" In *The Emergency of Black and the Emergence of Rap*. Special Issue of *Black Sacred Music: A Journal of Theomusicology* 5:1 (Spring 1991): 60–67.

Rule, Sheila, moderator. "Generation Rap" [discussion between Ice Cube and Last Poets member Abiodun Oyewole]. *The New York Times Magazine*, April 3, 1994, 40–45.

———. "Record Companies Are Challenging 'Sampling' in Rap." *New York Times*, April 21, 1992, sec. C:13.

———. "Rappers' words foretold depth of blacks' anger." *New York Times*, May 26, 1992, p. B1 (N) p. C13 (L).

Samuels, David. "The Rap on Rap: The Black Music that Isn't Either." *The New Republic*, Nov. 11, 1991: 24–29.

Sandow, Greg. "Taking a Bum Rap." *Entertainment Weekly*, July 10, 1992: 56–8.

————. "Fire and Ice" (on Ice-T and the "Cop Killer" controversy). *Entertainment Weekly*, Aug. 14, 1992: 31–2.

Scott, Michael. "Meditations on the Blues and Rap Music." Mississippi Folklore Register, 24 (1990), 17–33.

Shusterman, Richard. "The Fine Art of Rap." *New Literary History* 22 (1991): 613–632.

Simmons, Doug. "Gangsta Was the Case: Shaping Our Responses to Snoop Dogg" [includes reportage and commentary on the anti-gangsta congressional hearings]. *Village Voice*, March 8, 1994, pp. 63, 66.

Soocher, Stan. "It's bad, it's def—is it obscene? Rap music takes a bad rap from prosecutors" by Stan Soocher. *The National Law Journal*, vol. 12, no. 39 (June 4, 1990), p 1.

Sister Souljah. "S.O.S.: Souljah on Souljah." *Rap Pages* 1:7 (Oct. 1992): 54–56.

Small, Michael. *Break It On Down*. New York: Citadel Press, 1992.

Spencer, Jon Michael, ed. *The Emergency of Black and the Emergence of Rap*. Special Issue of *Black Sacred Music: A Journal of Theomusicology* 5:1 (Spring 1991).

————. "Rapsody in black: utopian aspirations." *Theology Today*, vol. 48, no. 4, (Jan. 1992) p. 444.

Stanley, Lawrence A. *Rap: The Lyrics*. New York: Penguin Books, 1992.

Stephens, Ronald Jemal. "The Three Waves of Contemporary Rap Music." In *The Emergency of Black and the Emergence of Rap*. Special Issue of *Black Sacred Music: A Journal of Theomusicology* 5:1 (Spring 1991): 25–40.

Stewart, Gary. *Breakout: profiles in African rhythm*. Chicago: University of Chicago Press, 1992.

Tate, Greg, "Hip-Hop is Here to Stay." *Village Voice*, Sept. 4, 1984, 73.

Thigpen, David E. "Not For Men Only" (on female rappers). *TIME*, May 27, 1991: 71–2.

Toop, David. *Rap Attack: African Jive to New York Hip-Hop*. Boston: South End Press, 1984. Second edition: *RAP Attack No. 2: African Rap to Global Hip-Hop*. London: Serpent's Tail, 1992.

Wallace, Michele. "Women rap back." *Ms.*, vol. 1, no. 3 (Nov.-Dec. 1990), p. 61.

Watkins, Mel. "The Lyrics of James Brown: Ain't It Funky Now, or Money Won't Change Your Licking Stick." In John A. Williams and Charles F. Harris, *Amistad 2* (New York: Vintage, 1971): 21–42.

West, Cornell. "On Afro-American Popular Music: From Bebop to Rap." Black Sacred Music 6:1 (1992), 282–294.

Williams, Todd. "Gil Scott-Heron and the Last Poets: Poetically Correct." *The Source*, 32 (May 1992): 42–44, 59.

Willis, Andre Craddock. "Rap Music and the Black Musical Tradition." *Radical America* vol. 23, no. 4 (1989), pp. 29–38.

Index

Academia, 22, 23

African-American culture, 16–17, 22, 121; appropriation of, 4, 103, 105; and authenticity, 104–5, 159 n. 22; and class, 94–97; and diaspora, 7, 20; identity, 136–38, 149; music, 26–28; and "white" culture, 64–65, 94–95

Antoinette, 93–94

Apache (rapper), 93

Archaeology, cultural, 13

Baker, Houston A., Jr., *Black Studies, Rap, and the Academy*, 150–51, 182 n. 23; *Blues, Ideology, and Afro–American Literature*, 55; concept of "deformation of mastery," 78–79, 144

Bakhtin, M. M., concept of chronotope, 18, 161 n. 29

Baldwin, James, 99

Bambaata, Afrika, 47–48, 99, 142, 145, 159 n. 22; "Looking for the Perfect Beat," 43; "Planet Rock," 48

Baraka, Amiri (LeRoi Jones), 21, 28, 71, 172 n. 25

Barthes, Roland, 78

Benjamin, Walter, "The Work of Art in the Age of Mechanical Reproduction," 46

Berman, Marshall, 84

Bernard, James, 96–97

Bhangra (music), 10

Big Daddy Kane, "Here Comes Kane, Scoob, Scrap," 82

Billboard, 112, 113

Black Panther Party, 44, 103, 173 n. 37

Black Vernacular English (BVE), 58, 62, 68–69, 170 n. 10

Boogie Down Productions (BDP), 52–53, 105; "Ghetto Music," 52–53; "Necessary," 85–86. *See also* KRS–One.

Bop, 70, 72

Bo$$, 71, 94; "I Don't Give a Fuck," 71

Broonzy, Big Bill, 42–43

Brown, H. "Rap," 174 n. 4

Brown, James, 40–41, 43

Butts, Calvin, 137, 138

B.W.P. (Bytches Wit' Problems), 93

Calypso, 142

Carmichael, Stokely, 180

Certeau, Michel de, *Heterologies*, 21, 148; *The Practice of Everyday* Life, 69, 107, 109

Chesnutt, Charles, 61

Chuck D, 15, 23, 73, 84, 114, 121, 141, 152; "The Sticka," 111. *See also* Public Enemy

Cleaver, Eldridge, 100

193